Soundings:

DOCUMENTARY FILM AND THE LISTENING EXPERIENCE

EDITED BY
GEOFFREY COX and JOHN CORNER

Published by University of Huddersfield Press

University of Huddersfield Press
The University of Huddersfield
Queensgate
Huddersfield HD1 3DH
Email enquiries university.press@hud.ac.uk

First published 2018
This work is licensed under a Creative Commons Attribution 4.0 International License

Images © as attributed

Every effort has been made to locate copyright
holders of materials included and to obtain
permission for their publication.

The publisher is not responsible for the continued
existence and accuracy of websites referenced
in the text.

A CIP catalogue record for this book is available
from the British Library.
ISBN 978-1-86218-154-0

Designed and printed by
D&M Heritage
Unit 7, Park Valley
Meltham Road
Huddersfield, HD4 7BH
www.dandmheritage.co.uk

Contents

Introduction   Geoffrey Cox   1

Part 1: The Promotional Imagination

Chapter 1   Stories from a stay at the *Arena* Hotel   17
Will L Finch

Chapter 2   *Weave Me a Rainbow*   37
'The march, the march of colour and pattern'
Music and cinematography at the service of the creative promotion of the 1960s Scottish woollen industry
Geoffrey Cox

Chapter 3   Sonicules - Designing drugs with sound: approaches to sound design for film, audiovisual performance and interactive sonification   69
Radoslaw Rudnicki and Jude Brereton

Part 2: Foregrounding the Aesthetic: Strategies and Practices

Chapter 4   Auralising Action Space: channelling a sense of play in documentary sound design   85
Simon Connor

Chapter 5   'The film looks like how Ornette sounds':   107
Shirley Clarke's music documentary *Ornette: Made in America*
Rosa Nogués

Chapter 6	Progress Music James Bulley	125
Chapter 7	Creative use of voice in non-fiction narrative film: an examination of the work of Peter Mettler Lars Koens and Demelza Kooij	151
Chapter 8	Documentary film as a backdrop for active thinking Ana Berkenhoff	173
Centrepiece	The unwanted sound of everything we think we want Andrew Kötting	183

Part 3: Nationhood and Conflict

Chapter 9	The 'Appassionata' Sonata in *A Diary for Timothy* Tsung-Han Tsai	203
Chapter 10	A 'Symphony of Britain at War' or the 'Rhythm of Workaday Britain'? Len Lye's *When the Pie Was Opened* (1941) and the musicalisation of warfare Anita Jorge	219
Chapter 11	Building a sonic image of a nation: Finnish documentary and propaganda films in the early decades of sound film Kaarina Kilpiö	239
Chapter 12	Raúl Ruiz's *Now We're Gonna Call You Brother* and the problem of the people's sonic representation Laura Jordán González and Nicolas Lema Habash	255
Afterword	John Corner	279
Contributors		285
Index		291

Introduction

Geoffrey Cox

Conceived at the Sound and Music in Documentary Film Symposium (SMDF) of February 2017, this collection of essays considers the ways sound as noise, music and speech informs the documentary form: noise as location sound, sound effects and concrete sounds that blur into musical expression; music as asynchronous score, diegetic performance and the musicality of the timbre of the speaking voice; speech as commentary (educative, poetic, surreal), witness testimony and expert exposition. All consider sound as a sonorous and resounding listening experience. Whilst any such collection must consider the audiovisual relationship as a primary concern, it is the special power of *sound* to generate profound feeling, employed in documentary to represent, inform, interpret, inspire and persuade, and ultimately to create powerfully affecting meanings to which the essays invariably return.

The purpose of this short introduction is to highlight the enveloping import of sound, to show how listening can generate great emotional as well as cognitive meaning and to outline the implications of both for the soundtrack of documentary film. In the following series of documentary case studies, the authors detail these powers of sound and listening. They articulate their implications and the meanings that are inherent, intended and can be extrapolated from the audiovisual relationships in the films under discussion.

Sound and Listening

The capacity for sound to be powerfully evocative is unquestionable. An old photograph, or even a silent cine film from one's childhood, brings back memories and can have strong emotional resonances. Listening to the 'unseen sound' of an old audio recording however, can almost without warning, engulf us in the feelings it triggers. The sound of a distant night-time foghorn or of close-by early morning chirruping sparrows can transport me back, as if through some mysterious portal, to my childhood bedroom in East London where I fell asleep and awoke to those sounds. The room itself and the very feeling of being there, and *listening*, is evoked. Delia Derbyshire has described how the sound of air-raid sirens during Coventry's wartime Blitz in her childhood engendered her 'love for abstract sounds', as did the 'percussive sound' of millworkers' 'clogs on cobbles' going to work at six o'clock in the morning in her later childhood home of Preston (Cavanagh, 1998). Listening is an intense, inner experience that can have lifelong resonances since 'there is nothing to stop' sound's 'penetrating enveloping presence from overpowering' (Rangan, 2017, p. 284); it has no bounding frame like the image, containing, defining and controlling it, and so is freer to generate deep affects that we have little voluntary control over. It is such a freedom that lies at the heart of the writing in this collection and its concern with the enveloping presence of sound in the context of documentary film. The photograph can show us things, even bring emotive responses but as all of the authors here show, sound's affectiveness can be deployed to generate deeper meanings beyond those provided by the frame of moving pictures.

This tendency of sound to break the frame makes it ambiguous and ephemeral. We talk of the 'soundscape', yet unlike its sister landscape, its content and especially its edges are far more blurred and ultimately, indefinable, even unknowable. Sound emanates from objects that in general, we can see, at least in one's mind's eye, but as Steven Connor suggests, the actual attachment of sound we make to those objects is dependent on whatever other thing is acting *on* them. There is in a sense, no sound of the object itself (2004, pp. 161 – 2). Anyone who has ever tried to record the sound of the wind will know that it appears to have no clear character or even sound unless it is blowing *through* something, such as the wires of a telephone line. We may not even make any attachment of sound to object. As Delia Derbyshire explains of the air-raid sirens, she did not know the source or meaning of their sound as a young child. Their power was both abstracted and metaphorical, like music, and this explains how they had such a profound effect on Derbyshire's future career as a composer of electronic and concrete music. Further, citing Lucy Donaldson, Simon Connor writes in this collection that unlike vision, in such listening, sound also 'makes a vital contribution to the evocation of other senses, for example, the sound of wind rustling leaves invites the feel of air on our skin, or the sizzle of food cooking conjures taste' (Simon Connor, 2018, p. 91). Sound seems to almost 'touch' us and then explode a multitude of responses, its sensual effect at once beguiling and unsettling. Compared to seeing, hearing is thus associated more with sensual *feeling* than understanding, since the experience of listening can be intense but without clear specificity (Steven Connor, 2004, p. 157). Sound comes towards us such that 'we cannot listen without taking into ourselves the sounds we hear' (p. 163). Sound thus has a very real physical power; it has a tactile, bodily effect despite this lack of materiality and specificity; it 'moves, shakes and touches us', yet remains 'mysterious' (p. 157).

Music and Noises as Music

It is of course the mysterious power of *musical* sound that can potentially move, shake and touch us the most. Traditionally, music operates on a generally non-referential, non-specific level in the first place, its power lying in its capacity to operate on a metaphorical and symbolic level, characterized by Pierre Schaeffer as the *comprendre* mode of listening. This has led to Friedrich Schlegel referring to music as, 'the highest of all arts' due to its apparent transcendent capacities and what Schopenhauer suggests is its relation 'to the true nature of all things' and its ability to 'express the metaphysical to everything physical in the world'. As Kulezic-Wilson perceptively suggests, Schopenhauer's idea that when played 'to any scene, action, event, or environment . . . music seems to disclose to us its most secret meanings, and appears to be the most accurate and distinct commentary on it', is a quite precise description of music's ascribed role in film (2015, p. 19). A deeper, non-cognitive *understanding* can thus result from this metaphorical transcendence.

However, as Schaeffer, and John Grierson before him explored, non-musical sounds of the everyday, organized in certain ways, can also take on the guise of music whilst partially retaining their links to their causal source. Boundaries become blurred between simple indexical recognition (Schaeffer's *écouter* listening mode), and Schaeffer's analytical *entendre* mode of objective, phenomenologically-inspired 'reduced' listening. The founders of modern documentary in the form of the British pre-war Movement, made films that employed the use of both music and sound in these ways. Examples such as *Coal Face* and *Night Mail* with their scores by Benjamin Britten are well known, but as early as 1930, Grierson was also suggesting

> [t]here must be a poetry of sound which none of us knows. . . . Meanings in footsteps, voices in trees, and woods of the day and night everywhere. . . . I have, like everybody else shut my eyes . . . and sat for hours trying to make something

of the door-bangings and footfalls and crazy oddments of conversation that broke the plush darkness of a London night (p. 13).

The result was films such as Movement directors Edgar Anstey and Harry Watt's *6.30 Collection* (1934) about mail sorting at the GPO, an early documentary that, along with the likes of Dziga Vertov's *Enthusiasm* (1931), explored the possibilities of the creative treatment of location sound recordings. Holly Rogers cites Ruoff's idea that the somewhat chaotic world of documentary location sound recording tends to abstract Grierson's 'crazy oddments' of sound from their sources as they 'coalesce in the aural middle ground'. This makes them both more confusing than sounds in everyday life and 'less realistic to ears attuned to the artificial sonic clarity of fiction film'. As a result, there is a tendency to push such sounds into the 'non-referential realm of music' (2015, p. 9), even before any creative manipulation of them. Once consciously and creatively organized, this tendency enables sound to enter the metaphorical realm as Grierson suggests:

> another curious fact emerges once you start detaching sounds from their origins, and it is this. Your aeroplane noise may not become the image of an aeroplane but the image of distance or of height. Your steamer whistle may not become the image of a steamer but of isolation and darkness (1934, p. 103).

Similarly, in a review of *Enthusiasm* Grierson extols its sonic potential: 'you will find most excellent passages of melancholy sound into musical sound: you will hear it distorted till it screams, and you will find feeling in it' (1931, p. 349). This is 'expanded listening' rather than Schaeffer's reduced variety and Grierson's direct listening experiences informed his understanding of the power of all sounds in documentary — synchronous and asynchronous and the myriad gradations in between the two. Such a listening experience is shared by the authors in this book. They examine sound in documentary from this perspective, following what Birtwistle suggests is film studies' 'increased interest in perception, embodiment and the senses' (2010, p. 6). They do so in a variety of ways: by interpreting their own listening experiences; by studying the listening experiences of other filmmakers, composers and sound designers; or by examining sound from the perspective of their own documentary creative practice.

Sonorous Voices

A further aspect of the documentary soundworld is, of course, the speaking voice. The 'voice of God' commentary (another legacy of the Griersonian tradition), the talking head, and the interviewee's testimony are traditionally seen as being at documentary's cognitive heart, the powerhouse of claims to any 'reality effect' and very much concerned with conveying specific information and ideas. Documentary has long privileged such an acquisitive listening, 'the fulfilment of a desire for understanding (something, someone)' (Leimbacher, 2015, p. 314). Watch almost any mainstream television documentary today and you will not find that the talking stops for very long, as if the audience cannot be trusted to think for themselves. It leaves little time for reflection. The dominance of often didactic commentary or interviewees acting like 'puppets conforming to [the] line' of the hidden voice of the filmmaker (Nichols, 1983, p. 27) is still common. There is sometimes a sense that one just wants the talking to stop: in critiquing the documentary work of the Films of Scotland Committee (discussed by Cox in this collection), film critic Allen Wright goes as far as to call for an 'embargo on wordiness' that if enacted for 'even a year would be the greatest blessing that could be bestowed on Scottish films' (1974, n. p.).

Yet, as several of this collection's authors reveal, in taking what Birtwistle describes as an 'affective turn' compared to the 'linguistic turn' of the 1960s (2010, p. 6), the 'sonorous voice' of such commentary can communicate through more ways than semantic articulation (see Kooij and Koen, Jorge, Tsai, Kilpiö, Berkenhoff). Even where the cognitively reliant, educative exposition of meaningful language is important (Rudnicki and Brereton, Connor), the sonic adornment of the voice can make meaning more *felt* and thus enduring. The voice can be 'the transient, transforming wave of sound through which we connect to each other' (Leimbacher, 2017, p. 293). Drawing on the work of philosophers Jean-Luc Nancy and Mladen Dolar, Leimbacher draws a distinction between 'listening, which attends to voice, and understanding or hearing . . . which seeks the meaning embedded in the language of speech' (2017, p. 296). Hearing attends to linguistic signification whereas listening is open to a more elusive sense that adheres to the voice's grain. In such listening, comprehending language may not be the final goal since our ears are more 'inclined toward affect rather than concept'. It is upon this affect that much of the discussion of voice in this collection focuses. The authors 'listen otherwise', as Lisbeth Lipari suggests is necessary in order to expand listening and go beyond conformity to something deeper, and so they are 'committed to receiving otherness' (Leimbacher, 2017, p. 297). This is manifest in their discussions of the speaking voice's timbre, rhythm, musicality and emotively human qualities that stretch well beyond language.

Listening *and* Looking

When it comes to the relationship between sound and image in film, the dominance of the visual is almost a given, although so much has been said in recent decades about the earlier neglect of sound's importance in the relationship, it can no longer be considered neglected at all. Whilst in much film there *is* still the sense that sound and music is essentially there to *support* the image, filmmakers such as Robert Bresson are willing to assert that sound is 'more evocative than an image, which is essentially only a stylization of visual reality' (Burch, 1985, p. 200). This returns to Rangan's idea of sound's 'penetrating enveloping presence' that in documentary film leads to its 'modes of interpellation lean[ing] toward the audial as much as if not more so than the visual' and the related idea that it uses our listening 'processes of auditory discrimination and discernment . . . to build second-order systems of meaning' (2017, p. 282). This presents a conundrum for documentary with its 'lingering imperative of objectivity' (p. 283) since such second-order meanings can easily be seen as being anything but objective. The imbuing of metaphorical meaning to diegetic sound and its inherent contribution to music, make sound's overall 'penetrating enveloping presence' a powerful conveyer of subjective meaning. As Michael Chanan points out with regard to music in documentary: 'it isn't factual, or neutral or even limited to the descriptive, but . . . is emotive, expressive and associative. It therefore inevitably functions as a form of commentary, sometimes all the more insidious for not declaring itself as such' (Chanan, 2007, p. 117). This is not so much André Bazin's 'window on the world', film's photographic transfer of 'the reality from the thing to its representation' (Nagib and Mello, 2009, p. xvi), as a mirror reflecting the agenda of the filmmaker or other inherent biases. As we shall see, this notion of an 'agenda' and how this can be bolstered by sound (and especially music) has legitimacy (Kilpiö, Cox, Jorge, Jordán González and Lema Habash), but the concept of 'the real' is also questioned, and the problem posed of how one might view attempts to reach at least, certain kinds of 'truth' or understanding via the deliberate creative exploration of the sonic (Tsai, Berkenhoff, Nogués). Such a delineation is however rather too stark as the authors show; the two positions are not mutually exclusive, since after all, one person's agenda is another's truth.

Dai Vaughan has written that documentary film is inevitably a construction, the editor reluctantly allowing 'the film to take on the form to which it seems to aspire' and that it is always distinguished from reality, because it is 'about something' (1999, p. 21). He points out that 'all events, at least in human affairs, are events perceived by somebody', but that documentary filmmakers attempt to 'prevent their own perceptions from intervening between the viewer and the pro-filmic' (p. 57). Transparency, objectivity and neutrality can be aspired to even if never fully attained. By contrast, Jay Ruby asserts that documentary filmmakers have a duty 'not to be objective' since they are essentially 'interpreters of the world' (2005, p. 45). Yet interpretation is not the same thing as representation, even though the two terms are sometimes closely interconnected in discussion of documentary. Grierson was of the view that documentary deals with the actual, and in that sense the real, but that what one should be aiming at is the 'really real' which 'is something deeper than that. The only reality which counts in the end is the interpretation which is profound' (Aitken, 1990, p. 109). Aitken suggests that Grierson privileges the notion of an abstract, 'poetic reality which existed beneath the rational' (p. 114) and that the 'intrinsic empirical naturalism of the documentary representation must become organized in order to express general truths, which exist at the level of abstraction, beyond the empirical' (p. 109). Schopenhauer's idea of how any 'scene' accompanied by music discloses 'to us its most secret meanings' (cited above), is echoed here and not surprisingly so given Grierson's university study and lifelong adherence to the Idealism of philosophers such as Schopenhauer. It also chimes with Lindsay Anderson's documentary work that, even when consciously realistic, sought deeper implications beyond the surface realities. For him 'the most important challenge is to go beyond pure naturalism into poetry [in order to] penetrate the reality of [a] particular world since as Brecht has said "realism [doesn't] show what things really 'look like' but how they really are"' (Sussex, 1969, p. 12). Herzog calls this a quest towards a mysterious and elusive 'ecstatic truth', only reachable 'through fabrication and imagination and stylisation' (Rogers, 2015, p. 5).

The penetrating force engendered by the creative treatment of sound and employment of music in documentary therefore can be embraced as a means of reaching such 'realities' and 'secret meanings', the 'really real'; the *poetic* truth. However, this appeal to 'sensual and intellectual' understanding that deliberately goes beyond the straightforwardly cognitive, tapping into what John Corner describes as the 'dreamlike potential for the indirectly suggestive and associative' (2003, p. 97), can also be harnessed to empower promotional persuasion (Finch, Cox, Rudnicki and Brereton) and bolster political ideology and propaganda (Kilpiö, Jorge, Jordán González and Lema Habash). It does, as Chanan said, 'inevitably function as a form of commentary'. In its audiovisual relationships, it can be less like Bazin's filmic window on the world and more like a mirror reflecting sometimes hidden purposes and ideas.

Soundings: Documentary Film and the Listening Experience

The 2017 SMDF Huddersfield Symposium came about through my own research-led creative practice as a composer and documentary filmmaker. As a result, the aim evolved to bring together practitioners and researchers via an open call for discussion on all aspects of sound and music in documentary film, including expositions of presenters' own creative practice (sometimes with film screenings). This led to talks ranging from discussion of the articulation of desired meaning through practical aesthetics and techniques, to theoretical analysis of such practice. It also brought together attendees from a variety of disciplines: musicology, film and media studies, filmmaking, art theory, art practice, theatre, composition, sound studies, sound design, social science, cultural history, philosophy and English literature. This eclectic mix has filtered down into the range of topics the authors discuss in this collection which was conceived at the closing discussions of the symposium.

Documentary is not a 'stable set of conventions [or] ethical motivations', but rather an 'evolving and heterogeneous constellation' (Rangan, 2017, p. 286). This is reflected in the range of disciplines that both examine and become involved in the practice of documentary filmmaking. Unlike fiction film, the theoretical and ethical questions posed by such interdisciplinarity have been part of documentary practice's story from the beginning with filmmakers, theorists and critics alike contributing to journals such as *Cinema Quarterly* and *Sight and Sound* from the 1930s onwards. Often such a filmmaker, theorist or critic was one and the same person and this is also reflected in the contributions here: practitioners discuss techniques, theory and idea in their own work (Bulley, Kötting, Berkenhoff, Connor, Rudnicki and Brereton), and in the work of others (Bulley, Cox, Kooij and Koen), whilst analysts consider the implications of both the detail of practice and wider philosophical and cultural questions of sound's role in documentary (Jorge, Tsai, Finch, Kilpiö, Nogués, Jordán González and Lema Habash). This blend of practice-based discussion and theoretical analysis can be seen as a complement to the growing scholarly interest in the role of sound in documentary film within the last decade. Gunnar Iversen and Jan Ketil Simonsen's edited collection *Beyond the Visual: Sounds and Image in Ethnographic and Documentary Film* (2010), *Music and Sound in Documentary Film* (2015) edited by Holly Rogers and the fall 2017 issue of *Discourse*, 'Documentary Audibilities', are recent key examples. *Soundings: Documentary Film and the Listening Experience* adds to this scholarship by linking both the technical and aesthetic aspects of practice and detailed analytical expositions, to sound's powerful affects, placing emphasis on its penetrating meaning-making in the documentary context.

Whilst the collection does not have a specific theme beyond that of the affective power of sound and music in documentary film outlined above, three broad areas emerged from the writing. These areas are linked and provide the structural foundation: 'The Promotional Imagination'; 'Foregrounding the Aesthetic: Strategies and Practices'; and 'Nationhood and Conflict'. The script of filmmaker Andrew Kötting's poetic and challenging SMDF keynote talk forms a centrepiece between the second and final sections. What follows is a brief summary of each chapter in the order that they appear in the book.

The Promotional Imagination

Will Finch's opening chapter looks at the *Arena* Hotel, a website used as a promotional archive and form of exhibition for the BBC's long running television arts documentary, *Arena* (1975-present). It uses the features of a virtual hotel to help browsers navigate the programme archive. Finch examines how sound, and especially the music of featured artists of the hotel's documentary extracts, is used to 'blur' figurative gaps between different subject areas and films in the hotel such that time and space become ambiguous, nostalgic memories are evoked and artificial juxtapositions elided. Promotion through a rootedness in the past is also a feature of the next chapter where Geoffrey Cox examines the industrial documentary *Weave Me a Rainbow* (1962), a film about turning wool into clothing produced by Films of Scotland and sponsored by Scottish wool manufacturers. Cox discusses how the collaboration between director Edward McConnell and composer Frank Spedding enables arresting cinematography, poetic commentary and especially jazzy, modernist-tinged music to suggest a forward-looking industry and a 'country on the move', at the same time as recognizing the importance of timeless tradition.

Radoslaw Rudnicki and Jude Brereton undertake a rather different promotional exercise; that of an interdisciplinary educational project (documentary video, computer game and audiovisual performance) to aid public understanding of how scientists are using sound to aid comprehension of the interaction of complex molecular structures in designing anti-cancer drugs. Synthetic electronic music and sound design are at the heart of their practice. They describe how both are made and then used to inform, engage and enhance the audience / participants' experiences, and how the scientists themselves are employing sound.

Foregrounding the Aesthetic: Strategies and Practices

Simon Connor is an electronic music composer who records and manipulates field recordings extensively in his work. Here he details the processes of recording the construction of a giant inflatable and the musical performances within it, for use in his soundtrack for *Action Space* (Wahl, 2016), a feature-length documentary about the work and ideas of the arts collective, Action Space (1968 – 78). His focus is on aesthetics, 'play' and how the inherent playfulness of the collective itself affected his own approach, helping to create the balance between informative interviewee testimony and highly sonically and visually evocative sections of the film. *Action Space* features performances by AMM and Henry Cow's Phil Minton, but we must turn to Rosa Nogués for discussion of music documentary proper in her analysis of Shirley Clarke's *Ornette: Made in America* (1985). Her premise is that the film looks how its subject, pioneering avant-garde jazz saxophonist Ornette Coleman, sounds: its structure, editing style and heterogeneous make-up, is driven by the freedom of form and expression of Coleman's featured music. She highlights the outsider status of Coleman *and* Clarke and, in detailing this, shows how Clarke conveys a political sense of irony about the American Dream, plays with the line between fact and fiction, and addresses Coleman's ostracization within the jazz community and his own questioning of his masculinity.

Music and the way it can drive visual structures is also at the heart of video artist and composer James Bulley's practice. Here he combines his creative work with research into the collaboration between electronic music pioneer Daphne Oram and experimental documentary filmmaker Geoffrey Jones in a project called 'Progress Music'. He uses textual historical analysis of their documentary film *Trinidad and Tobago* (1964) to inform his audio-visual, film-sound installation *Progress Music I*, and both are detailed here. His desire to 'unfold untold histories' of these underrepresented artists is realised through the 'liberation' of archival material, further 'activated' by the re-composition processes used in the installation. The analysis of creative practice from the perspective of other creative artists, is also exemplified by filmmaker Demelza Kooij and sound designer / composer Lars Koen's examination of the aesthetics of the voice in the documentary films of Peter Mettler. In doing so, they privilege techniques, intentionality, and creative and authorial issues. Mettler's use of interviews, radio announcers, crowds, and his own voice-over in conjunction with sound design and imagery is discussed through the filter of Michel Chion's ideas. These emphasize Mettler's tendency to separate voice from body, focus on its sonorous qualities and question the limits of language.

Introduction

Ana Berkenhoff, sound artist and theatre maker, also examines the use of the voice, in this case the voice-over commentary in *Cormorant* (2015), a short film by her and Ethan Folk that blurs the boundaries between documentary and video art. Shot in the City of London, the film is a 'movement and perspective study' questioning the life of people in the City's financial centres and asking 'what the poet is for'. In her desire to bring 'new realms of meaning into existence', she discusses the way the disembodied voice and music, in combination with almost banal everyday imagery, can be used as a possible 'call to action', a raising of possibilities in the audience's consciousness. Berkenhoff's ruminative, lyrical approach to her elucidation leads well into filmmaker Andrew Kötting's centrepiece, 'The Unwanted Sound of Everything We Think We Want'. He poses fundamental questions about the nature of documentary and explores his interest in 'the thin membrane between what might be called fiction and non-fiction' and how music and sound are key not just to his work, but to his life. Like his films, the highly poetic, stream-of-consciousness approach is rich and engaging, and underpinned by a deceptively logical flow.

Nationhood and Conflict

The sonorous voice of commentary, but here more a 'voice of God', is also explored in Tsung-Han Tsai's opening chapter of the final section of the collection with an examination of Humphrey Jennings' *A Diary for Timothy* (1946). Tsai provides a detailed analysis of the sonic 'polyvocality' of the film featured in the diegetic music of Beethoven (played by Dame Myra Hess), commentary spoken by actor Michael Redgrave and written by E. M. Forster, and diegetic sound (especially that of rain). On the surface, the film depicts a nation on the brink of wartime victory but uncertain of its future, but Tsai concludes that its sonic complexities actually elucidate a 'self-conscious examination of identity politics'. Anita Jorge continues the theme of wartime Britain with an analysis of Len Lye's *When the Pie Was Opened* (1941), a government-sponsored informational / propaganda film depicting a middle-class family dealing with rationing by the making of a suitably austere vegetable pie. Its soundtrack includes what Jorge describes as the official, reassuring discourse of the 'musicalisation of warfare' but, she suggests, concealed in its highly experimental juxtaposition and treatment of surreal, asynchronous mechanical and natural noises, is a political message of socialist Lye's own: it is the working classes that have made the meal possible at all. Kaarina Kilpiö offers a different wartime perspective in her analysis of Axis-aligned Finland's WWII propaganda films, as well as of those films that presented a cultural representation of

Finland into the 1950s. Both placed importance on musical soundtracks, especially the use of Sibelius's music and allusions to folklore, to bolster nationalistic feelings via the creation of a national 'sonic image'. More than any of the chapters in the collection, Kilpiö's critical approach articulates how documentary's truth claims can be warped and subverted by music, commentary and staged visual material such that any 'truth-value' is heavily compromised.

The collection closes by moving beyond the perspective of the West to Chile via Nicolas Lema Habash and Laura Jordán González's chapter on Raúl Ruiz's *Ahora te vamos a llamar hermano (Now We're Gonna Call You Brother)* (1971) about socialist President Salvador Allende's visit to the regional home of the Mapuche people. They present a nuanced reading of the film's political complexities inherent in the sonic tension set up between a speech by Allende and the voices, language and music of the Mapuche people. Uniquely to this collection, Lema and Jordán deal exclusively with 'direct cinema' and its concerns not to 'mystify its objects' but they show that even here, the film employs 'direct sound as a powerful creative and political device'. In doing so they highlight the richness of the broad theme running through this book: sound as a sonorous and resounding listening experience that can empower the documentary to reveal, imply and *create*, complex and nuanced but ultimately, powerfully affecting meanings.

Finally, John Corner concludes the volume with an Afterword that, in the light of the contributions, reflects broadly on aspects of sound in relation to the development both of documentary and of documentary scholarship, indicating some of the possibilities which the book opens up for future inquiry.

Bibliography

Aitken, I. (1990). *Film and reform: John Grierson and the documentary Movement*. London: Routledge.

Birtwistle, A. (2010). *Cinesonica: sounding film and video*. Manchester: Manchester University Press.

Burch, N. (1985). On the structural use of sound. In J. Belton & E. Weis (Eds.), *Film sound: theory and practice* (pp. 200 – 209). New York: Columbia University Press.

Cavanagh, J. (1998). *Delia Derbyshire: on our wavelength*, [first published in Boazine 7]. Retrieved from: http://www.delia-derbyshire.org/interview_boa.php

Chanan, M. (2007). *The politics of documentary*. London: The British Film Institute.

Connor, Simon. (2018). Auralising Action Space: channelling a sense of play in documentary sound design. In G. Cox & J. Corner (Eds.), *Soundings: documentary film and the listening experience* (pp. 85 – 105). Huddersfield: Huddersfield University Press.

Connor, Steven (2004). Edison's teeth: touching hearing. In V. Erlmann (Ed.), *Hearing cultures* (pp. 153 – 172). Oxford: Berg. Retrieved from http://voidnetwork.gr/wp-content/uploads/2016/09/Hearing-Cultures-Essays-on-Sound-Listening-and-Modernity-edited-by-Veit-Erlmann.pdf

Corner, J. (2003). Television, documentary and the category of the aesthetic, *Screen* 44 (1), 92 – 100.

Grierson, J. (1930, January 13). On the talkie horizon. *The Clarion*, p. 13.

Grierson, J. (1931, December). Russia's latest. *The Clarion*, p. 349.

Grierson, J. (1934). Introduction to a new art, *Sight and Sound* 3 (11), 101 – 104.

Iversen, G. & Simonsen, J. K. (Eds.). (2010). *Beyond the visual: sounds and image in ethnographic and documentary film*. Højbjerg: Intervention Press.

Kulezic-Wilson, D. (2015). *The musicality of narrative film*. Basingstoke: Palgrave Macmillan.

Leimbacher, I. (2017). Hearing voice(s): experiments with documentary listening, *Discourse* 39 (3), 292 – 318. DOI: 10.13110/discourse.39.3.0292

Nagib, L. and Mello, C. (2009). Introduction. In L. Nagib & L. Mello, Cecilia (Eds.), *Realism and the audiovisual media* (pp. xiv-xxvi). Basingstoke: Palgrave Macmillan.

Nichols, B. (1983). The voice of documentary, *Film Quarterly* 36 (3), 17 – 30.

Rangan, P. (2017). Audibilities: voice and listening in the penumbra of documentary: an introduction, *Discourse 39* (3), 279 – 291. DOI: 10.13110/discourse.39.3.0279

Rogers, H. (2015). Introduction: music, sound and the non-fiction aesthetic. In H. Rogers (Ed.), *Music and sound in documentary film* (pp. 1 – 19). Abingdon: Routledge.

Ruby, J. (2005). The image mirrored: reflexivity and the documentary film. In J. Corner & A. Rosenthal (Eds.), *New challenges for documentary* (pp. 34 – 47). Manchester: Manchester University Press.

Sussex, E. (1969). *Lindsay Anderson*. London: Studio Vista.

Vaughan, D. (1999). *For documentary*. Berkley: University of California Press.

Wright, A. (1974, August 26). Wanted: an embargo on film wordiness. [Review of Scotland on Screen event in unknown newspaper], n.p. University of Stirling: Forsyth Hardy Archive (H2.4).

Part 1:
The Promotional Imagination

Stories from a stay at the *Arena* Hotel

Will L Finch

I am grateful to Dr Guido Heldt for his help in improving this manuscript and to Dr Geoffrey Cox for his keen insight in editing the chapter. Thanks are also due to audiences at The Sound of Memory Symposium (London, 2017) and Music for Audio-Visual Media II conference (Leeds, 2016) for their questions and comments on early drafts of this research.

The BBC's arts and culture documentary series, Arena (1975 – present), has produced over 600 television documentaries on a diverse range of subjects. While prizing investigative and artistic rigour, Arena allows directors experimental approaches to subjects 'insignificant' and 'worthy', 'low' and 'high'. It is an approach earning Arena the descriptions: 'a maverick outfit' (Born, 2004, p. 97); a 'Panorama for the arts' (Seaton, 2015, p. 92); and 'our best arts programme' (Rees, 2016). Many of Arena's films do not give the didactic experience one might expect from public service documentaries, rather they provide cultural encounters that Arena's creators consider 'valid in their own right' (Walker, 1993, p. 108). Arena's documentaries vary in length and time slot and form a nexus of myriad directors, creative contributors, documentary styles, and subjects. Arena's audio profile is also diverse, using 'live', pre–existing, and specially commissioned music.

In 2012, Arena launched an online project, the Arena Hotel, hosted at: www.arenahotel.tv.[1] The Arena Hotel is an archive-cum-exhibition website using the ideas and features of a hotel to organise and present material pertaining to Arena. Rooms in the Hotel are linked web pages accessible via the 'lift'. In the rooms, visitors watch short (1 – 6 minutes), re-edited excerpts of Arena's documentaries that offer snapshots of several of Arena's subjects (see Table 1 for a full list). The simultaneous residency of these subjects makes the Hotel's position in time and space ambiguous. The Hotel is a concurrence of people and stories drawn from any *time* from the mid-twentieth century to 2012, and from any*where* within a broadly Anglo-American cultural sphere. This ambiguity enables Arena's films and the subjects they mediate to interact in the Hotel's simulated rooms and corridors.

Floor	Room	Artefact/object	Subject(s) of Film	Description of Subject
		Superman silhouette	Larry Niven	American science fiction writer
7	Rooftop	Kerouac's On the Road	William Burroughs	American writer
		Sign: 'Pool Closed: Positively No Swimming'	Pete Doherty	British musician
		Menu card	Andy Warhol (and W. Burroughs)	American artist
6	Restaurant	Trilby hat	Galton And Simpson	English comedy script writers
		Orange cricket	Cricket Bisque	Soup served in a dog bowl
		Crime scene	James Ellroy	American crime writer

5	Chapel	Stained-glass window	Amy Winehouse	British soul/jazz musician
		Sign: church services and information	Rev. Gary Howington	American evangelist
		Silhouette of a nun	Sister Wendy Beckett	British nun and art historian
4	Tea Room	Margaret Thatcher bust	Luck and Low	Creators of 'Spitting Image'
		Tea cup	Francis Bacon	British-Irish artist
		Round sunglasses	Ozzy Osbourne	British heavy metal musician
3	Health and Beauty Spa	Mirror/portrait of Ekberg	Anita Ekberg	Swedish actress/model
		Pair of trainers	Robert Crumb	American cartoonist/musician
		Inflatable pool chair	Luciano Pavarotti	Italian opera singer
2	Ballroom	Statue of George Formby	George Formby	The George Formby Society
		Leather jacket	Dancing in Texas	Country music and dance
		Sign: 'Robben Island Dancing Lessons'	Robben Island	Dancing in the South African prison
G	Lobby	Flat screen TV	*Arena* Hotel	Hotel's welcome video
		Stuffed panda head	Chi Chi	London Zoo's giant panda
		Portrait of Peel	John Peel	British radio DJ
		Portrait of Mandela	Nelson Mandela*	South African politician
		Portrait of Warhol	Chelsea Hotel*	Infamous New York hotel
		Portrait of Jesus	American South*	Country music and Christianity in America
		Photograph of Guthrie	Woody Guthrie*	American folk musician
-1	Bar	Neon Sign: 'Cocktails'	Luis Buñuel	Spanish filmmaker
		Photograph of Venables	Terry Venables	British footballer
		Cowboy hat	Kinky Friedman	American country singer
-2	Kitchen	Dinner trolley	Mary Langston	Elvis Presley's cook
		Meat and Yorkshire puddings	*Spitting Image*	British satirical puppet show
		Sign: 'Now wash your hands please'	Louise Bourgeois	French-American artist
-3	Nightclub	Guitar case	The Other Jimi Hendrix	Hendrix cover act
		Microphone stand and military jacket	Pete Doherty and Poly Styrene	Rock musicians
		Poster: Nigel Finch's film *Stonewall* (1995)	The Disappointer Sisters	Cabaret drag performers

Table 1: Contents of The *Arena* Hotel. * Takes visitors to external web page.

Arena's longstanding editor/director Anthony Wall has written a blog article titled 'Archive: Past, present, future' (2014). The article considers how *Arena's* film archive has been reused by *Arena* and introduces the Hotel as such a use. The Hotel is part of a complex non-linear flow between documentary films and archives. In one direction, archive footage moves into documentaries to serve myriad functions, the most prominent being as a primary source that supplies films with certain kinds of 'authority' (Kepley & Swender, 2009). In the other direction, documentary films are found in digital and analogue archives where they are open to interpretation as 'objective' evidence, indexical objects and personal mementos (Baron, 2014, pp. 2 – 4). Documentary practice is both *in* and *of* the archive. This deep-rooted movement shapes, and is shaped by, the *Arena* Hotel; it is central to the Hotel's genesis and to the way this chapter addresses the possible significance the Hotel holds for its creators, 'guests' and visitors.

This chapter comprises four sections. It begins with an account of how the Hotel operates and exposes the important position music is given within the hotel. Attention is drawn to how figurative gaps between subjects and films in the Hotel are blurred by the Hotel's use of sound and by its visual presentation. A second section gives two examples of this blurring in action and draws particular attention to two explicitly musical spaces within the Hotel. The third section frames the Hotel within the discourse of the so called 'archival turn' which was identified throughout the humanities during the late-twentieth-century (Simon, 2002). The final section draws these elements together to discuss how, by encouraging visitors to investigate gaps between *Arena's* archival materials through the use of sound and music, the Hotel acts as a (web)site of 'mediated memories' (van Dijck, 2007). In the Hotel, I argue, visitors can imagine the exhibition/archive space as, following Doreen Massey (2005), a simultaneity of stories. The encouragement and creation of these stories indicates a nostalgic desire to encounter the past, whilst understanding such a past is lost or never existed (Boym, 2001, p. 21). The music found within the Hotel acts both as a tool by which these feelings are conjured, and often as the documentary subject that focuses the Hotel's retrospective project.

But first, two caveats: my doctoral research explores *Arena's* wider relationship with music — how *Arena* constructs ideas about music, and what uses the series makes of music. This chapter, though, examines the *Arena* Hotel. It does not consider the Hotel in isolation, but it does so without extensive reference to *Arena's* televisual output. Similarly, although all films housed within the Hotel form part of my argument, this chapter limits its scope to a small number of examples. The selected films are identified both as examples of the Hotel's general approach and also as key films that focus the argument and best expose music and sound's roles within the Hotel.

An Audiovisual Guide to the *Arena* Hotel

Looking at the Hotel

The *Arena* Hotel is a series of highly stylised interactive photomontages. Its collage-like style gives the Hotel an appearance akin to British artist Richard Hamilton's iconic work, *Just what is it that makes today's homes so different, so appealing?* (1956). Considered as a catalytic work of the British Pop Art movement, Hamilton's is 'one of the most celebrated images in twentieth-century British art' (Stonard, 2007, p. 607). Hamilton's collage, as with the wider Pop Art movement, exposes a fascination (often ironic) with the objects and symbolism of popular culture, especially American popular culture (Ruhrberg, 2000, p. 303). For Karl Ruhrberg, *Just what is it* reveals the 'intelligence and sophistication of a composition rife with allusions and ambiguities' (2000, p. 303). Although not acknowledged as an influence on the Hotel's design, the debt to collages like Hamilton's is plain. By 2012, Hamilton's collage had become a well-known classic of British art and a cornerstone in the tradition of a 'high-art' take on popular culture. Considering Hamilton's work, (and similar works), as a point of reference for *Arena's* Hotel, positions it within the same venerable traditions. As well as the Hotel's use of a similar 'cut-and-paste' style, its allusion to Pop Art aesthetics points to comparable referential themes between Hamilton's collage and *Arena's* Hotel. *Arena's* wider project is also prompted by a fascination with popular culture, an area 'no [television] series before *Arena* entered with such energy and panache' (Wyver, 2007, p. 58). Popular culture offered fertile material for creating those documentaries for which *Arena* became famous. John Wyver described *Arena's* most celebrated films from the 1980s as 'irreverent, imaginative films colliding great characters with submerged skeins of cultural theory, boundless curiosity with a delight in every kind of surprise' (2007, p. 58). The films Wyver considers as contributing to this description occupy important places in the Hotel and the history of British television documentary e.g. *My Way* (1979), *Chelsea Hotel* (1981), and *The Life and Times of Don Luis Buñuel* (1984).

The films within the Hotel are housed in one of ten rooms. Visitors arriving in the lobby must enter the lift where buttons indicate the accessible rooms. Each room is framed by the lift's interior and a sign indicating the current floor; moving a mouse around the room causes the image to scroll left and right behind the static doors, giving the

Figure 1: The *Arena* Hotel's 'Tea Room'. Screenshot from <www.arenahotel.tv/floors/tea-room>. Reproduced with permission from BBC *Arena*.

impression of a three-dimensional space, much like a box diorama. The Hotel comprises an enviable number of amenities (see Table 1). Looking at these rooms, visitors find a straightforward treasure hunt (see Figure 1). Three or more glowing objects within a room can be clicked on to show short films from *Arena*'s archive.[2] The glowing objects — a guitar case, a pair of sunglasses, and a sign reading 'Now wash your hands please' — are artefacts relating to the films. Sometimes they offer simple associations. For example, a bust of *Spitting Image*'s Margaret Thatcher reveals the caption, 'Spitting Image' and a clip from *Arena*'s 1980 film *Luck and Flaw*, which profiles the show's creators.[3] The association of other objects is initially less clear. A large inflatable armchair floating in a swimming-pool takes visitors to footage of Pavarotti in the pool of his summer residence. In the Hotel's restaurant, a menu stand is captioned 'Andy Warhol'. Clicking on it begins a clip from *Arena*'s iconic film *Chelsea Hotel* (1981) in which Andy Warhol and William Burroughs sit at dinner discussing chicken fried steak.

As these brief examples show, the Hotel's rooms are, in the same way as Hamilton's collage *Just what is it,* littered with allusions and ambiguities. Visitors to the Hotel must 'decode' these objects and discover or imagine their meaning. At first visitors identify clickable objects which are marked by a subtle glow, and sometimes by a certain incongruity, the Hotel's restaurant contains a crime scene with the chalk outline of a body, for example. Once identified, objects can be hovered over to reveal a caption, in this case, 'James Ellroy'. This action also displays a small description in the lift's scrolling floor sign. For Ellroy's film this is 'Fine dining and murder.' Clicking on the murder scene, visitors join Ellroy and the L.A. Sheriff Department's homicide detectives for dinner. As the film begins, captions inform visitors about what is taking place, though limited meta-data or contextual information is provided. By making visitors investigate the 'cut-and-pasted' objects in such a way, Arena relies on visitors' critical engagement to explore and enjoy the archive. Withholding most of the expository information about each film until visitors have watched the first few seconds (11 seconds in the Ellroy film) forces visitors to construct meaning about what they are experiencing. In addition to meanings generated by the film itself, understanding also develops with regard to a visitor's initial reaction to the Hotel at large, the appearance of each individual room and the objects within them. This process blurs the gaps between films in each room and in the Hotel. Thus, it seems possible James Ellroy, the homicide detectives, William Burroughs and Andy Warhol, though not at the same table, simultaneously occupy the same virtual restaurant.

Listening to the Hotel
Paul Long has demonstrated that popular music lends itself readily to curatorial and archival practices in part because of its symbiotic relationship with the audiovisual technologies that 'capture it' (2015, p. 67). It is perhaps not surprising then that around 50% of films in the *Arena* Hotel engage with music, mostly popular music, as a documentary subject. Given the breadth of *Arena's* televisual output, of which less than 30% concerns music directly, it appears that the Hotel gives particular attention to music as a subject. It is notable, for instance, that whilst most rooms are expected parts of a Hotel, two of the more unusual rooms, the chapel and the nightclub, are reserved almost completely for films with music as one of their main subjects. Therefore, parts of the Hotel were probably created with music especially in mind. My primary interest in listening to the Hotel, however, is not the music in its films, but the Hotel's soundscape.

Sound within the *Arena* Hotel can be classified using the categories of video-game sound introduced by Mark Grimshaw (2007). At times sound takes the form of kinediegetic sound heard in response to a visitor's actions; sometimes exodiegetic sound, heard regardless of a visitor's actions, is used (Grimshaw, 2007, p. 227). For example, visitors are greeted in the lobby by concierge Noël Coward saying, 'Hello, how are you dear? Et cetera, et cetera' (exodiegetic). If visitors click on the reception desk's bell, a 'ding' is heard and Coward is likely to make another droll remark (kinediegetic). A range of atmospheric and location sounds accompany this welcome, including ringing phones, chiming lifts, muffled chatter, and street noise. Travelling to a chosen room requires pushing a lift button, waiting as the lift travels to the room (complete with appropriate sounds and synchronised audiovisual jolts) before the doors open. A layered stereo soundscape throughout the Hotel compounds its collage effect, drawing the visitor's attention to, for example, Gregorian chant, whispers, closing doors and footsteps in the Hotel's chapel. The materials and size of each room — in this case, vaulted ceilings and stone walls — are indicated by the quality and level of reverberation in the ambient soundscape. Within this, sounds are panned between channels to give further indication of the physical space and the impression that visitors occupy a particular spatial zone of audition (Chion, 1994, p. 89).

This sound design is undoubtedly intended to engender a feeling of presence within the Hotel. How we should understand and conceptualise sound's role in creating a feeling of immersion, presence or incorporation within a virtual-world is a fraught issue (Calleja, 2014). As Mark Grimshaw and Tom Garner explore, prevailing understandings suggest that such a feeling is 'technologically deterministic and directly related to the degree of simulation of reality provided by the technology' (2015, p. 7). Conversely, the authors argue, the extent to which a sense of presence is felt does not rely on technology's ability to produce stimuli that simulate reality. Rather it is simulation of the specific context of the virtual world that enables the immersive effects of music and sound (Grimshaw & Garner, 2015, p. 7). In *Arena's* Hotel, this seems to be the case. The context of the Hotel is an exaggerated, tongue-in-cheek world prompted by a fascination with the strangeness, humour, and ambiguity of culture, popular or otherwise. Whilst the Hotel's sounds position visitors spatially, they also act as part of the Hotel's Pop Art collage juxtaposing and exaggerating the everyday and the extraordinary. They position visitors in a symbolic zone of audition wherein sounds convey contextual information pertaining to the social function of the space as well as information about an extraordinary function of the space, to bring together an unbelievable and impossible group of people.

For example, although Gregorian chant is a suitable and reverent choice to accompany a chapel, hearing it with the image of a chapel only does so much to incorporate visitors within the space. Coupled with sounds of incessant shuffling, the image of Amy Winehouse in stained glass, and pink striped wallpaper above Gothic arches, the chant signifies the Hotel's stylised context. For visitors who recognise the chant, the 'strangeness' of the situation is only heightened; it is the sombre plainchant of the Dies Iræ, oft quoted in requiems and other works of great tumult or intensity (Gregory, 1953). Thus, the Hotel's soundworld offers visitors a feeling of incorporation into the Hotel's strange, fictional space. This sonic design, which follows visitors throughout the Hotel, concerns not only the visitor's enjoyment of the Hotel but also *Arena's* encouragement of visitors to explore its archive materials in a particular way. The attempt to include visitors within the Hotel via contextually realistic sound enables the Hotel's discontinuous elements — its short, seemingly unrelated film clips — to be conceived of by visitors as part of the same world, and thus to explore them with this referential frame in mind. Situating visitors and guests in the Hotel together blurs the gaps between the films presented. In doing so, the Hotel encourages the film's subjects, and the moments their films capture, to interact in the imagination of visitors.

Examples from the Chapel and Nightclub

This section explores two instances of this blurring of gaps between the films. The first instance gives an account of the possible gaps between the films housed in the chapel.

Film 1) Amy Winehouse performs in an Irish church. Her performance is intercut with footage of two interviews. In Winehouse's interview she discusses her musical influences and dwells upon Gospel singer Mahalia Jackson. Reverend Máirt Hanley's interview explores performances in his church as acts of worship (04:56).

Film 2) In Louisiana, Reverend Howington gives an evangelical sermon that includes his performance of country music during which the congregation clap, dance and appear to experience involuntary movements. An interview explores drug abuse in Howington's life and his playing/feeling of the blues (02:07).

Film 3) Sister Wendy Beckett goes about and talks about her solitary worship and wider beliefs. A narrator gives information about Beckett's life, and for 51 seconds of the film Gavin Bryars' arrangement, *Jesus' Blood Never Failed Me Yet* (1972), of an unknown homeless man's song underscores the footage, narration, and off-screen interview. Later, a choir begins their service in song (02:00). As with other films in the

Hotel, the gaps between these three films are drawn into the visitor's mind by the function of the room in which they are housed. In this case, religion acts as a referential frame for interpreting the films. Someone's attention might be drawn to the disparity between Beckett's solitary worship and Howington's tumultuous exclamations: 'We're not crazy!' Others might consider the films' varied depiction of religious spaces or types of congregation. Others still would identify the relationship between religious worship and musical practice as a key theme for the consideration of these films. As Winehouse makes clear: 'I'm not religious, but there's nothing more . . . pure than the relationship you have with God . . . apart from your love of music' (01:58). The films prompt similar themes in their own right of course, but juxtaposed in the chapel, each story is contextualised by the others. The different approaches to religion, and musical worship in particular, are brought into proximity in a way they are not when seen only as disparate parts of the *Arena* archive. The gaps between the films — from drug addict to evangelical country musician, and non-religious singer to an early death blighted by substance abuse — are blurred, increasing the potential for the Hotel's stories to interact as part of a multiplicity of stories seldom observed outside the virtual Hotel. In the above example, *Arena* prompts visitors to identify the similarities and differences in the stories, to make new and unlikely connections between the histories and lived experiences the films' mediate, and to acknowledge the wider context in which the stories were found.

There is one instance in the Hotel where stories are not so much encouraged into juxtaposition but forced. Although this is not the norm for the Hotel, I explore this second instance because, by Wall's admission, it is a concrete example of how he wanted the Hotel to operate: it 'encapsulates what I'm trying to get at', which is to 'reveal other meanings in [the] archive which could render it dynamic and creative in a way that suggests the future as much as the past' (Wall, 2014). In the Hotel's nightclub, a red military jacket hangs on a microphone stand. The image is captioned 'Poly Styrene and Pete Doherty'. Clicking on it takes visitors to what appears to be a performance of 'Albion' by Babyshambles. As their performance comes to an end however, footage turns to the outside of a club where another band enters the venue to the final few bars of 'Albion'. The new band takes the stage and performs Styrene's song, 'Art-I-Ficial'. It is an invented gig, but one partially successful in creating a club where Babyshambles, fronted by Doherty, and Styrene and her X-Ray Specs are forced to share a stage and interact across the decades.

It is the soundtrack that allows us to suspend our disbelief for a moment. Babyshambles finishing their song as Poly Styrene and her band arrive at the club helps us to make the journey in time despite changes in video quality and format. It is only when they enter the stage, or when on-screen captions give the game away completely, that we fully realise we are not where, or when, we were before. In this nightclub, meanings within Doherty and Styrene's songs are afforded added significance by their juxtaposition. Lyrically both present allegorical visions of society; Doherty's is a fable of Britain, filled with 'violence in dole queues' and 'gin in teacups', while Styrene protests 'the way a girl should be' in a 'consumer society'. The anti-idealistic, anti-consumerist and anti-authoritarian ideologies the artists present are reinforced by the presence of each other. Musically, Doherty's more melodically orientated indie-punk preceding Styrene's brash, fast-paced new-wave/punk-rock contextualises the artists and the roots and branches of punk's musical aesthetics.

It is not only the artists' *Arena* wants to bring together. 60% of the film is footage of the audience and our attention is drawn to what Styrene later in the film calls the 'hysterical' communities for whom this imagined gig is real. Shots of the audience are similar to the point where we might not be sure if one of Styrene's punks was actually one of Doherty's post-punk revivalists. The ambiguity of the audience's situation makes the existence of the impossible gig more believable; it also brings citizens of Doherty's Albion and Styrene's consumer society together to share the memory of the same 'gig' and a similar British society. The Hotel acts as a venue for this impossible interaction allowing music, musicians and musical communities to realise insights into their shared musical cultures.

This clip is an exaggerated example, but *Arena* employs music and sound throughout the Hotel to construct and organise its virtual world and to endow its fictional world with the hallmarks of a strange 'reality'. It is this ambiguity, resulting also from limited expository information, that helps present the gaps between the archive's materials as part of the archive itself. Rather than drawing attention to their separateness, the Hotel blurs gaps between the archive's materials. Thus, these gaps demand we consider objects on either side not as discrete objects but as ones in communication — a communication that can point to their differences and similarities. Visitors are encouraged to look for reasons as to why clips are presented together and to form stories that exist within the Hotel's fictional space and the real world. These gaps, and the narratives that occupy them, lead to the third section about the Hotel's relationship with the archive.

Secondary Narratives and the Archival Turn

The Curatorial Process

During visits to the Hotel I was surprised that *Arena* had not chosen to use an existing website already suited for the presentation of archival audiovisual material. A gallery's website or a social media site such as YouTube would offer advantages in terms of access, impact, and user discourse. Indeed, the Hotel's interactive elements feel limited by 2012's standards; visitors are able to pause films but not to jump between parts, for example. Nevertheless, the stylised world of the Hotel ties it to *Arena's* 'off-beat' brand. By avoiding platforms such as YouTube, *Arena* is able to control the space surrounding its films. In this way, *Arena's* Hotel follows the now highly problematised 'shift away from curating as an administrative, caring, mediating activity toward that of curating as a creative activity more akin to a form of artistic practice' (O'Neill, 2007, p. 22). This shift in curatorial practice began in the 1960s following attempts to demystify the art world and 'make visible the mediating component within the formation, production and dissemination of an exhibition' (O'Neill, 2007, p. 13). The Hotel's presentation of *Arena's* archive material is a purposive and artistic act of curation (Farquharson, 2003) that encourages visitors to explore its materials as something more than a series of independent, discontinuous elements; it is firmly concerned with the presentational function of the space. Encouraging a sense of incorporation for visitors establishes not only the sense of contextual realism that allows such exploration but also the visitor's importance to the construction of meaning about gaps between the Hotel's materials. Nevertheless, the *Arena* Hotel appears to engage in, at least partially, the opposite of the shift Paul O'Neill describes. Not wanting to delineate each film by providing metadata and other 'objective' information, the subjective acts of selection, editing, production and other curatorial processes are hidden. Although the Hotel serves as an exhibition of *Arena's* films, curatorial practices are only one side of the coin. The other side, archival practice, traditionally subordinated presentational functions to focus on the preservation and accessibility of material. Although the Hotel too subordinates the supposed 'objectivity' of the archive in favour of highly stylised presentational modes, archival practice is nevertheless important to an understanding of the significance the Hotel holds. To consider this aspect of the Hotel, I return to the film of Warhol and Burroughs.

In between footage of Warhol and Burrough's dinner, a guide takes a group around the real Chelsea Hotel in New York. Stopping outside the rooms Warhol and Burroughs stayed in, the tour guide evokes the Hotel's Bohemian mystique as a haunt of vanguard actors, writers, musicians and artists. It is not difficult to identify an inspiration for the

Arena Hotel's tag line: a rest stop for rare individuals. Indeed, as Wall recalls, the Hotel was based 'on the lobby of the Chelsea Hotel mixed with the back lifts of [BBC] Broadcasting House' (2014). I argue that a hotel serves as a uniquely suitable template for *Arena's* idiosyncratic exploration of its archive for several interconnected reasons.

Firstly, the Chelsea Hotel built a reputation as the semi-permanent residence of influential, famous, and eccentric figures of the twentieth-century cultural milieu who lived, died and conducted their personal and professional lives within its walls. *Arena's* archive, full of similar characters and stories, finds a felicitous association with the Chelsea Hotel's reputation and visitor book.

Secondly, the film *Chelsea Hotel*, through which *Arena* also became part of the Hotel's story by documenting and further mythologizing it, remains one of *Arena's* most well-known and acclaimed films. The film is cited as such in newspaper articles remarking on *Arena's* earlier years (e.g. Grant, 1988; Selway, 1981) and is repeated more often than the majority of *Arena's* other programmes, at least six times since 2000. It was described in 1982 as 'the best repeat of the week, compulsory if you missed it first time' (Fiddick 1982, p. 18), and 'fascinating' in a 2001 re-run (Mulvihill, 2001, p. 60). The film, and its reputation, are key parts in the cultivation of *Arena* as 'off-beat' (Selway, 1982, p. 48) but, 'vastly enjoyable' (Davalle, 1982, p. XVI).

Thirdly, Wall identifies the comedy value of hotel culture as a reason for *Arena's* choice of a hotel, stating 'everything about hotel culture is intrinsically funny' (2014). Though Wall makes no indication of what form this comedy takes, it is no doubt bolstered by the tropes of British hospitality comedies found in *Fawlty Towers* (1975 and 1979), *Carry on Abroad* (1972), and *Are You Being Served?* (1961 – 1970). The latter is not set in a hotel of course but is nevertheless an important hospitality comedy that continues many of the tropes found in the other examples e.g. style of humour, depiction of patrons, inter-staff relationships, and physical settings. This camp ironic tone resonates with the style for which *Arena* became renowned. The *Arena* Hotel is thus presented as an object that delights in, and artistically meditates, the funny and extraordinary nature of culture.

Though these reasons are important in understanding why *Arena* chose a hotel to re-present its archive, I suggest that a fourth reason is a principal factor in an examination of the Hotel and its relation to archival practice. This posits the Hotel, on the one hand, as an institutionalised space with well-known physical arrangements and expected behaviours. On the other hand, as with many real hotels (e.g. The Chelsea Hotel) and fictional hotels (e.g. *Fawlty Towers*), what happens in the Hotel is often considered as something outside everyday experience. In Wall's terms, using a hotel's blueprint 'was a way of randomising the archive but with a kind of acute organising principle' (2014). Hotels of this kind are known structures that are recognised as liminal spaces between public and private, banality and absurdity. The sonic experience of such a hotel is also layered with competing sounds and enforced silences made by the hotel's material features (a reception bell or a Do Not Disturb sign) and by those who inhabit the hotel. As suggested above, *Arena* apes this sonic world as a way to establish its fictional space and engender feelings of presence for the visitor. *Arena's* use of the audible features of a hotel also compounds the notion of the Hotel as a space between the expected and unexpected (a quiet chapel in which Gregorian chant and Amy Winehouse might both be heard, or a restaurant where clinking plates accompany a discussion of a homicide investigation, for example). Thus, these spatial, social, and sonic blueprints are presented in the Hotel as means to establish the *Arena* archive as part of an ill-defined 'third space' or 'third place', (evoking Bhabha (1994) and Oldenburg (1989) respectively), in which interactions occur between two or more cultures and between the private and professional. This contributes to the expansion of *Arena's* archive from a fixed series of objects to a nebula of stories of, and about, culture.

The Hotel as Archive

A central theme of Wall's article on *Arena's* archive is the changing nature of archives. For Wall, the changing meaning of archives has 'turned into every kid with a mobile phone constantly recording experiences to such an extent that you can't be clear exactly what archive [sic] is anymore' (2014). Wall conceived of the Hotel partly in response to this incorporation of the archival into the everyday. Jussi Parikka used the phrase 'information management society' to encapsulate this trend (2013, pp. 1 – 2). Technologically developed communities now 'archive' emails, tag digital galleries and rely on archival metaphors and processes to curate lived experience. The proliferation of digital technology has brought a challenge to previous conceptions of the archive as a concrete, institutionalised place of preservation — a place offering privileged access to authoritative texts, which occupies figurative spaces between knowledge and power, memory and truth and real spaces in the basements and backrooms of establishments. It is a challenge that continues to provoke post-modern ontological discussions of the archive, what has been termed the 'archival turn'. The turn problematized the archive's status in the light of changing socio-cultural conditions including the proliferation of visual and digital cultures, contemporary forms of nostalgia, and postmodern anxieties over time-space compression (Simon, 2002, p. 102; see also Cook, 2012). The archival turn reconsidered the archive's physical and privileged requirements and was driven by the work of critical theorists, especially Foucault (2012 [1969]), Benjamin (1968. [1939]) and Derrida (1998). Foucault and Benjamin's work reimagined the archive 'as a site of cultural power and social transformation, but one which is nonetheless abstract: an imaginary terminus wherein cultural expressions find meaning through contingencies, in allegorical associations and discursive formations' (Simon, 2002, p. 104). Later, in his famous work, *Mal d'Archive*, Derrida's psychoanalytic account (Steedman, 2001) of our preoccupation with archives drew attention to the nostalgic desires that drive and are driven by archival practice (Derrida, 1998, p. 91).

In many ways, the Hotel retains some of the principles of the 'modernist' archive: it has limitations to its access and how visitors may view material. Fashioning the website around the organising principles of a hotel certainly resonates with conceptions of the archive as a place with expected physical and social boundaries. Nevertheless, the *Arena* Hotel follows the archival turn. It takes the form of an imaginary space; it is certainly virtual and the rooms within it present imagined situations. The Hotel also undermines some sense of textual authority by chopping and re-cutting *Arena*'s footage and presenting it in new contexts. The Hotel necessitates a contingent experience of its materials and encourages visitors to engage with possible allegorical associations (as with Doherty and Styrene) discovered in the space between its clips. Wolfgang Ernst, argues 'the archive does not tell stories; only secondary narratives give meaningful coherence to its discontinuous elements' (2004, p. 3). He continues, 'there is no necessary coherent connection between archival data and documents, but rather gaps in between: holes and silence' (2004, p. 3). It is these gaps that *Arena's* Hotel attempts to draw into our consideration of the archive's materials. Through its ambiguity of presentation and immersive experience, both of which are enabled and intensified by the use of music and sound, the Hotel encourages the discovery of secondary narratives between clips and between the cultural formations documented by *Arena*. To conclude, I consider what purpose these secondary narratives might serve.

Cultural stories

Cultural memory has a complex theoretical history; it can be seen on the one hand as the practice of groups that construct versions of the past to document and recall national, institutional, or family histories (Erll, 2008, p. 5). On the other hand, cultural memory points to the neuropsychological act of an individual mind influenced by socio-cultural frameworks. The *Arena* Hotel engages with both interconnected meanings. The Hotel is built by the purposive selection of an institution (*Arena*) to create and present histories about *Arena* and certain parts of culture. At the same time, it relies on the particular experience of the individual to interpret this 'history' and owes its creation to nostalgic desires to experience the past in the full knowledge that such a past is lost or invented, what Svetlana Boym calls 'reflective nostalgia' (2001, p. 21). The role of music is paramount to the nostalgic desire the Hotel relies on and drives. Music, and popular music in particular, is recognised as sharing a complex and powerful relationship with nostalgic modes (for a summary see Dauncey and Tinker, 2017). Indeed, music serves in the Hotel as the means by which and about which the visitor's retrospective activity is often focused.

Following theories that consider cultural memory as inseparable from networks of mediated experience, Ann Rigney foregrounds new media technologies 'as an integral factor in the production of cultural memory today' (2016, p. 15). Such media, or technologies of memory (Plate and Smelik, 2009), 'operate within various symbolic systems' and 'broaden the temporal and spatial range of remembrance' (Erll, 2008, p. 12). Van Dijck takes this further to argue for 'the mutual shaping of human cognitive memory and media technologies in everyday cultural contexts' (2007, p. 150).

The memory practices and technologies conditioning Anglo-American understandings and enjoyment of the past have undergone great change as part of the so-called 'time-space compression' wherein the geographical and temporal gaps between communities and cultures become blurred as technologies speed up and disperse how and what we experience (Massey, 1994, p. 146). These changes resonate with new conceptions of 'space' as a product of global and local interrelations: a sphere, 'always under construction', 'in which distinct trajectories coexist' (Massey, 2005, p. 9). In the light of these conditions, Massey reimagines the notion of 'space' as a 'simultaneity of stories-so-far' (2005, p. 9). The *Arena* Hotel is such a space, created in response to the same conditions. The Hotel spatializes *Arena*'s archive and allows it to draw upon an extraordinary referential frame, which simultaneously includes the global and local; the past, present and future — a coexistence of mutable histories. *Arena*'s Hotel artistically encourages users to create alternative stories which provide added or meaningful significance to the Hotel's materials. These stories are generated within the gaps between films. Music and sound are employed as subjects and tools used to aid visitors' engagement with these gaps. Music affords the Hotel the means by which, and often about which, simultaneous stories surrounding cultural meaning and shared memories might be experienced, remembered or imagined.

Endnotes

1. The *Arena* Hotel is a collaboration between *Arena* director/editor Anthony Wall, Emma Matthews and several other *Arena* associates, Tony Ageh and Bill Thompson of the BBC, and The Space. The Space (funded by the Arts Council) supports online platforms for art. The Hotel's Software was designed by Klik. The original intention was to expand and update the materials housed in the Hotel. Apart from some minor additions and changes, this has not been carried out.

2. Although without the same goal-oriented function, the Hotel is similar to a 'point-and-click' adventure or treasure hunt video game, some of which are themselves indebted to twentieth-century collage techniques (Janik, 2015).

3. In 1992, Hamilton reworked his original 1956 collage. The remake was prompted by an invitation from the documentary series *Q.E.D.* to explore computer generated art. Hamilton produced the work digitally and included a bust of Thatcher (Manchester, 2007).

Bibliography

Baron, J. M. (2014). *The archive effect: found footage and the audiovisual experience of history*. Abingdon; New York: Routledge.

Benjamin, W. (1968). The Work Art in the Age of Mechanical Reproduction. In H. Arendt (Ed.), *Illuminations* (pp. 217 – 252). New York: Schocken Books.

Bhabha, H. K. (1994). *The location of culture*. London. New York: Routledge.

Born, G. (2004). *Uncertain vision: Birt, Dyke and the reinvention of the BBC*. London: Secker & Warburg.

Boym, S. (2001). *The future of nostalgia*. New York: Basic Books.

Calleja, G. (2014). Immersion in virtual worlds. in M. Grimshaw (Ed.), *The Oxford handbook of virtuality* (pp. 222 – 234). New York: Oxford University Press.

Chion, M. (1994). *Audio-vision: sound on screen*. New York: Columbia University Press.

Cook, T. (2012). Evidence, memory, identity, and community: four shifting archival paradigms. *Archival Science, 13*(2 – 3), 95 – 120. DOI: 10.1007/s10502-012-9180-7

Dauncey, D and Tinker, C. (2017). Popular music nostalgia, *Volume!,11*(1), 1 – 10. Retrieved from: http://volume.revues.org/4202

Davalle, P. (1982 February 12 – 18). Television. *The Times Preview*, p. XVI.

Derrida, J., (1998). *Archive fever: a Freudian impression*. Chicago: University of Chicago Press.

Erll, A. (2008). Cultural memory studies: an introduction. In A. Erll & A. Nunning, (Eds.), *Cultural memory studies: an international and interdisciplinary handbook* (pp. 1 – 18). Berlin; New York: de Gruyter.

Ernst, W. (2004). The archive as metaphor. *Open,* 7/(No)Memory, 1 – 8. Retrieved from http://www.onlineopen.org/the-archive-as-metaphor

Fiddick, P. (1982, February 13). Television/Radio: Next Week. *The Guardian*, p. 18.

Foucault, M. (2012). *The archaeology of knowledge*. London; New York: Routledge.

Grant, L. (1988, November 24). Regrets, they've had but few. *The Guardian*, p. 25.

Gregory, R. (1953). Dies Irae. *Music and Letters, 32*(2), 133 – 139.

Grimshaw, M. (2007). The acoustic ecology of the first-person shooter (PhD Thesis). Retrieved from http://hdl.handle.net/10289/2653

Grimshaw, M., & Garner, T. (2015). *Sonic virtuality: sound as emergent perception*. New York: Oxford University Press.

Janik, J. (2015). The Cluster Worlds of Imagination: the analysis of collage technique in games by Amanita Design. In Bártek, T., Miškov, J., Švelch, J. (Eds.) *New Perspectives in Game Studies: Proceedings of the Central and Eastern European Game Studies Conference*, 45 – 54. (Brno: Masaryk University). Retrieved from http://gamestudies.cz/odborne/ceegs2014/

Kepley, V., & Swender, R. (2009). Claiming the found: archive footage and documentary practice. *The Velvet Light Trap*, 64(1), 3 – 10. doi: 10.1353/vlt.0.0037

Long, P. (2015). 'Really Saying Something?' What do we talk about popular music heritage, memory, archives and the digital? In Baker, S. (Ed.) *Preserving popular music heritage: Do-it-yourself, do-it-together* (pp. 62 – 76). New York; Abingdon, Routledge.

Manchester, E. (2007, June) Just what is it that makes today's homes so different? *Tate*. Retrieved from http://www.tate.org.uk/art/artworks/hamilton-just-what-is-it-that-makes-todays-homes-so-different-p11358

Massey, D. (1994). A global sense of place. In *Space, place, and gender* (pp. 146 – 156). Minneapolis: University of Minnesota Press.

Massey, D. (2005). *For space*. London: Sage.

Mulvihill, M. (2001, August 4). Satellite and digital TV Choice. *The Times*, p. 60.

Oldenburg, R. (1989) *The great good place*, Cambridge, MA: Da Capo Press.

O'Neill, P. (2007). The curatorial turn: from practice to discourse. In J. Rugg and M. Sedgwick (Eds.) *Issues in curating contemporary art and performance* (pp. 13 – 28). Bristol: Intellect Books.

Parikka, J. (2013). Archival media theory: an introduction to Wolfgang Ernst's media archaeology. In W. Ernst, *Digital memory and the archive* (pp. 1 – 22). Minneapolis: University of Minnesota Press.

Plate, L., & Smelik, A. (2009). *Technologies of memory in the arts*. New York: Palgrave Macmillan.

Rees, J. (2016 July 24). Arena: the 10 films that defined our best arts programme. *The Telegraph*. Retrieved from http://www.telegraph.co.uk/tv/2016/07/24/arena-the-10-films-that-defined-our-best-arts-programme

Rigney, A. (2005). Plenitude, scarcity and the Circulation of Cultural Memory. *Journal of European Studies, 35*(1), 11 – 28.

Ruhrberg, K. (2000). *Art of the 20th century: painting.* London: Taschen.

Seaton, J. (2015). *Pinkoes and traitors: The BBC and the nation, 1974 – 1987.* London: Profile Books.

Selway, J. (1981, November 1). High art, low art. *The Observer*, p. 60.

Selway, J. (1982, February 14). Week in View. *The Observer*, p. 48.

Simon, C. (2002). Introduction: following the archival turn. *Visual resources, 18*(2), 101 – 107. http://doi.org/10.1080/01973760290011770

Steedman, C. (2001). Something she called a fever: Michelet, Derrida, and dust. *The American Historical Review, 106*(4), pp. 1159 – 1180.

Stonard, J. (2007). Pop in the age of boom: Richard Hamilton's 'Just What Is It That Makes Today's Homes So Different, so Appealing?'. *The Burlington Magazine, 149* (1254), 607 – 620.

van Dijck, J. (2007). *Mediated memories in the digital age.* Stanford: Stanford University Press.

Walker, J.A. (1993). *Arts TV*, London: Libbey.

Wall, A. (2014, October 7). Archive: past, present, future. *Arena Gazette*. Retrieved from http://www.bbc.co.uk/blogs/arena/entries/df8f8cc3-1a0f-3a96-83e8-f1ed498c762e

Wyver, J. (2007). *Vision on: film, television and the arts in Britain.* London: Wallflower.

CHAPTER 2

Weave Me a Rainbow
'The march, the march of colour and pattern'
Music and cinematography at the service of the creative promotion of the 1960s Scottish woollen industry

Geoffrey Cox

I am deeply indebted to Dr Fiona Ann Jardine of the Glasgow School of Art for ideas and information about the relationship between the Scottish textile industry, *The Ambassador Magazine* and the industry's desire to present a progressive image. This material informs much of the chapter's arguments, providing a crucial cornerstone upon which the chapter is built. Dr Jardine also provided information about a variety of examples of the industry's progressive approach as well as suggestions about similar films to *Weave Me a Rainbow*.

I

'Britain — Nation of Conservative Adventurers'! So claimed the December 1959 issue of *The Ambassador Magazine*, a British export journal for textiles and fashions run by German émigré Hans Juda. The issue features a photograph of a dashing young male model wearing a tartan kilt in a rugged highland scene (Fig. 1) and typifies the ethos of the magazine described as both 'one of the most bravely conceived and strikingly designed trade magazines ever to be published' and one that 'understood that progress in Britain was rooted in a sense of appreciation for the past' (Breward, 2012, p. 15). *The Ambassador* combined an increased post-war British patriotic stance with the internationalism of the modernist inter-war project. It privileged a radical approach that embraced promotional *creativity* (p. 10) and encouraged an 'alliance between the arts and industry', actively encouraging the involvement of young musicians and artists (Stapleton, 2012, p. 18). Juda's editorial for a bumper 'Creative Britain' edition of November 1964 claimed 'the Arts are not luxuries . . . they are a tough living force in our world' (Breward, 2012, p. 12). This is represented in the magazine by the Bauhaus-influenced radical fashion photography of Juda's wife Elsbeth, further abstract photography of textile designs, and editorials as much concerned with discussing creative endeavour as sales. This mix was also reflected in promotional industrial *film* of the post-war period where the emphasis on aesthetically driven cinematography, elaborate lighting and tracking shots was enhanced, and often shaped, by the commissioning of substantial orchestral musical scores and poetic commentaries with literary ambitions. These so-called 'prestige' documentaries were the living embodiment of Juda's art-industry alliance: they were funded by commercial companies or trade bodies that bought into the idea that big budgets and a potentially radical creative freedom (but one that still acknowledged tradition and the need for clear promotional exposition) could enhance their standing and ultimately increase sales. Russell and Taylor sum up post-war documentary as an '*applied art*, whose big political idea was less to critique society from without than to aid its humane and effective functioning by illuminating the interconnections on which it is built from within' (2010, p. 5), a trope that sprang naturally from the social democratic consensus of the period. This overall approach of an accommodation between contemporary artistic practice and commerce, modernity and a rootedness in the past had an enormous influence on the British textile industry generally. Beyond magazines like *The Ambassador*, this approach can be seen in the likes of the semi-abstract designs of William Mitchell's 'The Story of Wool' sculptural mural (1968) for the UK headquarters of the International Wool Secretariat (IWS) in Ilkley, as well as in experimental prestige industrial documentaries such as *Weave Me a Rainbow* (McConnell, 1962), sponsored by the National Association of Scottish Woollen Manufacturers (NASWM) and the main subject of this chapter.

Figure 1: Elsbeth Juda's photograph from the December 1959 issue of *The Ambassador Magazine*. © Elsbeth Juda/Victoria and Albert Museum, London.

II

The British woollen textile industry was one that was all too aware of the importance of the export market. The wool industry was essentially a luxury one with bodies like the IWS being formed in 1937 in Australia to fight the growing global threat of artificial fibres, a threat even more pertinent by the early 1960s with the decline of wool manufacturing in Britain in the face of much cheaper imports generally. In Scotland, the NASWM, a promotional trade body formed in 1924, was as keen as any to show that the woollen trade could also be a modern and scientifically-based industry as much as one which produced nylon and polyester fibres. It therefore embraced progressiveness in design and was receptive to the use of more avant-garde promotional practices to this end such as the artistic ambitions of Templar Film Studios who made *Weave Me a Rainbow*. This is also reflected in the numerous features and articles on Scottish textile production in *The Ambassador* such as 'Accent on Scotland' (1950, July), 'Ambassador from Scotland' (1954, July & 1955, November), 'Scotland's New Sophistication' (1959, August), and 'Scotland the Brave' (1967, August). The idea of *creative* promotion was therefore part of the thinking of bodies like the NASWM, that itself had an occasional voice in *The Ambassador*. The sometimes contradictory pull of modernity and tradition espoused by the magazine is arguably a particularly strong feature of the Scottish psyche, and one that has been open to much debate and question in terms of the nation's dominantly romantic or parochial representation in film and other media (see McArthur, 1982 and Blain, 1990). In terms of the selling of Scottish woollens around the world however, the NASWM saw the combination of the 'timeless' features of traditional skills and craftsmanship, and a modern, forward looking approach to colour, design and fabric technology, as crucial, a view espoused by *The Ambassador* in numerous editorials for Scottish features, such as in August 1959:

> What pinpoints the 1960 Scottish tweed, giving it its new sophistication, while retaining its traditional individuality? Coatings are still warm and luxurious but light to wear . . . [and] feature the smoother textures which are today at the avant-garde of fashion. . . . Colours, too, reflect the feeling for lightness in a luminosity that gives fabric a 'lift' without altering its tone value. . . . The Scottish weaving tradition, built on handicratfsmanship has changed to modern production methods without loss of individuality. The same applies to spinning and dyeing. Now carried out in the finest modern plants, this results in the production of new types of yarn as well as a reliable range in unlimited colours (Scotland's new sophistication, pp. 53 – 54).[1]

It is in this specific context that the NASWM's funding and ultimate approval of *Weave Me a Rainbow* for use as promotional material must be placed.

Much of the liaison with NASWM and promotion of the film was undertaken by Forsyth Hardy, Director of the Films of Scotland Committee, the government body under whose auspices the film was made and which had a remit to 'promote, stimulate and encourage the production and circulation of Scottish films of national interest' (Films of Scotland Committee, 1955).[2] The Committee had a particular interest in promoting Scottish *industry* but because it received no funding, relied on industry itself for sponsorship (except for a small amount from the Central Office of Information that helped part-fund the film's production and overseas distribution). Films of Scotland embraced the notion of documentary as an 'applied art' aiding society's 'humane and effective functioning', allying it to a Caledonian perspective and promoting its idea of 'Scotland on the Move'. Its publicity material describes *Weave Me a Rainbow* as containing 'outstanding colour photography' that 'opens a new perspective on fashion and design' (Scotland on screen, 1965, p. 105). John Grierson was a founding member of the Committee and a key player, writing film treatments (notably for the Academy Award winning *Seawards the Great Ships* of 1960) and advising young filmmakers such as Edward McConnell (1936 – 2018), director of *Weave Me a Rainbow*. Grierson's influence on British documentary generally, and especially on Films of Scotland in this era cannot be underestimated. McConnell describes how in the early 1960s 'great philosophical discussions' with Grierson over 'a few gins' in Glasgow's Royal Hotel were 'great learning times' (McBain, 2014). Grierson's belief in documentary's ability to reveal the poetry of the actual as a means of 'illumination and persuasion' (Grierson, 1962, p. 4) was deeply influential. He was trying to 'put the art' into the sponsored film according to McConnell, thus allowing the filmmaker to explore the aesthetics of industrial processes.[3]

The 'putting of art' into the sponsored documentary chimes with the ethos of *The Ambassador* and a network of associations seems to have been at play. *Weave Me a Rainbow* features animations by Halas and Batchelor who, by 1962, were renowned for their witty and sophisticated work, not least for Britain's first animated feature, *Animal Farm* (1954) but according to John Canemaker, it was Grierson who helped them get work with the Ministry of Information in 1941, effectively launching their careers (Halas and Wells, 2006, p. 214). Meanwhile, in August 1946, Halas and Batchelor had made a promotional film called *Export or Die* for the Ministry, promoting the need for British exports. The title is a phrase coined by Hans Juda as a mission statement for the first issue of *The Ambassador* in March of the same year; for Juda, only exports, and especially those of the textile trade, could help Britain to get back on its feet after the devastation of the war (Stapleton, 2012, p. 23). The network extends backwards too: Grierson championed the drawn film-stock animations of Len Lye in the 1930s for a series of Post Office promotions; and Lye's notion of 'freedom of expression' had a deep influence on Halas and Batchelor (Halas and Wells, 2006, pp. 92 & 158). This encouragement of young unknown talent (often with a radical bent), bringing their abilities to bear on his idea of the public consciousness-raising documentary film was typical of Grierson who famously employed the then little-known Benjamin Britten to compose the score for *Night Mail* (Watt and Wright, 1936). The commissioning of Frank Spedding's score for *Weave Me a Rainbow*, only his second film score following his work on *The Heart of Scotland* another Films of Scotland vehicle of the same year (Henson, 2001, p. 22), was thus a typically bold move of the Committee and followed in the footsteps of Iain Hamilton's work on *Seawards the Great Ships*. Neither composer was known for film scoring and their eclectic styles embraced both a contemporary expressive language and one steeped in musical tradition, almost the archetypical British conservative adventurers of Juda's imagination.

Figure 2: 'Tweed mills in the Hillfoots' (*Weave Me a Rainbow* production photograph). © National Library of Scotland.[4]

III

Weave Me a Rainbow is 27 minutes long and details the 'journey of wool' from a graphic depiction of the birth of a lamb on a Scottish hillside (with only a heartbeat as soundtrack), to trendily modelled high-fashion woollen clothing. Its working title was

'Scottish Woollens' and it was initially 'composed of six movements', according to the film treatment (Grant,[5] 1961, p. 7). These become 'Sequences' in the shooting script (McConnell,[6] 1961):

1. – The Miracle of Birth
2. – The Micro-Photography of Wool
3. – Yarn Manufacture
4. – Design
5. – Of Wool and Scotland
6. – Cloth and Clothing

In the final edit, Sequence 5, Of Wool and Scotland, was incorporated into Sequence 2, breaking up that section's detailed scientific exposition. From the start, the commentary emphasizes that 'wool is born, not made', but this initial appeal to the natural, and repost to those promoting artificial fibres, is immediately countered by Halas and Batchelor's cutting-edge animation depicting the scientific properties of wool, followed by Gordon Coull's quite radical and experimental cinematography of the working mill environment. Spedding's jazz-inspired score with classical and modernist-tinged leanings (to be discussed in detail later) is used throughout. The natural and traditional are never far away however, depicted through images of the Scottish landscape, its subtle winter and autumnal hues shown as the basis of the cloth colour palette; traditional Shetland hand-plucking of sheep's wool, and age-old, timeless textile patterns (all from the Of Wool and Scotland sequence). The commentary combines a quite poetic approach to names of places, cloth patterns and types of wool with a more hard-hitting factual style detailing cutting edge scientific understanding of the nature of wool, current dye technology and yarn manufacturing processes. The film finishes with a 'hard-sell' showing the finished *haute couture* wool clothing modelled by international members of what it calls the 'jet set' in rural and urban Scottish settings (Cloth and Clothing). It is accompanied by a wryly-humorous commentary that sounds dated and sexist today; the female models are treated to typical condescension.[7]

Weave Me a Rainbow certainly had international success in both aesthetic and marketing terms. Amongst several screenings at prestigious film festivals such as Venice (1962), it won first prize in the category of Technical-Industrial Films at the International Festival of Electronic, Nuclear and Teleradio-Cinematography in Rome in 1963, (Qualities to win awards — Scottish success, 1963), was purchased by the

Pittsburgh Board of Education Service Centre (Films of Scotland Committee, 1966, p. 1) and was 'in active use by the National Wool Textile Export Corporation in South Africa' where a Durban department store used it for a series of staff training exercises (Films of Scotland Committee, 1967a, p. 1). *The Times* describes the film as having 'an imaginative approach that lifts [it] out of the ordinary, a sense of sincerity and authenticity [that] immediately communicates itself to the viewer' (Qualities to win awards — Scottish success,1963).

In the context of this collection what is of especial note in the film is how the musical score in combination with the imagery, parallels the Judas's notion of *The Ambassador* as an 'experimental platform for presenting textiles in the context of a refreshingly modern approach' (Thomas, 2012, p. 46). This idea draws on the advertising stance of the *Neue Sachlichkeit* (New Objectivity) of 1920s Germany, influenced by the Bauhaus School and marked by precision and abstraction in reaction to the domination of 'pictorialism' (pp. 49 – 50). Both the 'refreshingly modern approach' and 'precision and abstraction' are apparent in John Grant's treatment for *Weave Me a Rainbow* which places emphasis on close-up and extreme close-up photography for long sections of the film that detail yarn production from wool sorting, scouring, carding and blending to spinning and weaving:

> [I]t is important to maintain a consistent film style. By eliminating all sense of the machine to concentrate always on what is happening to the wool itself we can aim at producing a hushed and dream-like impression, as though the eye were being stroked by a butterfly wing (1961, p. 9).

The lack of visual context combined with highly creative use of lighting, elaborate tracking shots and disorienting camera angles, makes the imagery vivid, abstracted and surreal. Director McConnell's time at Glasgow School of Art in the 1950s was also influential (personal communication March 15, 2017) and he has echoed Grierson's idea that 'cinema is like painting' (1968, p. 4), likening the work of Picasso, Cezanne and the Futurists to his approach:

> they were all trying to get dynamism and movement. They were pre-empting the movement of cinema. If you examine a Picasso — for example, a vase on a table — it is almost like an edited sequence from a film. A vase from above, the sides, looking down, looking up. Picasso had the totality of an image in an instant, and this is a thing that . . . film can do (Donald, 1964, p. 41).

As suggested, the yarn and cloth become a central focus, yet the processes to which it is being subjected can remain mysterious despite occasional explanation in the commentary. Occasionally, *all* that the viewer sees is 'objectified', to the point of complete abstraction such that one can only guess what the image might be showing (Fig. 4). The success of such visual strategies relies as much on the musical soundtrack as Coull's photography, its 'important contribution' presaged in the treatment (Grant, 1961, p. 11). The treatment and shooting script emphasize music's 'imaginative use' and are quite detailed in places suggesting, for example, the music should change 'to march tempo' on a cut to the 'military precision' of a '400-strong battery' (p. 9) of automatic spinning mules making the yarn, and later, as the focus shifts to machinery mechanisms, 'to an architectonic precision' (McConnell, 1961, p. 7) (Fig. 4).

However, this 'refreshingly experimental approach' to the presentation of textiles in the film also *embraces*, rather than rejects, pictorialism, something that has a long tradition in Scottish visual art and again, sound plays a key role. The claustrophobia of the mill and workshop interiors is interspersed at quite starkly drawn key structural points with more static picturesque panoramas of the beauty of Scotland's landscapes. In Sequence 4, Design, the driving music and location sounds of the mill are replaced with birdsong, a distant barking dog, sheep bleating and the hum of the wind, with the sparse voice-over taking on the form of what the treatment describes as 'verse commentary'. The action moves inside to a surprisingly long static shot of a still room. The sound of the wind is still present but it is now joined by a slowly ticking clock indicating thoughtful calm and reflection. A large country house interior is revealed[8] where the designers are shown thinking up their designs, inspired, as the commentary says, by 'the colours of Scotland . . . a landscape recaptured in wools'. Gentle dissolves between close-ups of pieces of cloth and heathers and grasses, trees and hillsides, bring home the point, but the discussion is also of the heat of summer in Tokyo and the need for new lightweight wool fabrics (a topic discussed in detail in the August 1959 *Ambassador* editorial cited above): innovation and the contemporary are addressed by drawing on the wisdom and strengths of the past.

The stark contrasts drawn in *Weave Me a Rainbow* apply to both its content and the way it is couched, its 'promotional creativity': modernity and tradition; the industrial urban and pastoral rural; the scientific and natural; the conservative and adventurous. These contrasts are also a key feature of Frank Spedding's compositional language which is in keeping with what Matthew Riley characterizes as the British approach to 'aesthetic modernity'. Technical innovation mattered but was not seen as 'the

Figure 3: Production photograph of mill machinery. © National Library of Scotland.

Figure 4: Production photograph of mill machinery: a twisting machine. © National Library of Scotland.

necessary and inevitable response to the contemporary situation in either music or society' and so, for some British composers, 'the new vocabulary of music took its place next to the old and could be drawn on freely and eclectically' (2010, p. 9). This arguably coincided with European musical modernism's general rapprochement with the past and rejection of the *tabula rasa* insistence of the immediate post-war avant-garde. In Britain this was pushing at an already open door.[9] Spedding was an admirer of Schoenberg and Webern, along with Haydn, Mozart, late Beethoven, Liszt and Kurt Weill: he 'was devoid of musical snobbery in a way which only those with an encyclopaedic knowledge of the repertoire seem to manage' (Inglis, 2001 and Boyle, personal communication January 31, 2017). A catholic mix of musical styles, often used in combination, results: jazz, classical tonality, modality, extended tonality, bi-tonality, serialism, atonality, and a fondness for musical quotation. Pupil and long-time colleague of Spedding, Rory Boyle, has argued that it is in Spedding's film music that we can hear him at his most radical. His work is also marked by a strong sense of the dramatic, rhythmic dynamism and an adventurous approach to instrumental colour. The widely varying styles and levels of dissonance that result rarely jar however; Spedding's skill is in seamless juxtaposition, combination and layering such that all seems of a piece. Along with *Weave Me a Rainbow*, his contemporaneous Films of Scotland scores for the industrial documentaries *The Heart of Scotland* and *The Big Mill* are prime examples (Henson, 1962 and 1963). They combine folk-like melodies, extended tonality, near-atonality and hints of jazz. His later score for *The Hand of Adam* (Grigor, 1975), about eighteenth-century Scottish architect Robert Adam, affectingly combines serialism with occasional 'windows' of classical tonality.

In *Weave Me a Rainbow*, a driving jazz style is very much at the forefront. This is reflected in the instrumentation of flute, clarinet, piano, vibraphone (with motor on), drum kit and double bass (played pizzicato). The specific rationale for the choice of jazz is unknown, but the precedent had already been set in both promotional and industrial film. Len Lye's 1930s work for the GPO under Grierson's auspices often employs trad jazz scoring, *A Colour Box* (1935) for example, and, probably most prescient, Bert Haanstra's Academy Award winning industrial film about a glass factory, *Glas* (1958), has a strongly modern jazz-influenced soundtrack. Unlike in those films however, Spedding's music uses the extended tonality of the jazz harmonies employed to slide easily into more dissonant and astringent textures that allude to modernist expression, aided by a subtle rhythmic shift from 'swung' triplets to 'straight' quavers. At other points the same technique is used but instead to move towards a more classical style, chiefly led by the piano in a way reminiscent of Jacques Loussier's use of J. S. Bach's compositions as a base for jazz improvisation (Loussier's innovative Trio had already released four LPs by 1962 so these may well have been a direct influence). The music that accompanies the titles sets up this ambiguity (Fig. 5): a fast walking bass line outlines a simple I-II-V-I progression in C# minor, with chord II altered to a secondary dominant D#7, a common jazz inflection. This simple four-bar harmonic progression repeats for most of the 40-second title sequence. However, the melodic material of the flute and clarinet clouds the progression with leaping chromatic dissonant tones reminiscent of eastern European klezmer music. The rhythms are simple crotchets and quavers, but the entry of the piano is heralded by their jaunty descending chromatic lines played with *notes inégales* (Fig. 5, bar 11). Though no score survives, it is reasonably safe to assume that any approximation of 'swing' is notated this way: Films of Scotland scores of this period were nearly all played by musicians from the Scottish Sinfonia conducted by Marcus Dods and there is an undoubted slight 'stiffness' to their version of swing. It is effective though because the instrumentation and general musical language signal it as an appropriate style. The ensuing piano music (Fig. 5, bars 12 – 18) has a baroque character in its melodic outline and reversion to quavers, and sets up a gentle bitonality in places (for example C# minor against the bass's D# major outline at bar 14). It then concludes with a recurrence of the triplets preceding a brief modulation to C# major (the last beat of bar 20). The overall effect is upbeat, quirky and slightly mysterious and, when combined with Halas and Batchelor's stylish but garishly 'rough' animated titles, encapsulates the whole tenor of the film to come.

The 'experimental platform for presenting textiles' will now be examined by focussing in detail on specific sections of the film that highlight the importance of music and 'verse commentary' as a means to showing a 'refreshingly modern approach' whilst also appealing to tradition.

IV

The verse commentary in the film may be described as a poetic approach that seeks as much to evoke feeling as to impart information. Although the verse form is used sparingly, its relative rarity gives it more impact. One such example is in the Of Wool and Scotland section (Sequence 5 but incorporated into Sequence 2 in the final cut) that shows traditional methods of hand-plucking wool in a rural Shetland setting. From 05:34 the commentary explains the unique soft quality of the Shetland sheep's wool. It then compares this to other types of wool found around the world that 'find their

Weave Me a Rainbow

Frank Spedding

Figure 5: Author's transcription of Frank Spedding's music accompanying the title sequence of *Weave Me a Rainbow*. All subsequent transcriptions are my own[10] and all instruments always notated at concert pitch.

way to Scotland' for use in cloth manufacture. The tone of Henry Donald's refined Scottish burr becomes wistful, the words savoured and slowly paced: 'like camel hair from Turkistan; or the soft and lovely vicuna from Chile, and Peru. Like mohair from the Cape and Turkey; and the alpaca and the llama, and Tibetan Kashmir'. As the words are intoned, the soundtrack of sheep bleating gives way to Spedding's quick and breezy, light 'swung' jazz in a generally major tonality with touches of the 'straight' baroque-like piano mentioned above. Drums excepted, the full ensemble is used and the vibraphone is prominent, leading the way through images of the sheep and shearers to a single long close-up of a lace shawl, gently blowing in the breeze. The commentary now focuses on the shawls made by the Shetland crofters, their names 'posses[ing] a magic' (Grant, 1961, p. 12) and again, savoured and drawn out by Donald: 'Rose of Sharon, Crown of Glory; Star of Bethlehem'. The treatment talks of the 'verse find[ing] its rhythm in the sounds of names and place-names' and of the 'music in names' that acts in 'counterpoint' to the shearing scenes: 'let the sounds purr in the ear' (pp. 12 – 13). The imagery is of timeless rural scenes and practices. The subject matter discussed reflects this but is then extrapolated to an exotic, international realm that is couched a little mysteriously, all the while accompanied by cool, upbeat jazzy music, the 'classical' couching of which exudes sophistication. The attempt to show the importance of age-old practices, but ones that are far from just parochial, is clear and entirely led by the 'music' of both words and score.

The section ends with a startling cut to an eerie, washed-out shot of the winter sun through some bare trees, the music concluding in typically jazz-like harmonic ambiguity, the oscillating vibraphone resounding. The commentary suggests: 'colour is gifted by the sun, it's great light a radiant source and origin'. An arresting close-up image of a single blinking eye ensues as Donald comments that 'like beauty, colour lies in the eye of the beholder. All nature's colours are reproduced in wool from dyes perfected by colour chemistry'. And so the film switches back to the scientific examination of dyes and wool of Sequence 2, The Micro-Photography of Wool, with a series of surreal shots of brightly coloured dyes dripping into clear liquids filling the frame. The following 30 seconds of film is commentary-free. The music takes centre-stage beginning with a simple oscillating two-note flute motive, C-Db against the clarinet's C joined by a near atonal 10-note descending piano arpeggio that mirrors the falling dyes. The dissonant, modernist-tinged music follows on from the commentary's talk of 'colour chemistry', the appeal to science and modernity clear. However, it is then softened by a return to a jazzy modality alternating between G dorian and Bb aeolian (indicated by the changing key signatures from bar 6, Fig. 6) and with chords extended to include flattened 7th, 9th and 11th creating familiar jazz bitonalities. The common time and steady quavers are replaced by complex triple time measures, including embedded triplets and quasi-improvised virtuosic woodwind lines (bars 9 – 12). The clarinet acts as an intervallic binder between the opening dissonance and jazzy section with its accompanying movement in seconds, as does a rapid, dissonant chordal piano passage that leads convincingly to a return of the dissonance of the opening that accompanies a concluding animated section. The modernity and *connections* between both musics are highlighted, with mystery and familiarity juxtaposed *and* combined (Fig. 6).

This alternation between jazz and more modernist musical expression is a strong feature of the following Sequence. Sequence 3, Yarn Manufacture, is set within the mill environment (08:12 – 11:53) and details dyeing, carding (the initial making of threads from the wool) then spinning. Commentary is sparse with long sections of music and image alone. It employs the close-up, creatively-lit cinematography mentioned above throughout, exemplifiying the Griersonian 'poetry of the actual' and the bringing of beauty to industrial processes. Occasional faces of the mill workers are seen through the yarn and steaming vats, their faces surreal in the lights. In keeping with the continually moving camera, fairly rapid editing and dynamism of the moving machines and bubbling dye liquids, the music runs at an extremely fast, bebop tempo (crotchet = 290) with the clarinet and vibraphone often leading with mellifluous and flowing melodies strongly reminiscent of 'improvised' jazz solos. The modernist passages feature a ponderous, serialist-inspired vibraphone melody, doubled two octaves lower on piano, that uses eleven tones of the chromatic scale (08:54, Fig. 7), and pounding

Weave Me a Rainbow

Colour is gifted by the
sun, its great light a
radiant source and origin.
Like beauty, colour lies in
the eye of the beholder.

All nature's colours are reproduced in wool

from dyes perfected
by colour chemistry.

Figure 6: Transcription of Frank Spedding's music for *Weave Me a Rainbow* Sequence 2, The Micro-Photography of Wool, from 06:35.

Figure 7: Transcription of Frank Spedding's serialist-inspired melody for *Weave Me a Rainbow* Sequence 3, Yarn Manufacture, from 08:54.

piano dissonances that flow out of the extended jazz harmonies. The rhythms alternate between 'swing' and classical 'straightness' as before. They often take on an overtly stiff and mechanical bent, changing in tempo in direct correspondence with the movement of the machines. The drum kit is featured in this section, its brush-driven rhythms often following the fast movement of the carding machines, whilst trills on woodwind and piano, along with flutter tonguing on the flute, allude to factory processes with their 'mechanical' oscillation of major and minor seconds. The final section of the sequence features the dynamism of the spinning machines with their wide arc of back and forth movement, introduced sonically by a highly dissonant strumming up and down the strings inside the piano (that sounds electronically treated towards its end).

The visual similarity between the internal workings of the piano and the complex vibrating lines of yarn and spinning bobbins is pinpointed in sound (Fig. 8).

As the strumming fades the commentary describes how in order 'to give wool strength the yarn has to be drawn out, twisted and wound. Wool gets its muscles by binding the fibres tightly together, making each length of thread narrower; narrower and stronger'. With the rest of the ensemble silent, a free and fast, virtuosic drum solo ensues (10:58 – 11:49) over various shots alternating between rapidly wavering threads from various close-up perspectives and vividly-coloured spinning bobbins, the camera zooming out occasionally to show a little more context. The treatment asks for the music to change to march tempo, 'with military precision' (Grant, 1961, p. 9) and Spedding employs sharp bass drum 'stabs' and all manner of syncopated rim-shots, flams and rolls played with hard sticks on a tight snare, strongly suggestive of the growing strength of the yarn and 'military precision' of the process. The shooting script instructs the solo to build to a crescendo 'as colour potentially grows' (McConnell, 1961, p. 5) and the commentary begins to talk about the colours depicted as a 'paintbox' of the designer 'who now takes over'. After a brief return of the full ensemble, the film moves on to the pictorial rural calm of the Design Sequence 4 described above.

The latter half of the Design Sequence (from 16:16) returns to the mill but this time to concentrate on weaving. It employs similar audio-visual tactics as before though begins with a sudden brief focus on the ethereal sound and image of threads being spun off bobbins for weaving, the treatment instructing a 'plunge from a two-fold consideration of design theory into the practical workings of . . . the power loom. Make a crash entrance by reproducing in realistic sound the shock motif of the motion of the weft projectile' (Grant, 1961, p. 11). The commentary states: 'colours are chosen, patterns decided. The production of all kinds of cloth is in full swing' and what follows

Figure 8: Production photograph of mill machinery: a twisting machine. © National Library of Scotland.

is one of the more extraordinary sequences in the film where the correspondence between the music and visual depictions is so close that the two almost become one. Before falling silent, Donald informs the viewer they are to see 'warp lines first' (as in the warp and weft of the weave) heralding a completely abstracted and mesmerising shot of coloured threads from below that fills the frame, the brightly-coloured yarn vibrating and oscillating. Gradually the camera pans and zooms out revealing the yarn being drawn onto the revolving wheel of the 'warping' machine in which 'the correct colour sequences of yarn are wound . . . to form the entire length of a piece of cloth' (McConnell, 1961, p. 6) before being sent to the loom. This is followed by regular alternating close-ups of the wheel turning and threads being drawn, with one arresting pull-focus shot of a worker seen through the threads from below. All through this sequence, the music, which seems to evolve directly from the oscillating location sound of the weft projectile, consists of a simple two-note repeating flute figure, Eb-F, strongly reminiscent of the earlier flute minor second figure in Sequence 2 (Fig. 6, bars 1 – 4) but now using flutter tongue articulation. This is doubled by the vibrating sound of the vibraphone played tremolando with the motor on, whilst a bass flute intones a low F (Fig. 9). This short phrase is repeated sixteen times. There is a literal correspondence between the close musical interval of a second and the parallel closeness of the threads. The oscillating tones of the vibraphone are similarly paralleled by the vibrations of the yarn which are almost magically haloed by the creative lighting. The repetition matches the mesmerizing quality of the photography, the mechanical nature of the yarn being drawn, the wheel turning, *and* the deliberately mechanistically regular editing. The colours of the imagery are 'matched' by the musical 'colour' of the orchestration that in turn mirrors the detailed arrangement and subtle movement of the threads.

The yarn is now ready for weaving and a kind of audio-visual culmination ensues (from 17:38) with the closest rhythmic correspondences of the film drawn between the regular movement of the loom mechanisms and a simpler, downbeat blues-inflected groove.[11] The music, led by a catchy if moody vibraphone then flute melody in F minor, is underpinned by a walking bass line outlining a relatively simple and familiar chord sequence, repeated twice. It is strongly reminiscent of a 'cool' 1960s jazz-blues film theme, though maintains its vaguely mechanical feel via slightly awkward syncopated piano chords. The tempo, led by the visual suggestion of machine rhythms, is much more stately than before (crotchet=112), allowing extended and repetitive crunching piano dissonances to have great force, tension and grit. The groove opens at 17:38

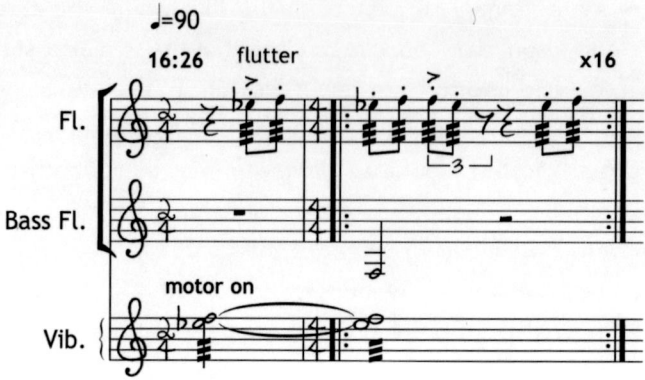

Figure 9: Transcription of Frank Spedding's music for *Weave Me a Rainbow* Sequence 4, Design, from 16:26.

with a syncopated and vigorous seven-bar solo drum break that almost *lurches* into the 'two beats to the bar' feel of this dirge-like march (from 17:52, Fig. 10), the heart of which lies in a repeated and highly pregnant dominant C7b9 chord that on its repeat closely follows a chain clicking regularly round a cog as the visual focus shifts to a loom's driver mechanism (18:12, Fig. 10, bar 10). The dissonance points to the blues and also, in its repetition, to the unfeelingly mechanical. This shift is the shooting script's instruction for a tempo change 'to an architectonic precision — warp and weft always at 90°. The march, the march of colour and pattern' (McConnell, 1961, p. 7). Spedding's faithful realization of McConnell's instruction is a highpoint of the whole film, the aesthetic pleasure generated, paramount.

The creative experimentation in *Weave Me a Rainbow* shows a strong freedom of expression and capacity to immerse the audience into the world of the mill and ultimately that of wool, yarn and cloth — the cinematography in all the mill sequences uses close-up and mid-shots relentlessly, ultra-vivid lighting and surreal angles. This serves to deepen what Patrick Russell describes as industrial documentary's concern during the post-war era for recapturing 'for adult eyes and ears the excitement a young child might feel when taken inside a factory whose vivid sights and sounds envelop and overwhelm' (Russell, 2010, p. 35). At the same time, the creative audio-visual strategy also still fulfils the promotional purpose championed by the likes of Hans Juda and his notions of creative Britain as a nation of conservative adventurers, and of an art-industry alliance. Factory weaving had never looked or sounded so 'cool' and 'happening', the fabrics more colourful, desirable and trendly modern; but with the practices that led to their creation ultimately shown to be rooted in time-honoured traditions, designs and with an emphasis on quality. The NASWM and the Films of Scotland must have been delighted: Scottish woollen textiles *could* compete with artificial fabrics, employ equally scientific methods in their production and development of new lines, whilst drawing deep on the age-old rural basis of both the very development of the craft and its ultimately natural, and thus superior, basis.

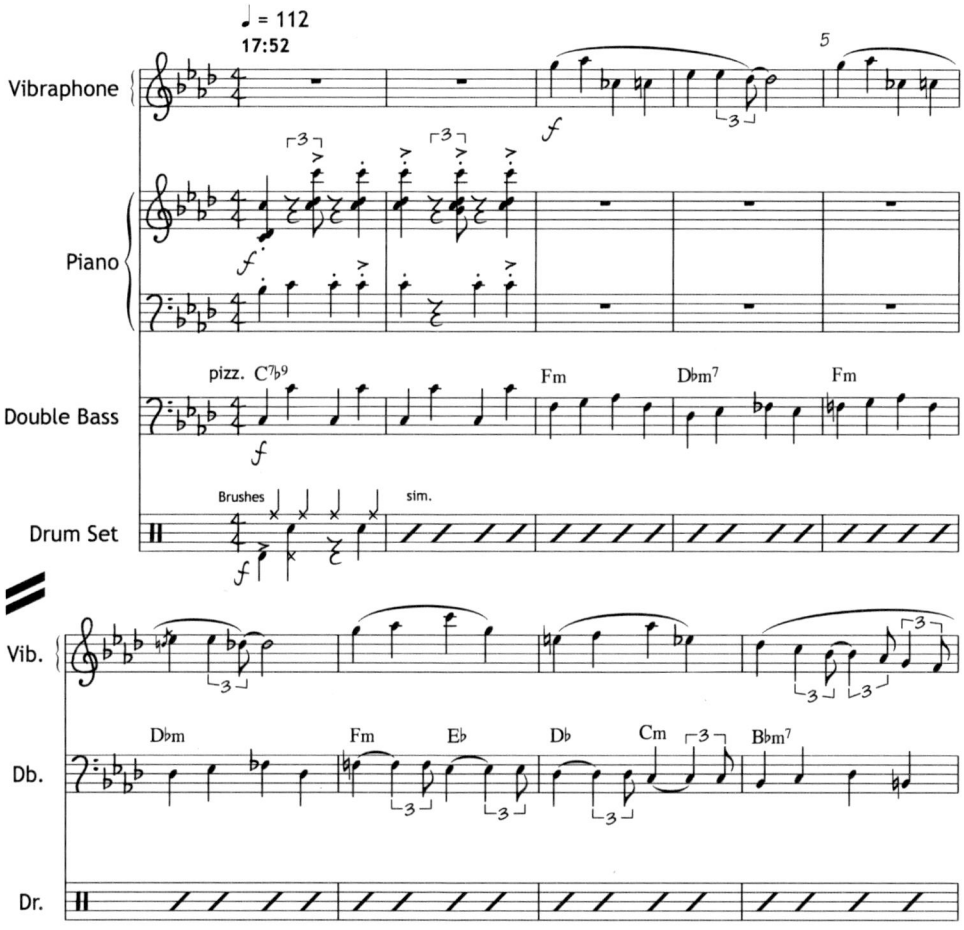

Figure 10: Transcription of Frank Spedding's blues-inflected groove for *Weave Me a Rainbow* Sequence 4, Design, from 17:52.

V

As Free Cinema documentary filmmaker Karel Reisz pointedly said in 1958, for all their polished achievements, filmmakers responsible for work such as *Weave Me a Rainbow* were little more than 'poets making a living in the advertising industry discuss[ing] their advertiser's copy as [if it were] poetry' (Russell and Taylor, 2010, p. 9). Even Laurence Henson, McConnell's fellow director at Templar Film Studios, conceded that 'too many of our films are flawed because they go to pieces selling something' and that the need to include 'qualifying passages [in *The Big Mill*] . . . weakened the thing as a dramatic piece' (Donald, 1964, p. 41). It is hard to argue with either and no amount of artistry, either visual or sonic, makes up for the at best, 'qualifying', and at worst, rather crass ending to *Weave Me a Rainbow*. Its play on national stereotypes, sexist portrayal of women and somewhat empty appeal to trendiness, jars considerably by contemporary standards. Yet as McConnell points out about the film:

> I was given the chance to do the thing I wanted with colour and form. I had freedom . . . but [f]reedom is a thing that has got rules to work by, and the rules that I was given were that I was to show wool in the best possible way. To show that it is born and not made. But as it happened, I had the opportunity to do a thing that pleased me as a filmmaker, visually, *in certain sequences* [my italics] (Donald, 1964, p. 41).

It is of course the music and to a lesser extent, the commentary, in combination with the photography that makes those sequences so powerful and aesthetically pleasing. Indeed, compared to say *Cashmere is Scottish* (Goddman, 1973) that has a similar purpose and tenor and contains some superficially similar mill photography, *Weave Me a Rainbow* is in a different league of artistic prowess. The bland musical accompaniment and incessant factual and dull commentary of *Cashmere is Scottish* cannot hope to match the ingenuity of Spedding's score and Grant's evocative and restrained commentary, just as the flat lighting and cursory nods to arty photography cannot match McConnell and Coull's vivid, skilful and arresting depictions. So whilst *Weave Me a Rainbow* is unconcerned with specific social matters or the problems of the industrial workplace, resulting in a 'failure to accommodate analysis and contradiction' (McArthur, 1982, p. 62), it offers instead, what Grierson termed the potential 'magic' (1968, p. 5) of documentary representation as a means of 'illumination and persuasion'. By engaging the audience in a 'sensual journey' of music and image, woollen textile production is made strange and beautiful *and* promoted as drawing on the strengths of Scotland's national past, whilst all the while looking to the future.

However, as with advertising of even the greatest integrity, it is largely a fantasy world that is 'depicted' — textile mills, whilst fascinating and dynamic workplaces, do not look as good as this, they do not have engaging musical accompaniment and in fact, by the early 1960s, were in serious decline, undermining any sense of 'Scotland on the move'. Mills were workplaces of deafening noise, danger, long shifts, low pay and little job security. What is left of significance in the film is therefore the *art*, the *creative* promotional aspects that exemplify Juda's notion of the conservatively adventurous British approach to mid-late twentieth-century modernity. In certain sections of *Weave Me a Rainbow*, the aesthetically driven audiovisual evocations of industrial processes that were a mainstay of post-war documentary, reach a creative peak in McConnell and Spedding's collaboration. The correspondences drawn between music, verse commentary and cinematography have the capacity to *affect* broad feelings about modernity and tradition as well as making highly detailed subliminal and overt connections between musical and visual detail: musical and visual 'colour' almost become one. 'Export or die' was Juda's clarion call in *The Ambassador*, surely understood too by the NASWM's concern to counter the onslaught of artificial fibres and overseas competition by sponsoring the film. In the end, even *with* the partial death of the British woollen textile industry since, their openness to such an experimental and artistically modern approach to promotion has happily left behind a film that endures, representing very well Juda's belief in the arts as a 'tough living force in our world'.

Endnotes

1. Further examples are July 1954's 'Ambassador from Scotland' feature: 'In its local distribution throughout the country and in its standards of quality, the Scottish woollen industry might be seen to cling to tradition. That there is nothing old-fashioned about it, however, is demonstrated by the continual research carried out (p. 71)'; and the same titled November 1955 edition: 'If the River Tweed is eternal, tweed is eternal, too. . . . However, the fabric is no more at a standstill than is the stream — and that goes for the Scottish textile industry as a whole' (p. 72).

2. Archive research for this chapter was carried out at: The National Library of Scotland (NLS) Moving Image Archive at Kelvin Hall, Glasgow; the John Grierson and Forsyth Hardy archives at the University of Stirling (G and H codes respectively in the bibliography); and the Archive of Art and Design, Victoria & Albert Museum, London (AAD).

3. Robert Flaherty's *Industrial Britain*, made in 1931 for the Empire Marketing Board (a body that Grierson led), remains a benchmark for both its poetic and naturalistic approach to photography of industrial scenery. Grierson greatly admired Flaherty's flare and capacity to transform promotion into art via his photography and the operation of what Dziga Vertov called the 'camera-eye'.

4. The exact filming location of *Weave Me a Rainbow* is unknown, but the photograph strongly suggests a mill in the Hillfoots region. The Hillfoots are the villages and small towns that lie at the base of the southern scarp face of the Ochil Hills in Stirlingshire and Clackmannanshire, central Scotland. Many owe their development to eighteenth and nineteenth century textile mills driven by waterpower derived from fast flowing streams that drop down from the hills.

5. The treatment is an anonymous Films of Scotland Committee document, but Scotland on Screen (1965) publicity material cites Grant as author of both the film treatment and commentary.

6. The document is signed by the Committee and Templar Films, but McConnell states the 'shooting script would follow my visual "recce" and talking to wool experts and designers' (personal communication, October 27, 2017).

7. This final section was filmed in May 1968 and replaced the original 'international parade of tweed' (Scotland on Screen, 1965, p. 105) when additional shared funding of £2000 from the Central Office of Information (COI) and NASWM became available (Films of Scotland Committee, 1968, p. 1). McConnell states that

'the earlier Templar Films' version is the original that won the prizes. The ending of this original consisted of various shots in European capitals of people wearing Border tweeds, and library shots of the Far East where lightweight tweeds would be suitable. Motivation for redoing the ending was the availability of new funding' (personal communication, October 27, 2017). This appears to be related to rather heated exchanges between Forsyth Hardy and John Bewg, Director of the Films Division at the COI, in which Hardy accuses the COI of being tight-fisted and London-centric (Films of Scotland, 1967b, p. 4).

8 The house is in Langholm in the Scottish borders, once home to a thriving woollen milling trade that still employs people in the town today. The high street chain, The Edinburgh Woollen Mill is based in Langholm.

9 Manifest not only in the work of composers such as Peter Maxwell Davies and his exploration of music of the middle ages but also in popular music. After its own *tabula rasa* of the brash new rock and roll, groups like The Beatles, and psychedelia generally, became steeped in nostalgia for music hall, childhood and authors such as Lewis Carroll, for all its otherworldly innovative studio experimentations.

10 The exact manner of notation cannot be known but, despite the music often sounding quite improvised, Boyle, whose knowledge of Spedding's concert music is probably unsurpassed, suggests that he 'was incredibly thorough with his scores and I would think it highly unlikely that he would not write out everything in his scores even if they sound improvisatory . . . I don't ever remember seeing any aleatoric techniques (despite him being an admirer of Lutoslawski)' (personal communication, October 6, 2017).

11 Apart from the biting flattened ninth, Db, on the dominant C7 in the piano, this is mainly characterized in the flute melody by the use of the flattened fifth, Cb, over the tonic F minor and the sharpened ninth, E, over Db major

Bibliography

Accent on Scotland (1950, July). *The Ambassador Magazine*, pp. 108 – 131. (AAD 1/22 – 1987).

Ambassador from Scotland (1954, July). *The Ambassador Magazine*, p. 71. (AAD 1/30 – 1987).

Ambassador from Scotland (1955, November). *The Ambassador Magazine*, pp. 72 – 3. (AAD 1/32 – 1987).

Blain, N. (1990). A Scotland as good as any other? Documentary film 1937 – 82. In E. Dick (Ed.), *From limelight to satellite: a Scottish film book* (pp. 53 – 70). Edinburgh: Scottish Film Council and British Film Institute.

Breward, C. (2012). Introduction. In C. Breward & C. Wilcox (Eds.), *The Ambassador magazine: promoting post-war British textiles and fashion* (pp. 6 – 15). London: V&A.

Donald, D. (1964, January). Business lunch. *Scotland Magazine* (pp. 40 – 43). (NLS 4/11/317).

Films of Scotland Committee (1955, November 1). 'Industrial Film' (n.p.). (H2.2.2).

Films of Scotland Committee (1966, December 1). Production and distribution report. (G7.7.36).

Films of Scotland Committee (1967a, February 3). Production and distribution report. (G7.8.7).

Films of Scotland Committee (1967b, July 21). Meeting notes. (G7.8.34).

Films of Scotland Committee (1968, January 12). Production and distribution report. (G7.8.11).

Grant, J. (1961, May 5). 'Scottish Woollens part II: draft outline treatment for a two-reel film in Eastmancolour' (pp. 7 – 14). (NLS 4/11/180).

Grierson, J. (1962). 'Art and Revolution' (pp. 1 – 12). (G7.56.6).

Grierson, J. (1968) Script for *I Remember, I Remember* (pp. 1 – 6). (NLS 4/11/476).

Halas, V. and Wells, P. (2006). *Halas and Batchelor cartoons*. London: Southbank Publishing.

Henson, L. (2001, November 16). Frank Spedding. *The Herald*, p. 22.

Inglis, R. (2001, November 5). Frank Spedding: an acclaimed composer, a gentle and original teacher, and a witty friend. *The Herald*. Retrieved from: http://

www.heraldscotland.com/news/12135770.Frank_Spedding__An_acclaimed_composer_a_gentle_and_original_teacher__and_a_witty_friend/

McArthur, C. (1982). Scotland and cinema: the iniquity of the fathers. In C. McArthur (Ed.), *Scotch reels* (pp. 40 – 69). London: BFI Publishing.

McConnell, E. (1961, November 6). Scottish Woollens: shooting script. (NLS 4/11/180).

McConnell, E. (Director). (1962). *Weave me a rainbow* [Motion picture]. United Kingdom: Templar Films. Available at: https://movingimage.nls.uk/film/2245

McBain, J. (2014, November 12). Interview with Eddie McConnell. (NLS 8/317).

Ministry of Information, *Export or Die* (1946). Retrieved from https://www.britishpathe.com/video/export-or-die

Qualities to win awards — Scottish success (1963, August 26). *The Times*, n.p. (H2.14.4).

Riley, M. (2010). Introduction. In M. Riley (Ed.), *British music and modernism, 1895 – 1960* (pp. 1 – 11). Farnham: Routledge.

Russell, P. (2013). The shadow of progress — documentary and post-war industry. In *Shadows of progress* DVD booklet (pp. 34 – 6). London: BFI Publications.

Russell. P. and Taylor, J. P. (2010). The long tail. In P. Russell & J. P. Taylor (Eds.), *Shadows of progress* (pp. 4 – 10). Basingstoke: Palgrave MacMillan.

Scotland on screen. *Weave me a rainbow* (1965, April 5). [screening booklet]. (H2.P7).

Scotland's new sophistication (1959, August). *The Ambassador Magazine*, p. 53. (AAD 1/40 – 1987).

Scotland the Brave (1967, August). *The Ambassador Magazine*, pp. 37 – 83. (AAD 1/60 – 1987).

Stapleton, A. (2012). Hans and Elsbeth Juda. In C. Breward & C. Wilcox (Eds.), *The Ambassador magazine: promoting post-war British textiles and fashion* (pp. 16 – 43). London: V&A.

Thomas, A. (2012). Photography and graphic design: 'just a job lot'. In C. Breward & C. Wilcox (Eds.), *The Ambassador magazine: promoting post-war British textiles and fashion* (pp. 44 – 101). London: V&A.

CHAPTER 3

Sonicules - Designing drugs with sound: approaches to sound design for film, audiovisual performance and interactive sonification

Radoslaw Rudnicki and Jude Brereton

This work was part-funded by the Wellcome Trust through the Centre for Chronic Diseases and Disorders at the University of York. Grateful thanks to: Paul Walton for advice with scientific aspects of the project; Calum Armstrong for help with data collection; Andrew Chadwick who implemented the audio programming and Jakub Hader for generative visual system and visual design; Alastair Munday who helped to design the game and organise public engagement events; Darren Reed for advice on interaction design and analysis; Brian Katz for advice on audio interaction, spatial audio and general inspiration; Chris Power for help with gameplay data analysis and statistics.

To access sound files discussed in this chapter, please visit http://eprints.hud.ac.uk/id/eprint/34505/

Introduction

The key to effective design of new anti-cancer drugs is the ability to target specific biomolecules by carefully engineering the 3D shape of the drug molecule to allow for optimal docking between a drug and target enzyme. 'Sonicules' is an interdisciplinary project involving a variety of multi-modal media for public engagement. This includes an audiovisual computer game with interactive spatial sonification, an audiovisual performance and a documentary film. Each of these is designed to engage the public with the challenges inherent in drug design processes.

In this chapter, we will discuss how sound is used as the subject of the video, game and performance to engage audiences in an effective way. Furthermore, we will discuss the use of sound and its potential impact in health sciences research.

The game involves a number of staged interactive sonification tasks that incorporate complex non-linear multi-parameter mapping. Numerical data from over 100 gameplays was collated at several public engagement events and analysed in order to investigate whether the interactive sonification provided improved player accuracy and/or efficiency in completing the drug-docking task. The audiovisual performance takes the sound design system and soundworld used in the project (modular synthesis), using it in a creative way for live performance outside of the bounds/constrictions of scientific parameter mapping, adding additional rhythmic elements. Visual aspects of the performance are based on the biomolecules used in the game (i.e anti-cancer drug Tamoxifen). The abstract performance engages the public in a musical and artistic way, creating an immersive experience using spatial sound where the audience is presented with molecular docking from a first-person perspective. The performance showcases four scenarios that envision future drug design processes using immersive auditory and visual display. The video documentary tells the story of the project and its development. Its focus is on spatial sound and its use in the drug design process. It includes interviews with members of the research team. The video was designed to engage with the wider public via social media to allow engagement in a variety of places and times, unlike the game and the performance that were time and place specific. The sound design used in the film is, by its nature, linear and therefore distinct from the other parts of the project. Spatial sound is driving the narrative of the story, through its dynamics and density, and its connection to the spoken word that brings focus to specific aspects of the project.

The Use of Sound

The process of designing anti-cancer drugs is so complex that achieving an effective solution through computational "brute force" alone has been found to be, as yet, still slower than reaching the solution through human manipulation of visual representations of molecular structures. Furthermore, even with the aid of state-of-the-art visualisation software such as PyMol (Schrödinger, 2017), the lengthy process is imperfect, slow, and often misses some of the principal electronic interactions between the atoms of each molecule, which form the basis of drug-enzyme docking. Recently, researchers have started to investigate whether displaying such complex molecular interactions through sound can aid comprehension of the structures involved, and support chemistry researchers to design more effective drug molecules. Garcia-Ruiz & Gutierrez-Pulido (2006, pp. 853 – 868) showed that the auditory display of molecular structures and bonding aided better understanding of complex biomolecular relationships, which chemistry researchers and students found difficult to grasp solely through visualisation. Férey, N. et al (2009) have also investigated continuous provision of multi-modal (visual, aural and haptic) feedback during protein docking manipulations. Initial work at the University of York on a spatialised sonification system to display drug enzyme interactions (McIlraith, Walton, Brereton, 2015) demonstrated the potential of sonifying molecular interactions using binaural beats to represent molecule positional information. The Sonicules project built on this work to develop an audiovisual interactive molecule docking computer game, complemented by a live audiovisual performance and a documentary film in order to engage with the wide public on the challenges inherent in drug design processes.

This chapter describes the interactive sonification used in the Sonicules audiovisual computer game, the soundworld created for the audiovisual live performance and its adaptation for use in the documentary film. It investigates briefly whether the use of a staged interactive sonification improves accuracy and efficiency of task completion, and reflects on naive user engagement with non-linear, musically informed complex auditory display. Furthermore, it discusses how the soundworld is used as a subject in the different media reinforcing the impact and engagement with the audience in an effective way.

Sonicules: Game

The Sonicules game presents a number of increasingly difficult molecule docking tasks, based on anti-cancer drug molecules and their target enzymes. Representations of the molecular structures are presented on screen, and the player is able to manipulate the position (translation) and rotation of the drug molecule in order to fit it within the active site of the enzyme. After an initial tutorial level to allow the player to become familiar with a 3D mouse controller (SpaceMouse) and numerical keypad, the game includes a number of staged levels in which the user has to find a known target position (known solution). A complex set of auditory mappings are introduced to the user in stages, so that during the tutorial levels of the game he/she may become gradually more aware of the target 'sound' signifying the correct solution.

Levels

Level 1 is a simple translation and rotation task with the correct solution displayed in gold (left side of screen in Figure 1).

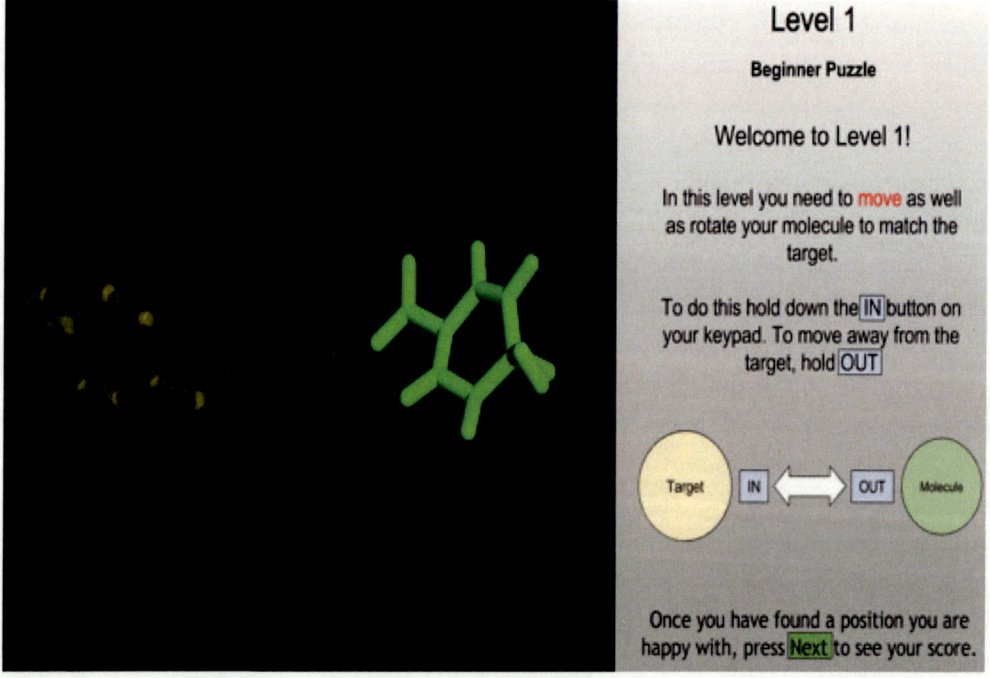

Figure 1: Screenshot of Level 1 gameplay - the drug molecule manipulated by the player is pictured on the right-hand side, and the target position pictured in gold on the left-hand side of the screen. Reproduced with permission of the Sonicules Project Team.

Sonicules

In Level 2 the player must rotate and translate the drug molecule (green) that is initially placed at the right-hand side of the screen (Figure 2 below). The correct solution is displayed in gold (within red circle in Figure 2) and is nestled within the target biomolecule structure (pictured in blue). Level 3 of the game is similar to Level 2 but the correct solution is not displayed in gold, and the player must find the correct solution using visual and aural means alone.

In the final, and most complex, level, a visual representation of a real anti-cancer drug (Tamoxifen) is presented, but the outline of the correct solution is not shown. When the correct position is reached the green drug molecule is visually partly obscured by the structure of the target biomolecule (the large blue molecule as pictured in Figure 3).

Sonification

[Audio files to illustrate the auditory display accompany this submission rendered as stereo files.]

The game incorporates interactive spatial sonification, presented binaurally over headphones, which aids the player in probing the 'physical' and 'electronic' space of the interaction between an anticancer drug and the active site of its target biomolecule. Sonification is also referred to as 'auditory display' and is the process of translating quantitative data into sound to enable investigation and understanding through auditory, rather than visual, means.

Ambient Harmonic Chord

In effect, two main phases of auditory display are heard. When the drug molecule is outside of the nominated 'target-zone' (see Section 4) an 'ambient harmonic chord' (Audio File 1) is heard which does not change even when the drug-molecule is rotated on the screen by the player.

Once the 'target zone' is reached the auditory display alters according to the overall accuracy score that incorporates measures of rotational accuracy on the X, Y and Z planes together with translational accuracy. As the position of the drug molecule becomes more accurate the ambient harmonic chord becomes increasingly 'present' in the mix by increased volume, reduced reverberation and opening of low pass filter that brings high frequencies and harmonics to the mix.

As the positional accuracy of the drug molecule 'homes in' further on the correct solution, beats are heard which gradually reduce in frequency as the accuracy improves.

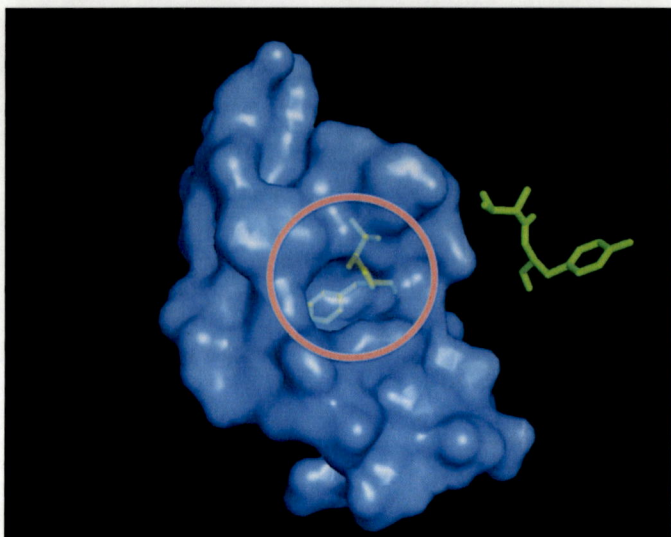

Figure 2: Screenshot of Level 2 gameplay - the drug molecule manipulated by the player is pictured on the right-hand side (green), and the correct target position (gold) within the target biomolecule (blue) on the left-hand side of the screen. The 'target zone' is indicated by the central orange circle. Reproduced with permission of the Sonicules Project Team.

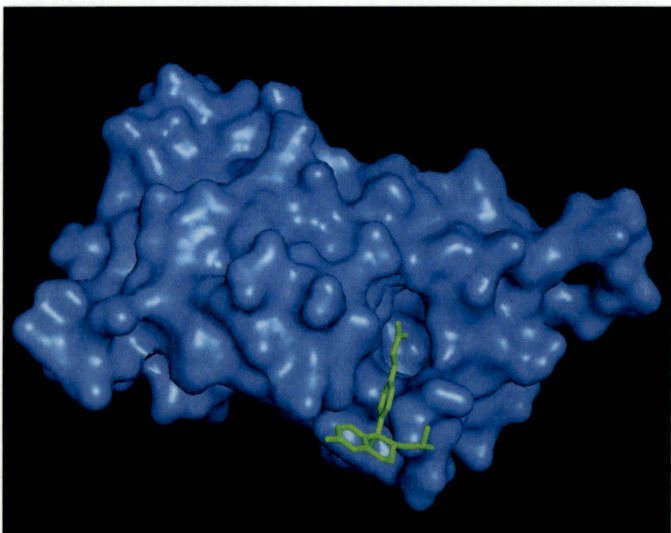

Figure 3: Screenshot of Level 4: the drug molecule (green) is pictured off-centre right in the lower part of the screen; the player must translate and rotate the drug molecule to fit inside the larger target molecule. Reproduced with permission of the Sonicules Project Team.

In addition, the width of the stereo field narrows as positional accuracy increases, meaning that the whole of the auditory sound field narrows and focuses to a central point as the player's accuracy relative to the position of the ligand, the molecular structure which creates a bond to the target enzyme

Collisions

Collisions, where the drug molecule's structure overlaps with the target enzyme molecule, are represented visually by red dots, and are sonified via repeated samples of 'crunchy' sounds, spatialized in the auditory environment according to the centre of gravity of each group of collisions.

Sound Design

The aesthetics of the soundworld for each element of the project were designed on a Eurorack and Serge modular synthesizer (James, 2013).

The aesthetics are reminiscent of the work of Post-Digital composers (Cascone, 2001) such as Sasu Ripatti's *Anima* or Autechre's algorithmic sound design work (Muggs, 2016), incorporating irregular rhythms, dense textures and ambient soundscapes using sound synthesis. Similar generative strategies in composition are used through signal processing and sampling using hardware devices, as well as algorithms for sound synthesis and signal processing. The difference here is the use of data, spatial sound, audiovisual material and interaction with a visual artist as well as scientific concepts.

Three layers of sounds were created and taken into account.
1. Ambient harmonic chord
2. Glitches / irregular rhythmic material
3. Collisions

Ambient harmonic chord sounds were designed using a wavetable oscillator (Intellijel Shapeshifter) in chord mode that uses eight parallel oscillators to form a chord (Intellijel, 2017). This was processed through a Cwejman DMF-2 low pass filter. This particular combination gives a smooth and easy-to-listen-to sound, ideal for creating a pleasant sound to indicate successful task completion in the game. It was also used to create the low background hum with the DMF-2 filter closed, as well as to create movement in sound at the start of the game, performance and film.

The sound was modulated by LFOs and random voltage generators (SSF Ultra Random Analog) to achieve a sense of movement and frantic instability. This was achieved by changing filter parameters such as modulating the cut off of the filter and animating waves in the table. Both methods allowed for timbral manipulation of the sound.

'Glitchy' sounds were produced using the Harvestman/Industrial Music Electronics Piston Honda MK2, a wavetable oscillator where waveforms are organised into 16x16x16 cube giving a total of 4096 choices (Industrial Music Electronics, 2017). In addition, each axis can be modulated by control voltage (CV). The oscillator uses 8bit waveforms creating raw and 'edgy' sounds. The oscillator was processed with Modcan Dual Delay with modulated delay time and feedback to produce an irregular and almost granular sound of delayed particles. These sounds were recorded before and during the live performance, in real time to an Elektron Octatrack sampler containing multiple audio tracks of different lengths. This created polyrhythms and evolving patterns during the performance, portraying the complexity of the molecular data.

Collisions were designed on a Serge Modular System using an STS X-fader VCA for 'punchy' and dynamic sounds clicks. These sounds were achieved by sending gate signals and waveforms from a VC Timegen Oscillator, modulated by Dual Universal Slope Generators, creating irregular patterns of clicks that were used to present collisions between molecules. To make this sound we used 'punchy' and with high dynamic range Serge Modular Synthesiser Voltage Controlled Amplifiers that with modulated amplitude created distinct 'crispy' and clear click sounds.

The sound design utilised a trial-and-error process to find aesthetically interesting combinations of various modules within the system in order to create the desired sounds which provided perceived ecological validity for molecule docking tasks in the game. All three layers of sounds are mixed in the performance and the film. They fade in and out and morph through control voltage modulations. The combination of hardware and software systems during the live performance was utilised for flexibility in sound design and sound spatialisation. The series of sound design ideas associated with each sound were provided for the programmer to utilise in the game. Each sound was sampled and resynthesized in NI Reaktor and then used in a Max/MSP-based game system. This made it easier for the users to understand and interact with the system, as the interaction/gestures had a more obvious effect on the sound and therefore made the interactive data sonification system more intuitive.

Sonicules: Audiovisual Performance

The Sonicules audiovisual performance is inspired and informed by the game. It takes the game's sound design, as well as visual aspects of the data visualisation into an

Sonicules

artistic and aesthetically challenging environment. It showcases, in an abstract way, how sound and visual display of information can work together, aiding one another. It is performed by a duo comprising a visual artist (Jakub Hader) and a sound artist (Radek Rudnicki). The visual artist uses the vvvv programming environment (vvvv group, 2017) for generative visualisations and the sound artist uses a modular synthesiser system, sampler and send effects. Mixing, sequential switching and modulations management create complex shapes and irregular sound patterns.

The performance is based on four molecules that are represented as separate 'movements' of the piece. The visual artist performs molecule docking while the music follows his actions in real time and vice versa, so that the visual performer also follows the sound changing position of the ligand while docking. The interplay between the two artists represents the interaction between machines, software and chemists using the system to dock the molecule. It also places the audience in the position of a spectator as well as mimicking the viewpoint of user-interactive molecule docking software. Furthermore, the audience experiences the molecule in a first-person perspective, since any movement of the ligand is represented on a seven-loudspeaker array with two subwoofers. The immersive soundfield needed for this effect was achieved via custom-made software using an Max/MSP IRCAM Spat package. It was used to pan three stereo mix buses.

1. Dry modular synthesiser signal.
2. Sampled and processed modular synthesiser signal.
3. Send effects.

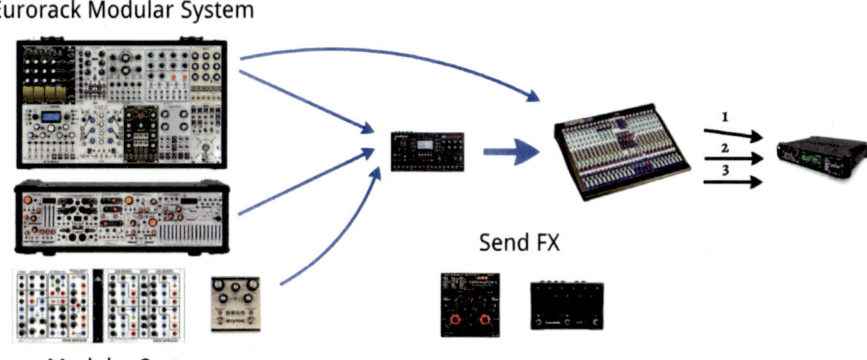

Figure 4: Graph showing the live performance audio setup and signal flow. Reproduced with permission of the Sonicules Project Team.

The molecular visualisation was controlled by the visual artist using a SpaceMouse controller, as used in the game system. What is more, one audio channel, with a stereo effects mix (delay and reverb effects), was linked to the molecule interaction performed by the visual artist. Whenever the image zoomed in visually this effect was enhanced by sending the sound towards the rear speakers in order to give the audience a sense of movement in space. Additionally, visual aspects of the live performance were audio reactive through amplitude and spectral analysis of the master stereo mix which affected the shapes, shaders and graphic textures in the visual content. This audiovisual reactive approach allowed interplay, not only between the performers, but also between the audio and visual systems used and resulted in unified aesthetics for sound and image.

Sonicules: Video Documentary

The video documentary focuses on the sound itself and its use in health sciences and the development of anti-cancer drugs. As a narrative, each member of the research team is interviewed describing their role. They present their views on the impact of using sound in public engagement, health science research, and work in multidisciplinary projects. The film shows this as an example of successful collaboration and combination of arts and science research. It features the views of scientists and artists working together collaboratively and exchanging their knowledge and expertise.

The sound design and music used in the film were generated during rehearsals and preparation for the live performance, as well as in the sound design process for the game. Since the author both filmed and edited the video, as well as designing the sound composition, the creation of the documentary was unified and holistic. There is a synergy between the video and audio material as both were generated from the very start of the project. The sound design uses non-linear generative patches that had been made on the Eurorack synthesizer. These were too complex for use in the game where simplicity and accuracy of aural detail was crucial. In the video these recorded modular patches are edited bringing a focus to specific parts, for example the ambient parts at the beginning and end of the task and the beat-based material used between the spoken parts in the video. There are parts where the video determined what sound material is used; for example when Radek Rudnicki is talking about the collisions, they appear in the background (04:21) and the collision sounds are heard. Similarly, at the film's ending (08:25) the ambient chord sounds are used again to provide a calm resolution to the film. The same source material was used at the end of the game once the docking task

Sonicules

has been successfully completed. On the other hand, at 03:07 the video is paced to the sound in order to make a bigger impact, once louder and more intense sound material is present. This happens right after Andrew Chadwick is talking about the challenge of designing the software and computational effort required in that task.

Figure 5: Sonicules performance at Stockholm Tech Fest 2017 Reproduced with permission of the Sonicules Project Team.

The role of the video was to engage the public online via social media and also to document the project development process. It was successful in that sense as it contributed to the overall promotion of the project resulting in additional live performances outside of the UK e.g. at the Stockholm Tech Fest 2017 in Sweden and in the Copernicus Science Centre, Warsaw, Poland.

Analysis / discussion

The Sonicules project engages audiences of all ages not only with health science and biochemistry research, but also with auditory display, spatial sound and data sonification. It raises awareness of the scientific, engineering and artistic aspects involved in the project and allows users to interact (via the game), experience (via the performance) and to find out more about drug design (via the film). In that sense, the film plays an educational role. The importance of sound and its impact for public understanding and engagement is showcased in every aspect of the project. Sound is the main subject of the project and is treated differently in each part, bringing the audience a different angle, point of view and method of engagement.

The video is the only linear part of the project containing non-linear material that was used in rehearsals and the sound design process of the game. The performance was semi-structured and improvised, while the game was based on interactive sound design giving the player a hands-on, tactile feel. This multi-modal and diverse way of addressing the audience is an effective means of engagement, especially when used in combination, because it allows the project to target multiple senses and, by multiple media use, can engage with a wider audience. Furthermore, the game and the sonification system (mapping and interaction) as well as live performance (aesthetics) work as proof of concept. These parts of the project show how, in the future, sound can be used in scientific research and be part of actual antidrug design process.

Future Work

The audiovisual performance is still evolving by the nature of the medium. For example, the artists experimented with the size of the physical setup, venue, duration of the piece, different scenarios, the number of loudspeakers and the type of sound system used. Future work will include more extreme dynamics and density of sound material. The simplicity, duration and ease of transportation are crucial factors in the performance's life cycle. Keeping the hardware setup as an entirely modular system makes it easier to transport and will be worth exploring further, not only to experience the logistic, but also the artistic implications. Furthermore, linking the visual artist (who controls the visual parameters) with the sound parameters simultaneously could be explored further in order to bring an element of gameplay to the performance.

Finally, incorporating augmented reality, virtual reality and 3D environments within the project seems to be a natural development and a perfect fit to enhance the immersive surround sound and visual experience in the future.

Since all gameplays were undertaken during public engagement events, conditions of the playing environment were not controlled and varied considerably during the day, so that at some points background noise levels would have been reasonably high, and as such may have affected a player's ability to attend fully to the interactive auditory display. It will be interesting to assess the learning curve in relation to the Sonicules game performance: further analysis of gameplay data across the staged levels, leading from Level 2 (solution given on simplified molecular structure) to Level 4 (real molecule, no solution given) is planned. Furthermore, systematic testing under controlled experimental conditions will be undertaken in order to better assess the validity of providing spatial sonification in comparison with completing the task with visual display alone.

Conclusion

The sound design used in the project is primarily non-linear, complex and musically informed. Created for three parts of the project including game, performance and video, it engages with audiences of all ages and addresses audiences with different media and environments. Using such diverse methods and engagement outputs, is effective, as it widens the audience and targets diverse interests.

The video not only allows documentation of the project, but also helps with its promotion. It is a key aspect of future development, funding acquisition and generation of additional outputs. It is an effective way of telling the story and showing what the project is about. Furthermore, it allows engagement with the wider public online and via social media, therefore helping to boost the impact of the project.

Bibliography

Cascone, K. (2000). The aesthetics of failure: 'post-digital' tendencies in contemporary computer music. *Computer Music Journal, 24*(1), 12 – 18.

Férey, N., Nelson, J., Martin, C., Picinali, L., Bouyer, G., Tek, A., Bourdot, P., Burkhardt, J.M., Katz, B.F.G., Ammi, M., Etchebest, C., Autin, L. (2009). Multisensory VR interaction for protein docking in the CoRSAIRe project. *Virtual Reality 13*, 273 – 293.

Garcia Ruiz, M.A., Gutierrez Pulido, J.R. (2006). An overview of auditory display to assist comprehension of molecular information. *Interacting with Computers 18*, 853 – 868.

Hermann, T., Hunt, A., Neuhoff, J.G. (2011). *The sonification handbook.* Berlin: Logos Verlag.

Industrial Music Electronics. (2017). Piston Honda MK2. Retrieved from

http://www.industrialmusicelectronics.com/products/4

Intellijel. (2017). Cylonix Shapeshifter Dual Complex Morphable Wavetable VCO. Retrieved from https://intellijel.com/eurorack-modules/cylonix-shapeshifter/

James, A. (2013). The Secret World of Modular Synthesizers. Retrieved from https://www.soundonsound.com/reviews/secret-world-modular-synthesizers

McIlraith, R.J., Walton, P.H., Brereton, J.S. (2015), The Spatialiased Sonification of Drug Enzyme Interactions, in: *The 21st International Conference On Auditory Display (ICAD 2015)*, Graz, Austria, 323 – 324.

Muggs, J. (2016). Joe Muggs goes deep with the seminal Warp Records duo. Retrieved from https://www.residentadvisor.net/features/2756

Schrödinger. (2017). Pymol. Retrieved from https://pymol.org/2/

vvvv group. (2017). vvvv - a multipurpose toolkit. Retrieved from https://vvvv.org/

Part 2:
Foregrounding the Aesthetic: Strategies and Practices

CHAPTER 4 85

Auralising Action Space: channelling a sense of play in documentary sound design

Simon Connor

Many thanks to Ken Turner for giving his time and personal interviews regarding the sound of Action Space and Alan Nisbet, and for permission to use the included archive photos. Also thanks to the University of Sheffield for giving access to these photos and to the Action Space sound archive referred to within this article.

Walter Murch's traditional sense of the the sound designer working within cinema was responsible for ensuring sonic consistency through every stage of the production process, in short 'sound from start to finish' (Wright, 2013, p. 139). The role extended beyond the technical responsibilities of the soundtrack to more artistic and aesthetic considerations, famously exemplified by his work in Francis Ford Coppola's films of the 1970s such as *The Godfather Part II* (1974) and *Apocalypse Now* (1979) (Buhler, Neumeyer, & Deemer, 2010, p.391). This required a successful coordination of the main components of the 'multiplane soundtrack'; the dialogue; sound effects and music, or what could be identified as Rick Altman's *'mise-en-bande'* system (2000, p. 341).[1] The definition however has increasingly been resisted and, according to Wright, become more diversified in modern day Hollywood (2013)[2], with what Jeffrey Ruoff describes as having inherent 'mass production techniques and precise divisions of labour' (1992, p. 221). Alternatively, the financial restrictions and minimal crew typical of low budget documentaries or guerrilla-style filmmaking can require those with responsibility of sound to take a more holistic approach to the sonic world of the film (Jones and Jonliffe, 2006). This encompasses both technical and creative practices, embracing the notion of play and experimentation, and requires an overarching understanding of the entire soundtrack. *Action Space* (Wahl, 2016) is such an example of this guerrilla-style of documentary filmmaking, with a small budget and skeleton crew. The film explores the work and ideas of the arts collective Action Space, between the years 1968 – 78, and how their work in education, the arts and cultural and public uses of space are relevant today. With a particular focus on *Action Space*, this chapter explores the importance of play in documentary film sound design from a practitioner perspective. My role as sound designer and recordist covered several responsibilities including production sound, recording the featured musical performances, archive digitisation, sound collage and the final film mix. Here I aim to reveal how the Action Space's do-it-yourself (DIY) ethic, and ethos of learning through play, influenced my approach to shaping the sound world of the film.

Action Space Collective: 1968 – 78

Founded in 1968 by artists Ken and Mary Turner; Action Space aimed to bring art out of the exclusive gallery system to the general public and everyday communities. This coincided with a broader movement, during the late 1960s and early 1970s, by many anti-establishment artists who were dissatisfied with elite institutions, galleries and the art market, and wanted to reach out to previously ignored audiences such

Auralising Action Space

Figure 1: Music in Action Space. © Ken Turner

Figure 2: An early Action Space inflatable. © Ken Turner

as underprivileged groups or local communities. This was coupled with a search for creative forms of expression beyond traditional methods of drawing or painting (Walker, 2002). Artist collectives such as Fluxus, founded by George Maciunas and largely based in New York, used music, performance art and participatory events to engage with the masses whilst rallying against notions of 'high art' (Higgins, 2002). In London, the collective Inter-Action founded by Ed Berman 1968, used a range of alternative theatre, workshops, film and the travelling Fun Art Bus to bring arts closer to the community (Unfinished Histories, n.d.). Though other artists at the time were exploring participatory pneumatic works, such as Graham Stevens' *'Walking on Water* series in 1966, or Jeffery Shaw's *Pneutube* in 1968, the Turner's approach was to emphasize the act of play, education and the arts through engaging with the public in these extraordinary inflatable environments. (Chau, 2012, Shaw, 2018, Turner, 1971). These were simply constructed, mobile and easily erected. The group could quickly and easily set up in council estates, parks and other public spaces to engage with communities, as explained by founder member Mary Turner:

> We took what we had, structures, pneumatic and rigid; techniques were developed in sound, movement and drama, and we created outlets for ourselves in parks, streets, and playgrounds. The work was an experiment in living as well as striving to find an art relevant to wider public. (Turner, 1971, p. 12)

Engagement with the public was facilitated through the creation and erection of these inflatables, they were structures to enter and explore. The domed and arched structures of PVC (polyvinyl chloride) created an otherworldly environment, leading to a heightened perception of space, colour and sound. As members of the group were mainly artists and musicians, sound and music were an integral part of the experience.

Action Space (2016): The Documentary

Action Space the documentary is a film by Huw Wahl, son of one of the founding members of the group; Ken Turner, and explores the beginnings and ideas of Action Space. Archive film and audio material are key components of the film and are combined with present day footage and commentary from contemporary theorists and the group's key members. A major part of the film is the design and building of a new inflatable structure which acts as a conduit to house four key performances relating to the act of play.

Auralising Action Space

Figure 3: During production of *Action Space*: the documentary. © Huw Wahl

The film's modest production budget was £7,500, with most of this being allocated to the building materials of the new inflatable. The core crew totalled three people; director Huw Wahl; producer Amanda Ravetz and myself as sound designer. *Action Space* was a 'passion project', in that we were each attracted and motivated by the project's creative appeal. Unlike a large budget or Hollywood production; no crew member received payment for their contribution, there were no strict divisions of labour, job descriptions, contracts or union restrictions. My personal interest stemmed from the vast potential for sound exploration through recording unique spaces and performances and unearthing the treasures of the Action Space reel-to-reel audio archive. Being free of bureaucratic or supervisory restrictions allowed an unburdened freedom to explore, enabling a more creative approach to capturing and shaping the sound of the film.

Though we were both accustomed to working with short film, the director and I were relatively new to the world of feature length film, having previously worked together on only one feature; *To Hell With Culture* (Wahl, 2014). We had developed a good collaborative working relationship and the lack of industrialised regime in *Action*

Space allowed a more fluid experimental approach. We were almost 'learning through play' ourselves, an approach very much in the spirit of the founding of the Action Space collective.

In the first instance, my role covered the typical technical responsibilities for sound commonly found in documentary, involving location sound, working as boom operator, striving to record dialogue as closely and as cleanly as possible, and capturing the unfolding events that appear in the frame of the camera (Ruoff, 1992, pp. 224 – 225). This tethering of camera and sound person can often require a 'highly choreographed' dance in order to capture the unfolding events but remain out of each other's way, as highlighted by both Raymond (1973, in Ruoff, ibid) and Rogers (2013, p. 5). However, it was also necessary for me to untether myself from this partnership and to go beyond the strictly technical role of audio reinforcement in order to seek out other sonic perspectives for the film. As Grierson highlights as far back as 1934, 'the microphone, like the camera, can do better things than merely reproduce' (1966, p. 158). Sound in documentary has much creative potential beyond the technical requirement of synchronously reinforcing the unfolding action. During pre-production for *Action Space*, discussions about the soundtrack were formulated and the director encouraged a more abstract process to recording the production sound. To bring alive the multisensory world of *Action Space* it would be important to capture aspects of the tangible, the materiality of the sounds of making, the unique spatial characteristics of the inflatable structures and to evoke the sensation of being inside such a place.

The remainder of this chapter will address the following key processes that contributed to the finished soundtrack from a technical and creative perspective, before attempting to explore the desired and achieved effect on the viewer-listener:

- Capturing the sounds of making.
- Exploring the acoustic space of an inflatable structure.
- Capturing the musical responses of play and improvisation.
- Sounds from the Action Space archive.

Capturing the Sounds of Making

The film's main shooting period focussed on the planning and building process of a new inflatable in Ambika P3 Gallery, a huge warehouse size space hidden under Westminster University. Involved in the build were 12 student volunteers, original members of Action Space including Ken and Mary Turner, and members of the inflatable company Architects of Air. The space was alive with activity during this filming period, a multisensory experience of vibrant colour, the buzz of conversation, the cutting of scissors, the unrolling of PVC, and the smell of glue as the inflatable began to be assembled. One of the sonic themes of the film was to represent the tangible — the sound of pencil put to paper, and the cutting, rolling and gluing of materials. These sounds of making were collected throughout the building process: the scoring, and slicing of scissors; the pressing, folding and squeaking of plastic; the drag of heavy vinyl across the coarse concrete warehouse floor; the ripping and unrolling of tape; and the smearing of glue. Alongside this could be heard the excited chatter and murmur of voices, collaborating, deliberating, designing and refining the ongoing process. The gallery floor was alive with an orchestration of all these simultaneous sounds, awash with reverberation from the surrounding bare walls and high ceilings, blurring all into a din of activity.

Sounds were recorded individually at close distance with a highly directional shotgun microphone to capture the nuances and sonic details. Recording at such close distances captures an unnatural level of detail, almost hyper-real, a perspective usually unavailable to the naked ear. This is made easier through digital technology that allows one to easily capture footage that is ripe for malleability, transformation and processing (Rogers, 2013, p. 3) and allows one to enhance the details, reinforcing what Chion calls the 'Materializing Sound Indices', defined as:

> . . . the sound details that cause us to 'feel' the material conditions of the sound source, and refer to the concrete process of the sound's production, They can give us information about the substance causing the sound, — wood, metal, paper, cloth — as well as the way sound is produced . . . (Chion, Gorbman, & Murch, 1994, p. 114).

It was important to capture this heightened sense of the tactile, the physicality of the building materials and tools, to evoke the experience and environment. As highlighted by Donaldson, sound 'makes a vital contribution to the evocation of other senses, for example, the sound of wind rustling leaves invites the feel of air on our skin, or the sizzle of food cooking conjures taste' (2017, p. 32). The power of such detailed sound can often enable a multisensory experience for the audience. It was also important to capture the sense of the reverberant and busy atmosphere, a working, social and creative environment. Perhaps imbued with the sense of play and creativity that surrounded me during the build, I experimented with placing the shotgun microphone inside a roll of PVC, waiting to be cut to size, pointing towards the busy factory-like floor. The slight movement of the microphone within the tube created a pulsing modulation in pitch and timbre, a low drone, punctuated by bursts of activity into the reflective and reverberant space. In the film's final edit this brief moment allows us to attune our ears to the unique *spatial signature* (Altman, 1992, p. 24), awash with the sound of ripping tape, the cutting of scissors and chatter of excited voices. These actions came from an opportunistic sense of play, seeking out new perspectives, experimenting, playing with the sound world of the film. This was perhaps imbued subconsciously with the ideology of the Action Space collective, who championed the importance of discovery through play and experimentation.

This approach is akin to that of Hollywood sound designers of the 1970s who often found their iconic sounds through unusual resonances and unique sonic phenomena in the real world. Sound designer Ben Burtt used very similar processes of recording through lengths of tubing to create some of the iconic sound effects for *Star Wars* (Lucas, 1977) (Lo Brutto, 1994, p. 235). Likewise, Murch would experiment by recording in various spaces, such as bathrooms or the Museum of Natural History, to capture the unique reverb, which could then be processed, distorted, time stretched and layered afterwards (Lo Brutto, 1994, p. 86). He termed this technique as 'worldizing', a means of capturing the surrounding environment as much as the specific cause of sound:

Figure 4: Capturing sounds of making at Ambika P3 Gallery. © Huw Wahl

Auralising Action Space

> My general principle of recording sound is never to think of recording just the sound itself. To record a telephone ring I think of recording the space between myself and the telephone. What I'm really recording is the relationship between that telephone and the space around it (Lo Brutto, 1994, p. 88).

These are techniques that are still relevant in sound design today, even with the vast array of sound manipulation easily available via computer software and digital audio plug-ins, the ideas of physical play are still essential practice, as illustrated by sound designer Gary Rydstrom:

> The trick to a lot of sound effects recording is to experiment with different mike placements and different ways of recording. . . . It's just a matter of experimenting. So much of what happens in sound effects recording is unexpected. You just have to be open to finding something different than you originally intended. . . . It's a time of discovery (Lo Brutto, 1994, pp. 235 – 6).

So the techniques of sound design in Hollywood or low budget documentary film are not mutually exclusive. But being free of industrial, bureaucratic and financial implications can encourage an avant-garde, radical or explorative approach to sound in low budget film, just as it did with Murch and his contemporaries in the 1970s, the heyday of the American Zoetrope (Thom, 1999). In a similar period, on the other side of the Atlantic in London, the same could be said of Action Space and their approach to engaging and educating audiences. Unbound from the restrictive elitism of the gallery-based art world, their DIY approach required them to learn as they went, as described by Ken Turner:

> We could only see that parts were beginning to fit together in a new way: we had to feel intuitively that things were right; there's no grand master plan to work to. It often happens by accident or force of circumstance, which I think is sometimes exactly that, accidental (Turner, 1971, p. 14).

Exploring the Acoustic Space of an Inflatable Structure

Entering an inflatable structure for the first time is an otherworldly experience: it is a fabricated vessel that breathes and swells with air as its only structural support. The internal surfaces respond to touch, encouraging one to lean, lie, bounce or roll against them. It is a space that provokes a childish reaction to run, jump, roll and bounce. The bold slashes of red, yellow and blue transparent PVC that adorn the structure allow the internal space to flood with light and colour, reminiscent of a stained-glass window. At several points in the film, the finished structure is inflated and 'brought to life'. With the inflatable as almost a central character, it was important to sonically capture the expanding space and corresponding change in acoustics within. This was achieved through the use of several piezo contact microphones and condenser microphones placed within the folds of plastic, capturing the gradual metamorphosis from its chrysalis like state into its full bloom. This process of inflation and deflation was completed several times, for the purpose of the audio takes, and allowed every nuance, creak and flap to be captured. At semi-inflation there was enough room to allow me to explore inside and capture sound from within the folds of the structure. Armed with a mobile recorder and pseudo-binaural recording setup I could gravitate towards the areas of most interest. Such sounds were collected with the final mix in mind, and were later subjected to time stretching and filtering in order to reinforce the size and weight of the structure.

This sense of the 'otherworldly' is highlighted in the film's opening scene. Sensitivity to sound here is particularly heightened, in darkness the only sound heard is the initial powerful rush of air from the fans, then the gradual unfolding and crinkling of PVC. Close-up detailed shots come into focus: slowly shifting, creased plastic surfaces begin to take shape; and the occasional waft of air allows glimpses of exterior light to bleed into the space. The detailed material sounds were blended with the exhalation of the human voice to reinforce the idea of new life as the scene transitions into the film's first featured performance — 'Expanding Space' by vocalist Phil Minton. Minton has been an active vocal improvisational artist since the late 1960s with an illustrious solo career, as well as being a regular collaborator with other influential performers such as the band Henry Cow. As one of the artists invited to perform inside by director Wahl, he reacted and respond sonically to the unique space. Using several extended and unorthodox vocal techniques, Minton focussed primarily on breath, breathing life into the inflatable. This metaphor was heavily emphasized in the post production stage, as the heavy structure begins to heave and sigh in synchronisation with Minton's inhalation and exhalation, the plastic crinkles as the folds expand and stretch outward like lungs filling with air.

Capturing the Musical Responses of Play and Improvisation

Alongside Phil Minton, the other key performances featured an improvised musical set by AMM, 'The Space of Play'; a performance theatre art piece by founder member

Auralising Action Space   95

Ken Turner, 'The Folds of Time'; and a live sound collage by myself, 'Sounds of the Action Space Audio Archive'. In each of these performances, artists were encouraged to improvise and channel the idea of playful expression, responding to the unique space surrounding them.

Like Minton, AMM also emerged from the mid-1960s avant-garde and free improvisational scene in London. They initially started as an unnamed ensemble with founder members Lou Gare, Eddie Prévost and Keith Rowe playing sessions at the Royal College of Art. AMM's formative years were in the same era as Action Space's, and the group even performed during one of Action Space's summer residencies at Wapping Graveyard between 1969 and 1970. AMM have gone through several incarnations since their first album *AMMMusic* (1967) and past members have included the composers Cornelius Cardew and Christian Wolff. Since 2005, and at the time of filming, the main line up consists of percussionist Eddie Prévost and pianist John Tilbury. The duo were ideal for performing inside the inflatable, both in terms of their links to the past of Action Space and their emphasis on improvisational experimentation using extended and traditional techniques to explore the possibilities of their instruments and collectively create new sonic textures. As highly proficient improvisers, AMM

Figure 5: AMM: The Space of Play. © Huw Wahl

were quickly at ease in playing and experimenting, testing out the acoustics, casting out harsh, percussive strikes into the space followed by softly subdued, low-register resonances that radiated through the inflatable, resounding around the curved surfaces. Low-register fluid piano figures blended into the low groans of the bass drum, whilst sporadic trills in the high notes alternated with eerie drones produced from bowed gong and cymbal. Their performance in the film is a heightened sensory one with its exploration of texture and timbre, the scratching and scraping of surfaces, the friction of bow hair against metal, and the heavy drag of wooden beaters across stretched drum skin. The resultant reverberation of these sounds was also important to capture, but the inflatable's unusual acoustics made for challenging recording. As much of the structure is perfectly curved or domed, sound reflects in highly unpredictable ways and is constantly reinforced or cancelled depending on one's pinpoint location inside the space. Suitable microphone placement was key to capturing these performances successfully, using distant ambient microphone techniques had the undesired effect of inadvertently capturing a high level of the attached fans required to keep the structure inflated. Conversely, closer microphone placements on the piano and percussion allowed a much more detailed sound, but lost some of the spatial character. In the end a compromise was made: both close and distant capture microphones were utilised and then mixed accordingly later, depending on the nature of the shot.

Sounds from the Action Space Archive

The Action Space audio archive totals approximately 80 hours of reel-to-reel analogue tape. These are recordings of documented meetings, radio interviews, and several musical contributions from members of the group including Richard Harper and Jon Trotter, featuring electric and acoustic guitar, flute, vocals and clarinet. Many of these pieces feature in the film and were digitised prior to the edit, with some recordings requiring additional audio restoration to reduce noise, or to enhance the clarity of dialogue and music. Most of the documented meetings were in poor condition, through years of neglect and inadequate storage, resulting in the raw content being almost inaudible. Through digitisation and restoration, several stories were uncovered that may have otherwise been lost, such as one key recording from 1976 featured in the film (01:07:49). The visual focal point here is the reel-to reel tape recorder, playing back the original tape as the inflatable begins to deflate around it. The crackly, distant but heated discussion between the members about the direction of the group, reveals the internal frictions of Action Space, hinting at the inevitability of its ultimate fracture.

Auralising Action Space

A substantial amount of the Action Space archive comprises the sound collages of Alan Nisbet, one of the group's founder members. Nisbet was an active musician and sound artist, his home tapes contain intricate compositions created from manipulated textures, nature recordings and everyday objects, in the vein of Pierre Schaeffer's *musique concrète*. Many of these pieces are chaotic, percussive and abrasive; struck pots and pans, motor engines and industrialised sounds are all merged and mashed into complex and relentless rhythms. Some sounds are much more mesmeric, long-form drones that subtly evolve, modulate and morph over time. It is clear that Nisbet was skilled at manipulating tape to create these pieces, often through his use of looping. This would have required the physical cutting and splicing of several tape loops, which would then be re-recorded onto a second tape and multi-tracked over several layers. By all accounts Nisbet only had access to limited recording equipment and resources, rendering this all the more impressive. During Action Space's most active period these pieces were played over a public-address system inside and outside the inflatables to entice and engage the public as part of the group's happenings and interventions in the parks, streets and council estates; wherever the group happened to be. As Ken Turner reminisced:

> The sounds he built for the outdoor pieces, the inflatables, were truly amazing, they held the whole environment together, he put out speakers, about four or five speakers in surround and he'd operate these heavy reel-to-reel recorders, and those large tapes they'd last quite a long time. We couldn't have done it without them, they gave an added depth to the atmosphere (K. Turner, personal interview 16th Oct 2017).

As the vast majority of the Action Space archive was still on ¼ inch analogue tape, it needed to be digitised for use in the film. Spending time actively listening to and cataloguing this material helped me to gain a healthy appreciation and respect for the work of Nisbet, Trotter et al. and the wealth of creative music-making within Action Space. Notes were made on each tape, based on usability and quality (some had partly perished over years) and on the featured musical qualities ('slow drones', 'frantic percussion' etc.). Some of these digitised pieces would be incorporated 'as is' into the film's edit, whilst selections were also catalogued and curated to be used in 'Sounds from the Action Space Archive'; a live tape piece performed by myself as one of the film's featured performances. In the spirit of Nisbet's original approach I limited myself to a completely analogue setup, with two ¼ inch tape machines, a mixing desk, and an analogue delay unit. The limitations of such a setup, though at first restrictive, became extremely liberating. I had to think creatively to maximise the limited resource of sounds and with only variations in levels, pan, filtering, tape speed and delay to create variation. This was not an exact replica of Nesbit's setup, but an attempt to channel his tactile approach and add some authenticity that harked back to the sound worlds of Action Space's heyday. Engaging with the physical and malleable properties of sound was important to his creative process, as highlighted by fellow member Ken Turner:

> I don't think anybody actually saw him putting the tapes together, you know, collecting the sounds or how he did it, it's all a bit of a mystery. So he would turn up one day and say 'here I've made another tape', a reel-to-reel tape. He had these two very old tape recorders, well they were old because they were slung out by the BBC and he just got them for nothing practically. It was like handling a big digger or something, because you had to sort of yank the handle to make it move, or switch it on, or reverse it and so on. . . .
>
> What he would have done with a computer-generated sound system, I don't know. Maybe he wouldn't have liked it; it wouldn't be real enough for him. He loved the reality of material to make sounds and maybe the tape recorders being heavy and having to wrench them as though they were a mechanical tool, rather than an instrument, [was what] he really enjoyed (K. Turner, personal interview 16th Oct 2017).

As Donaldson highlights, these familiar physical approaches to sculpting, wrenching and playing with sound are an integral process to the world of sound design:

> . . . the processes of creating film sound requires physical activity and involvement, play and experimentation, which might be literally physical, or have a kind of tactile analogy (to weaving, sculpting and so on) (Donaldson, 2017, p. 31).

In this regard, Nisbet was indeed a sound designer. He took a tactile, avant-garde and experimental approach to sound, sculpting, layering and weaving strands together, using sound to evoke atmosphere, entrance and entertain, working together with performers to enrich the visual spectacle and ultimately enhance the overall experience. In the late 1960s to late 1970s Nisbet and Action Space were rallying against the art elite, incorporating a DIY approach to attracting and educating audiences in London and around the UK. At the same time Murch and contemporaries in California, US

Auralising Action Space

Figure 6: The Action Space audio archive. © Huw Wahl

were reacting against established Hollywood film protocols, seeking new creative and aesthetic applications of sound in film. Despite their different applications, sound was, and still is, essential to create atmosphere, mood, and to engage audiences. This was understood by Murch and the American Zoetrope as much as it was by Nisbet and Action Space. And although the tools may have changed, traditional roles may have been blurred or redefined, and film budgets and their available resources vary wildly; play, risk taking and experimentation are still integral skills to successful sound design.

Sound and Affect

Whilst this chapter highlights the vital importance of play and experimentation in the various contributions to the soundtrack, an immediate response from the viewer-listener could well be a visceral sense of the surreal or otherworldliness, created through the use of archive material, production sound and featured music when combined with the visual.

The audio archive excerpts and sound collages are often coupled with idealistic visual imagery from archive film footage — children playing, bouncing, laughing, enjoying the structures. Occasionally the footage becomes more surreal, huge looming inflatable shapes sway with the force of activity around and inside them, adult characters appear to lead the action dressed in theatrical costume, dancing, singing, chanting or writhing on the floor. The participants in these scenes are lost in the moment, absolutely absorbed, the music seeming to heighten the trance-like or instinctive behaviour. These scenes are accompanied sonically by evolving drones, distorted and ambiguous voices, sporadic percussion, steel drums or woodwind textures. At several moments, the camera catches everyday passing onlookers appearing bemused, curious and somewhat suspicious — 'What on earth is going on?' — a reaction that may in fact be similar for the film viewer at these points. Although history and context are given in the film, much of the archive material is unaccompanied by voice-over to allow the viewer to take in the full spectacle for their own interpretation. Sounds drift in and out, often asynchronous with image, the combination resulting in a bewildering audio-visual experience.

This dreamlike effect is partly evoked through the nature of the sounds themselves; abstracted and contorted beyond recognition. The source material of Nisbet's tape loops becomes unidentifiable through filtering, reversing and time warping processes. These are mixed and woven together to create further indistinguishable layers. The film's location sound is sometimes subtly shaped in a similar vein, as with the tubing effects described earlier, or emphasized through post-production layering and experimentation. This abstraction is also true of the featured musical performances through the use of extended instrumental techniques. Minton uses the most primordial instrument available, the human voice, yet he uses it in an unconventional way. His opening performance of yelps, cries, screams and two-tone throat singing, along with the emphasized inhalation and exhalation of breath, give a very impressive yet unsettling performance. AMM feature a fairly orthodox musical combination of piano and percussion, but applied with a completely experimental approach. The bass drum groans, resonances, scratches and scrapes, bowed cymbal shrieks, and fluid atonal piano figures create a mesmerising but mysterious performance.

This sense of the surreal, or even unease, for the audience is heightened further by the musical structures that contain these sounds. The film does not feature a 'composed' soundtrack and, although extracts of AMM's performance are woven throughout the film, the source material is improvised through musical and sonic responses to the uniqueness of the surroundings. There is no clearly identifiable melodic material, no reused musical cues nor recognisable themes, thereby shunning conventional approaches to the film score. The featured music, whether archive or featured performances, is mainly responsive and reactive, leading to a sense of uncertainty for the film audience. This embodied sense of risk, experimentation and play, an unwillingness to remain rigid or commit to conventional structures, is very much in the ethos of Action Space. Sound and music, like theatre and performance, were used to push and provoke audiences and to disrupt accepted opinions of culture. It is only in fleeting moments, such as the film's conclusion, that equilibrium is found through a more stable sense of sound. Here, the second main extract from AMM is featured non-diegetically; the piano now employs more major tonalities, bolder chords, clearer cadences and rhythmic progressions. The occasional minor chords lend an edge of melancholy, reinforced by bowed cymbals that ring out like whale song, echoing around the inflatable. Gradually the texture becomes sparser and the sounds more delicate, accompanying a more intimate moment, the final scene where Ken Turner plays amongst the folds of the semi-inflated structure as it eventually deflates around him. The metaphorical 'death' of the inflatable signifies the end of Action Space, the time lived and left for Ken in his advanced years, and his relationship with his son the filmmaker. This change to a more fragile and intimate sensitivity, in both sound and image, signals the end of the film.

This sense of the otherworldly emerges from within the inflatable structures. As Turner states, the created structures enabled 'an imaginative understanding of the world more sensually. A difference in sound, colour, space awareness and movement. One could say that a new dimension of life was being unfolded' (Turner, 2016, p. 78). The overall effect of the soundtrack is an attempt to bring alive that heightened sensory experience, to express, through whatever creative means necessary, the sensation of being inside these spaces. In the film, philosopher Johan Siebers describes the newly made inflatable structure as having 'a kind of enchanting appeal as if it leads you into a different world. A world that is somehow real, or more real even than the world in which we normally live but you can't capture it.' (Wahl, 2016). Nisbet, AMM, Phil Minton and myself are all striving to express this sonically; be that through instinctive play, experimentation, seeking new sounds via extended techniques, or via the abstraction and accentuated materiality of sound and its dynamic, timbral and spatial characteristics. These facets are coupled with the visual of perspective, colour, shape and movement in an attempt to recreate the heightened sensory and otherworldly experience for the viewer-listener.

The permission to play granted to the documentary sound designer opens up critical arguments around authenticity (Rogers, 2013, p. 1). As detailed here, such practices might seem more aligned to those of fiction film. One may need to strike a balance between using sound for aesthetic or embellishment purposes and providing a sense of actuality. *Action Space* treads the line of primarily telling the story and history of the group and the impact on the family unit found at its core. However this story is acknowledged to be 'a re-presentation' rather than a 'clear window onto reality' (Nichols, 2005, p. 18). As in all documentary, there is a subjective shaping of aesthetics throughout — decisions when to record, when to stop, and choices of length and combinations of shot during the editing stages. As Dai Vaughan states, attempting to try and achieve exact impartial truths would not only be 'practically impossible but absurd' (1999, p. 88). These influences are acknowledged in *Action Space*: it is also a personal story, the filmmaker is part of the extended family of Action Space, a potential 'fabricator of meaning' (Nichols, 2005, p. 18) and this interest is declared to the audience through the voice of the filmmaker in one of the film's first scenes. This central story however occasionally needs to transcend the 'real', to blur into the otherworld, to give important glimpses of a non-reality, of another time, other possibilities — new spaces in which to start anew. All of which were dreams of Action Space's alternative culture, to 'move out' and 'do something different' (Wahl, 2016). Representing both the 'real' and 'unreal' have equal authentic importance in the film which requires the audience to 'hold together two worlds at once' and simultaneously engage and suspend our disbelief (Rogers, 2013, p. 12).

Conclusion

Reflecting on the process of *Action Space* as sound designer, it is evident that I became completely absorbed by the whole process. The vibrant creative energy present during the production and inflatable build was indeed infectious and inspiring, it wasn't enough to stand on the side lines as an objective observer. As Turner stated in 1971: 'You can't get much from Action Space just by looking at it; it is meant to be joined in' (Turner, 1971, p. 24). As a passion project this wasn't simply a job, but an experience that I became truly immersed in, discovering the history and ethos of Action Space for myself, which in turn influenced my approach to the sound design. This is true whether exploring the archive material, playing with the production sound, recording the musical performances or shaping the final mix. Working as sole sound designer on a small budget documentary film does have many limitations including not having enough time, resources, or even hands to do the job. However, it also comes with an unencumbered freedom to explore, to seek out creative opportunities, and allows one to learn through play, enabling a more artistic and holistic application of the soundtrack.

Endnotes

1 '*Mise-en-bande*' is Altman's analytical approach to understanding the interrelationships between dialogue, music and effects that contribute to the complete soundtrack. This is akin to the visual sense of *mise-en-scène*, where we consider the significance of what is 'put onto the stage', *mise-en-bande* requires we consider the importance of what is 'put onto the track' (2000)

2 Wright identifies at least three interpretations of the sound designer in modern day Hollywood:

i) those who undertake the administrative role of managing the various sound departments on a film production

ii) those who create special sound effects through recording, processing and layering audio

iii) a combination of these roles, both administrative and creative (2013).

Bibliography

Altman, R. (1992). The material heterogeneity of recorded sound. In R. Altman (Ed.), *Sound Theory, Sound Practice* (pp. 2 – 31). New York: Routledge.

Altman, R., Jones, M., & Tratoe, S. (2000). Inventing the cinema soundtrack: Hollywood's multiplane sound system. In J. Buhler, C. Flinn, & D. Neumeyer (Eds.), *Music and cinema* (pp. 339 – 359). Hanover, NH: University Press of New England [for] Wesleyan University Press.

AMM. (1967). *AMMMusic*. UK: Elektra EUK-256.

Buhler, J., Neumeyer, D., & Deemer, R. (2010). *Hearing the movies : music and sound in film history*. New York: Oxford University Press.

Chau, C. (2012). *Now history repeats itself with Graham Stevens' pneumatic art*. un Magazine 6.1. Retrieved from http://unprojects.org.au/magazine/issues/issue-6-1/now-history-repeats-itself-with-graham-stevens-pneumatic-art/

Chion, M., Gorbman, C., & Murch, W. (1994). *Audio-vision : sound on screen*. New York: Columbia University Press.

Coppola, F. F. (1974). *The Godfather Part II*. USA: Paramount.

Coppola, F. F. (1979). *Apocalypse Now*. USA: Zoetrope Studios.

Donaldson, L. F. (2017). Feeling and filmmaking: the design and affect of film sound. *The New Soundtrack, 7*(1), 31 – 46. https://doi.org/10.3366/sound.2017.0095

Grierson, J., & Hardy, F. (1966). *Grierson on documentary*. London: Faber and Faber.

Higgins, H. (2002). *Fluxus experience*. Berkeley: University of California Press.

Jones, C., & Jolliffe, G. (2011). *The guerilla film makers handbook*. New York; London: Continuum International Publishing Group.

Lo Brutto, V. (1994). *Sound-on-film : interviews with creators of film sound*. Westport, Conneticut: Praeger.

Lucas, G. (1977). *Star Wars*. USA: 20th Century Fox.

Nichols, B. (2005). The voice of documentary. In A. Rosenthal & J. Corner (Eds.), *New challenges for documentary* (Second Ed, pp. 17 – 33). Manchester; New York: Manchester University Press.

Rogers, H. (2013). Composing with reality: digital sound and music in documentary film. *In Zdok. 13* From: https://blog.zhdk.ch/zdok/talk-video/2016-talk-video/english/2017/composing-with-reality-digital-music-and-sound-in-documentary-film/

Ruoff, J. (1992). Conventions of sound in documentary. In R. Altman (Ed.), *Sound theory/sound practice* (pp. 217 – 234). New York: Routledge.

Thom, R. (1999). Designing for sound by Randy Thom. Retrieved 3 November 2017, from http://filmsound.org/articles/designing_for_sound.htm

Turner, K. (1971). Discussion: Action Space. *Theoria to Theory*, 5(2), 10. From: https://babel.hathitrust.org/cgipt?view=image;size=100;id=mdp.39015024593041;q1=turner;page=root;seq=120;num=10%0D

Turner, K. (2016). *Crashing culture: an artist notebook from 1954 to 2016*. UK: Imaginative Eye and Eye Projects.

Unfinished Histories (n.d.). *Inter-Action*. Retrieved from http://www.unfinishedhistories.com/history/companies/inter-action

Vaughan, D. (1999). *For documentary : twelve essays*. Berkeley: University of California Press.

Wahl, H. (2014). *To hell with culture*. UK: Distrify.com.

Wahl, H. (2016). *Action Space*. UK: Distrify.com.

Walker, J. A. (2002). *Left shift : radical art in 1970s Britain*. London; New York: I.B. Tauris.

Wright, B. (2013). What do we hear? The pluralism of sound design in Hollywood sound production. *The New Soundtrack*, 3(2), 137 – 157. https://doi.org/10.3366/sound.2013.0043

CHAPTER 5

'The film looks like how Ornette sounds': Shirley Clarke's music documentary *Ornette: Made in America*

Rosa Nogués

Shirley Clarke's documentary film *Ornette: Made in America* (1985) is no ordinary music documentary. The film — a portrait of the free jazz music legend Ornette Coleman — follows the jazz musician over the course of 20 years, and yet, it offers neither a biographical narrative nor a celebration of his musical achievements. Clarke, the American independent filmmaker responsible for films such as *The Connection* (1961) and *Portrait of Jason* (1967), came to prominence in the 1950s for short experimental dance films and documentaries made in collaboration with Willard Van Dyke, D. A. Pennebaker and Richard Leacock, proponents of what would become the direct cinema movement. This experience would prove instrumental in Clarke's life-long approach to filmmaking, which was concerned with the critical examination of the limitations of representation and the claim to truth of documentary filmmaking. *Ornette: Made in America* is thus framed by the question as to the nature of the documentary process itself, as well as that of the relationship between film and music, questions which permeate all of Clarke's filmmaking practice. Her particular approach to documentary was especially critical: 'no such thing [as a documentary] exists' (Rice, 1972, p. 22), making *Ornette: Made in America* a particularly unusual type of film, lying as it does within the realm of documentary filmmaking, yet at the same time clearly problematizing its place within it. In addition, although the film centres around the figure of Coleman and his approach to music and provides a lot of footage of one particular performance, the film is neither a strictly biographical exercise, nor an inquiry into Coleman's oeuvre and musical achievements, and least of all, a film about the performance that opens and closes the film. And yet, it is the music of this performance, which underlies the whole length of the film. Not only do we hear this music through most of the film, but it is also the skeleton around which the film takes shape.

Music is naturally the central element in *Ornette: Made in America*, but rather than having an expository or diegetic function, music is that which drives and frames the film. And given that Coleman's music is based on freedom of form and improvisation, Clarke's film attempts to do exactly that with its non-linear structure, quick editing style, and jumps between documentary and staged sequences, as well as between film and video footage. The object of the documentary is thus the music itself, and the ongoing question and objective in the film is precisely how to reflect, portray and document the nature of Coleman's music. In an interview with Jacques Derrida in 1997, Coleman described his approach to music in the following terms: 'the idea is that two or three people can have a conversation with sounds, without trying to dominate it or lead it' (Murphy, 2004, p. 322). Clarke's film reflects precisely this collective and spontaneous ethos, as a disjunctive unity of images, narratives, sounds and music.

Coleman was an outsider in the jazz world: the innovation that he introduced into jazz, rejecting the traditional harmonic structures that had characterized it up until the post-war bebop era, completely freed improvisation and provoked as much animosity as admiration amongst fellow musicians. Clarke, like Coleman, also never escaped her position as an outsider in cinema. A pioneer filmmaker whose work anticipated important trends in both film and artistic practice in the second half of the twentieth century, she was a central figure in the New American Cinema and the wider independent film scene that emerged in New York in the 1950s and 60s. And yet her name has been relegated to a minor position in the historical accounts of the period (in relation to a male pantheon of figures such as Jonas Mekas, John Cassavetes and Ken Jacobs, for example). Even when her name is mentioned, the central role that she played both in the foundation of the Filmmakers Cooperative (what would become the New American Cinema) and its development — in terms of activism for wider distribution and screenings of independent films — is not acknowledged.

Made in America: Questioning the American Dream

Ornette [Coleman], Archie [Shepp] and Cecil [Taylor]. Three versions of a contemporary Black Secularism. Making it in America, from the country, the ghetto, into the gnashing maw of the Western art world. The freedom they, the music, want is *the freedom to exist in this.* . . . The freedom of the given. The freedom to exist as artists. (Jones, 1969, p. 197).

Ornette: Made in America centres around the 1983 performance of Ornette Coleman's symphonic piece *Skies of America*, written in 1965 for symphony orchestra and jazz ensemble. The performance was part of the inauguration of the Caravan of Dreams Performing Arts Centre in Fort Worth, Texas, Coleman's own hometown. The film begins, before we even see the title sequence on screen, with a shot of a young black boy leaving 'Felix Bar', immediately followed by a quick scene of the dramatization of a cowboy stand-off in the streets of Fort Worth. Then comes a longer scene where Coleman, in the middle of a small gathering outside, is being handed the keys to the city by the mayor. After this, the title of the film is shown on an LED scrolling sign in the middle of the city: 'Ornette: Made in America'. This introductory sequence initiates the blurring of the boundaries between document and fiction, reality and dramatization, which are going to determine the rest of the film. In addition, it offers a clue as to the ironic character of the film's title *Made in America*, and the particular critique that the film is going to perform in relation to it. In this sequence, the mayor of Fort Worth, as is typical in these types of events, grandiloquently proclaims the merits, success, and importance of Coleman, praising him and claiming it as evidence of the reality and reach of the American Dream, that is, that, in the mayor's own words: 'success is possible for all who take advantage of the opportunities of our country'. This bombastic and misguided rhetoric about the virtues of the American social and cultural context, what he calls 'the American way of life', and its role in forging Coleman's musical career, success, excellence and virtuosity, will contrast starkly with the reality of Coleman's life and musical development as the film progresses. Despite the fact that the viewer is not provided with much detailed information about Coleman's upbringing or adult life, it becomes clear that he grew up with scarce resources in an impoverished part of town by the railroad tracks and that he encountered obstacles grounded in racism and prejudice every step of the way to the pedestal that Fort Worth's mayor is raising for him in 1983. Thus the title *Made in America* holds a particularly ironic resonance throughout the film.

The complex and conflictual nature of this notion of 'making it in America', which Jones' quotation above fully conveys, was not lost on Coleman. And, although he exemplarily plays his part during the commemorative key-giving ceremony, he was fully aware of both the process of reification and commodification that this 'made in America' entailed for him as a black musician, as well as the racist social, political and cultural context that produced it: 'The insanity of living in America is that ownership is really strength. It's who owns who's strongest in America . . .in jazz the Negro is the product. The way they handle the publicity on me . . . it gets to be that I'm the product myself.' (Spellman, 1967, pp. 130 – 31).

Not surprisingly, despite the celebratory welcome extended to Coleman, there are quite a few very visible empty seats in the auditorium during the performance, laying bare the fact that, despite his stature as, in the words of the mayor, 'a widely acclaimed figure in the jazz world', he remained an outsider for most of his career, especially in his hometown. Another interesting contrast is the fact that, as Coleman revealed in his interview with Derrida in 1997, writing *Skies of America* was a tragic event for him because of his poor relationship with the music scene. Since his early days in Texas playing the saxophone in rhythm and blues bands, Coleman attracted attention for his particular and innovative style of playing — 'the first truly original concept of saxophone playing since Charlie Parker' (Spellman, 1967, p. 79) — and encountered hostility from both fellow musicians and punters every step of the way to his residence at the Five Spot Cafe in New York City at the end of 1959, which was extended from two to ten weeks. The freedom with which he approached the music, the dissonant nature of his sound, and the fact that he defied all previously accepted conventions about jazz, made him into a controversial figure within the jazz establishment at the time. This contrasts starkly with the humility and generosity with which he played and spoke about his music, as *Made in America* reveals. The difficulty and complexity of Coleman's relationship to the jazz world is only briefly alluded to in the film, and not by Coleman himself, but rather by his ex-wife, the poet Jayne Cortez, the musician James Clay, and his sister, Truvenza Leach. They bear witness to his position as outsider from the very beginning of his career as a musician: drawing suspicion from fellow musicians; provoking violent rejection (musicians would sometimes leave the bandstand when he sat in at club performances and he was physically attacked on a number of occasions, most famously by Max Roach); getting his instrument broken; and being considered mentally unstable (by Miles Davis for example) (Litweiler, 1992 and Spellman, 1967). Clarke clearly chose not to dwell on these infamous moments in Coleman's biography although they are well known and part of what Clay refers to as the 'Ornette mystique'. She was actively avoiding the kind of biographical exercise which would focus on these — 'I wasn't trying to make a "documentary" of Ornette' (Snowden, 1986).

It is worth dwelling for a short moment on the specific conditions that brought *Ornette: Made in America* to life because Clarke faced similar difficulties throughout her career as a woman filmmaker, that is, she was always considered an outsider and thus found it increasingly difficult to get her projects funded. Although the film was finished and released in 1985, Clarke's first proposal for a film about Ornette Coleman was submitted in 1968 to the Public Broadcasting Laboratory (PBL). The main terms of her proposal were to focus on the relationship between Coleman and his son Denardo, who at 11 years of age at the time, had been included by Coleman in his band as the drummer. The controversy that this decision generated was the first motivation for Clarke to document the relationship between father and son. She was granted a limited budget, shooting started, and not before long, PBL cancelled the project. After several attempts to get additional funding (from the BBC and a German television company, for example), Clarke gave up on the project, but managed to keep the footage shot thus far.

15 years later, when Coleman was asked to perform at the inauguration of the Caravan of Dreams Performance Arts Centre in Forth Worth as the returning prodigal son, Clarke got her chance to finish the film. The Centre's director, Kathelin Hoffman, after viewing the earlier footage, decided to employ Clarke to document the inaugural performance. The film thus spans almost 20 years, with varied footage from various sources and in

different formats (both film and video) and both high and low resolution. This includes: 16mm reversal film from the material shot in the 1960s; several formats of video gathered from television broadcasts, home video recordings and club performances; and the Super 16mm used in 1983. In addition to this, the film combines documentary footage with staged dramatizations of Ornette's childhood memories.

The heterogeneous and eclectic nature of the original footage is one of the foundations of the film. Rather than attempt to disguise it and unify the visual language under an overarching narrative (of musical achievement or a biographical journey), the film emphasizes and dwells on the disjunctive character of the images on screen, self-reflexively bearing testimony to its own conditions of production. The film's visual fragmentation echoes the temporal disjunction that constitutes it, bringing to the fore the indeterminate and dispersed nature of the film. Flutter cutting, video effects, and frames within frames are used throughout the film, constantly frustrating the viewer's expectations of a stable and unified narrative. Early on in the film, it is made clear that it is the relationship between images and music that is the main driving force of the film, rather than that between images and narrative content. There are several thematic threads weaving the film together which function as archival records of the film's own heterogeneous constitution. As Hoffman remarked: 'Ornette and I were focused on making a film about the creative process of a pioneering artist. Shirley was focused on continuing the story she had begun in the '60s, of a musician and his relationship with his son. We wove these themes together in the shooting along with John Dolphin's interest in the story of a poor black kid returning home as a symphony composer; a classic "rags to riches"' (Milestone Film and Video, 2014).

Blurring the Lines Between Fact and Fiction

As if to underline the fictional nature of any attempt at narrative representation in documentary filmmaking — as in the 'classic rags to riches stories' alluded to above — Clarke intersperses staged dramatizations of scenes from Ornette's childhood throughout the film. And rather than aim for naturalism in these sequences, Clarke emphasizes their artificiality, with awkward acting on the part of the child actors and the constant acknowledgement of the presence of the camera, as subjects on screen are continuously breaking the fourth wall. For example, in the scene where young Ornette is leaving home to make a living as a musician, we see the present-day residents of Coleman's childhood neighbourhood look at both the child actor and the filming taking place, breaking the narrative pulse and forcing the viewer to consciously oscillate between both levels of representation.

By juxtaposing these stylised sequences with the documentary footage, Clarke is again exploring an ongoing concern in her film practice, the ambiguous relationship between the factual and the fictional at the core of cinematic representation. This was a fundamental problematic for Clarke that she gradually developed along the three feature films that she made between 1961 and 1967: *The Connection* (1961), based on the Living Theatre's off-Broadway production of Jack Gelber's homonymous play; *The Cool World* (1963), based on Warren Miller's novel of the same name; and *Portrait of Jason* (1967), a documentary portrait of Jason Holliday, a middle-aged gay black hustler longing for a slot in Greenwich Village's cabaret circuit. In *The Connection* Clarke offers a critical examination of the limitations of representation and the claim to truth of documentary film-making. This was seven years before Jim McBride's *David Holzman's Diary* (1968) was made, the film considered to have started the tradition of self-reflexive critical pseudo-documentary. Clarke's first feature is presented as the edited collection of the footage recorded by Jim Dunn, a documentary film director, and J. J. Burden, a cameraman, who at the beginning of the film informs us that he is the one responsible for putting the film together. In true *cinéma vérité* fashion, it purports to offer us a glimpse into the lives of a group of New York drug addicts waiting for their 'connection', the dealer with the drug supply for the day. It is this notion of film being able to capture an authentic experience of reality that, along the film, Clarke lays bare as fundamentally a misconstruction. In the same way as the play on which it is based, the film continuously blurs the boundaries between the factual and the fictional, leaving the spectator to negotiate the different levels of reality presented. Clarke turns the camera on itself, revealing how it is the camera that creates the reality it depicts, provoking and producing the action on screen. In her second feature, *The Cool World*, Clarke further explores the ambiguous relationship between the factual and the fictional at the heart of cinematic representation. The film combines fiction and documentary to portray a few days in the life of a black Harlem teenager at the start of the Civil Rights Movement. The highly stylised documentary depiction of Harlem, which serves as both the cultural and the political backdrop for the film's narrative, reflects a self-critical examination of the technologies of representation. In *Portrait of Jason* we find again a self-reflexive exploration of the question of cinematic representation, with the materiality of the filmmaking process coming centre stage. On screen, Jason Holliday's performance before the camera oscillates between humorous camp sketches — he plays part of his cabaret act to the camera — and overly dramatic scenes of emotional vulnerability. With few narrative transitions in between, it is again up to the spectator to negotiate who the real Jason Holliday is, where his act ends and he himself begins.

As Clarke put it: 'I was very curious about the whole discussion of documentary and dramatic films and what was truly true. I had a lot of ideas about what was *cinéma vérité*, what was real, what was documentary, and what was fiction' (Rabinovitz, 1983, p. 10). Having made documentary films during the 1950s in collaboration with Willard Van Dyke, D. A. Pennebaker and Richard Leacock, proponents of the direct cinema movement — characterized by a 'hyperbolic insistence on objectivity, spontaneity and non-mediation' (Green, 2006, p. 69) — it is not surprising that Clarke's filmmaking practice articulated such a sharp critique of the claim to truth of documentary filmmaking. *The Connection* was in fact the first film in a long tradition of documentaries, which appropriate the visual and stylistic conventions of documentary filmmaking to highlight the limitations of the documentary conceit, that is, that reality can be captured objectively and without mediation.

The Visualisation of Sound

Ornette: Made in America is likewise determined by the question as to the nature of the documentary process itself, yet more specifically, it is addressing the question of the relationship between film and music. Music is without a doubt the central motif in the film, but rather than having an expository or diegetic function, the music drives the film forward and frames it. It is, as advanced earlier, the skeleton around which the film takes shape. Clarke said the following about her approach to the editing of the film: 'I knew I was connecting to the way [Coleman] sounded because the first thing I laid down was the sound. . . . Then I decided what images were going to go with that particular sound. I shot every single piece we used without knowing what I was going to do with it' (Snowden, 1986). After transferring all the footage to video, Clarke edited the film on U-matic, 'playing the machine like one plays the piano'. Her editing pulsates to the rhythm of Coleman's music, the visual style is completely in tune with the music soundtrack. And Clarke acknowledged using improvisation in laying down the images in the editing process. She said: '[h]aving laid the spine down, which was his music, I edited to the music. That's where the rhythms and energy came from. The film looks like how Ornette sounds and has the same basic thinking' (Snowden, 1986).

It is not just in terms of the editing of the film that Clarke attempted to reflect the nature of Coleman's music. Her decision to maintain and emphasize the heterogeneous nature of the footage, and the disjunctive quality of the images on screen, clearly mirrors the tonal and rhythmic eclecticism at the heart of the one musical piece at the centre of the film, *Skies of America*, and Coleman's music more generally. The eschewal of visual harmony evident in the film is clearly determined by Coleman's own theory of 'harmolodics' which dictates that 'harmony cease to exist as a primary concept' (Litweiler, 1992, p. 54) and that hierarchies be rejected to make all three basic musical elements, melody, harmony and rhythm equal in significance and prominence. Despite the obvious complexity of Coleman's conception of harmolodics — his definition of it as that which 'allows a person to use a multiplicity of elements to express more than one direction' (Litweiler, 1992, p. 131) — it resonates perfectly with Clarke's strategy in *Made in America*. By highlighting the heterogeneous nature of the different elements making up the film, she was clearly echoing Coleman's understanding of harmolodics, as well as his own approach to composition in *Skies of America*. The music was composed by Coleman in 1965 and recorded in London in 1972 with the London Symphony Orchestra, yet, due to contractual problems with the musicians' union in the UK, he was the only improviser on the album. In *Made in America*, it is Coleman's original vision for the piece that is revealed. Orchestral passages alternate with sections played by Coleman's band at the time, Prime Time, which comprised two electric guitarists, two electric bassists and two drummers. The jagged and disjunctive nature of the transitions between the two is evident and intensified rather than downplayed, and the symphony itself is a collage of new compositions and reworked old themes, a heterogeneous collection of music and sounds, which Clarke's film reproduces visually. One of the most recognizable tunes in *Skies of America* is 'School Work' (which appears on the album *Broken Shadows*, recorded in 1971), whose playful sax riff we hear again and again in countless variations throughout the film.

In the 1968 proposal to the BBC, Clarke referred explicitly to the experimental nature of the project, declaring her aim to be the exploration of the way that new film techniques and electronic media can contribute to the visualisation of sound. The main concern, she stated, was how to film music successfully (Cohen, 2012a). Unfortunately she didn't get the funds, as Coleman was not sufficiently well known at the time. Later she said that, had she made that early film, it would not have been anything exceptional. Given the primary role that video experimentation and visual improvisation play in *Made in America*, in terms of attempting to capture and reflect the free and heterogeneous nature of Coleman's music, it is not difficult to conclude that Clarke would not have achieved the same results with film in 1968. It was only after spending over a decade experimenting with video that she was able to approach the filmic process in the truly improvisational manner that her vision for the project required. Video provided an immediacy that film lacked in order to experiment with the image in real time, enabling the spontaneity in improvisation necessary to replicate Coleman's approach to music which 'should require no mediation' (Mandel, 2008, p. 126). Video also 'allow[ed] for an emotional response on the part of the person editing' (Snowden, 1986). This focus on the emotional engagement with the image again reflected Coleman's own 'emotionalism' in his improvisation (Litweiler, 1992, p. 54).

Between 1969 and 1983, when the latest footage of Made in America was shot, Clarke stopped making films and turned her attention to video. According to legend, the switch was the result of a chance encounter on the street. After learning that PBL had pulled the plug on the Ornette project, Clarke bumped into an acquaintance of hers who was carrying a Sony Portapak, the first video camera to be made widely available to consumers in 1969. With help from a grant from the New York State Council on the Arts — which at the time saw its budget multiplied from two to 20 million dollars as part of Nelson Rockefeller's re-election campaign to be New York State governor (Ryan, 1988, p. 42) — she bought cameras, monitors and tape decks with which she filled her penthouse apartment at New York's Chelsea Hotel. There she organised events and workshops and set up a collective that would come to be known as the Tee Pee Video Space Troupe which included members of video collectives Videofreex and Raindance, as well as Bruce Ferguson, Andrew Gurian, Frank Gillette, Dee Dee Halleck, Susan Milano and Clarke's own daughter Wendy.

Her workshops were attended by artists such as Nam June Paik, Shigeko Kubota, Yoko Ono, Harry Smith, and Steina and Woody Vasulka, amongst others. Figures such as Andy Warhol, the actress Viva (who was a neighbour), Alan Watts and Arthur C. Clarke also visited regularly. Central to these workshops was the imperative to experiment with the new technology, to play around with the cameras, synthesizers and monitors, to try things out, to improvise, and to play. Video was in these workshops a performative practice and not a recording medium. The emphasis was on the process and not on the production of a final object. In fact, tapes were mostly discarded. Thomas Cohen has likened the atmosphere and working ethos of these workshops as that of a jazz jam session which privileges improvisation and experimentation, an engagement with the expanding musical form and response to it — as well as to the other musicians — in real time, rather than the completion of a finished piece of music (Cohen, 2012b, p. 59).

Clarke was not just a jazz enthusiast; she had a lifelong commitment to jazz. The soundtrack for The Cool World (1963) was scored by Mal Waldron and performed by

Dizzy Gillespie and his quintet, and the quick editing style of the documentary scenes shot in Harlem clearly indicate the integrative approach taken to the relationship between soundtrack music and image, which is also evident in *Ornette: Made in America*. In *The Connection* (1961), the jazz musicians on screen — the Freddie Redd quartet, which included Jackie McLean — are playing themselves, and form an integral part of the on-screen action. Given that the film presents a film within a film — within a scathing critique of the direct cinema documentary style — the music is, on one level, strictly diegetic and does not betray the documentary ethos. Yet on another level, it is clear that it is the musicians' improvisations that in effect drive the dramatic development of the film forward and play a vital role in the denouement of the film.

Yet this concern with the relationship between music, particularly jazz music, and film is at the heart of Clarke's filmmaking practice since her early days. Her characteristic quick and rhythmic montage style in *The Cool World* and *Ornette: Made in America* emerges in her experimental film loops of the 1950s. In 1958 she was one — the only woman — of a number of filmmakers (including Van Dyke, Leacock, and Pennebaker) commissioned by US State Department to shoot and edit a number of short film loops which were bound to be part of the US pavilion at the 1958 Brussels World's Fair. The social and political context for the commission of the loops was that of a US government eager to present the image of a free, democratic, forward moving and modern society, and to dispel the image of a country still permeated by racism and riddled with racial conflict (which had been reinforced by the incidents in Little Rock, Arkansas, only a few months previously). With this aim, and after having closed down the one section in the pavilion which directly addressed the problem of racism in US society, the US Department relied on a roster of mainly black performers (Harry Belafonte being one of the better known participants at the time) to counteract the perception that the US was still the racist and segregated country that the crisis in Little Rock had revealed (Nilsen, 2011, pp. 126 – 135). Jazz was part of the ideological warfare, as it not only evoked the idea of freedom that the US State Department wanted the country to be associated with, but it also offered an image of racial integration that, again, the State Department was hopeful would help extricate any accusations of racism.

It is important to situate Clarke's film loops for the American pavilion within this context of racial conflict. Formally, these quickly edited film loops anticipate in important ways not only Clarke's visual style in her ensuing film work, but also her approach to montage as a kind of improvisation, an exploration of movement and rhythm in the image, as a 'visual equivalent of jazz' (Auerbach, 1998, p. 82 in Nilsen,

2011, p. 149). Indeed, her aim was to make them all 'jazzy' given that the State Department had instructed her that the one subject matter that she could *not* portray was precisely jazz (Rabinovitz, 2003, p. 100). Although these loops were made without sound, as wall decor rather than films to be watched, later experimental films such as *Bridges Go Round* (1958) (a loop that was rejected by the US State Department) and *Skyscraper* (1959), co-directed with Van Dyke, were edited to non-diegetic music and asynchronous sound. *Skyscraper* used the off-screen voices of the construction workers featured in the film. The film critic Henry Breitrose described *Skyscraper* as displaying an 'astonishing lyric quality . . . shots edited dynamically . . . the changes of tempo, the pauses, accelerations, retards and even visual glissandos . . . work with a remarkably complex correctness and grace. One is tempted to suggest that, like jazz, 'Skyscraper' simply "swings"' (Breitrose, 1960, p. 58).

Ornette: Made in America clearly reflects the development of Clarke's improvised and rhythmic approach to montage which she began to explore with the Brussels film loops, those 'little, jazzy, dance-like films'. And although her concern with the relationship between film and music spans her whole career, it is with *Ornette: Made in America* that Clarke's ideas about visual experimentation and improvisation, and the role of music in relation to cinematic representation all come together. The film openly defies the conventions of documentary and ironically reflects on them. The camera is often acknowledged and sometimes it is actually shown on screen. The footage, both film and video, was heavily manipulated at the time of shooting and in post-production, emphasizing the mediated nature of the documentary images. There are crude early video-game graphics and video effects, and at one point we witness a bizarre surrealist-like scene of Coleman riding a space rocket in outer space. Talking heads are enclosed in cartoon-like drawn television sets in a sort of childish defiance of the authority reserved for the speaker in this documentary convention. On several occasions we can hear Clarke's own voice giving directions or conversing with Coleman, asking him to discuss something in particular. And throughout the film, the intimate nature of the relationship between Clarke and Coleman leaves no doubt as to the subjective nature of that which is being represented onscreen. In the final scene of the film, although only Coleman is on screen, it is as if we were watching the two of them looking into each other's eyes. Coleman looks straight at the camera for what feels like hours: the intimacy that both his eyes and smile reveal leads our gaze behind the camera to Clarke herself.

'I'd rather be a man than a male'

One of the moments most revealing of this intimacy between Clarke and Coleman is located towards the end of the film, when offscreen Clarke asks Coleman to 'tell the castration story'. It is a significant sequence showing that Coleman is comfortable enough with Clarke to tell the story, to discuss his issues with sex — something that many of us would only do on the therapist's couch — and to reveal such an intimate aspect of his life and personality. Interestingly, this is the only moment in the film when the music we hear is not Coleman's own, rather it is the song 'AOS - Emotional Modulations' by The Plastic Ono Band, drawing attention to the special significance of this sequence. Whilst we hear Yoko Ono grunting and moaning to an atonal instrumental backdrop, Coleman recounts how in his early thirties, having always found it frustrating not knowing whether the many women who desired him and approached him did so just because he was a musician, he decided to ask a doctor to castrate him to do away with those kinds of distractions. The doctor dissuaded him and suggested circumcision instead, 'symbolic castration'. When Coleman finishes by saying that he decided that he was going to be a man rather than a male, it is clear that the nature of his struggle has to do with his sense of masculinity and how this is determined by a specific (white) fetishising and objectifying gaze. The castration story sequence resonates during the final scene in the film, when, after the performance of *Skies of America*, woman after woman (mostly white) come to Coleman in their fancy clothes, with big admiring grins on their faces and stars in their eyes, hug him and kiss him with little restraint. Ironically, when one woman in particular, claiming to be a journalist, asks to see him in his hotel room with the excuse of interviewing him, Coleman gives her the number of his room without any hesitation.

It is significant that, out of the many exchanges in the aftermath of the inaugurating performance that the film could have finished with, Clarke decided to finish with this one. It reveals one of Clarke's ongoing concerns in her filmmaking practice: the construction and performance of masculinity, and specifically, black masculinity, as determined by a white supremacist society. In the case of *Ornette: Made in America*, the focus is on another paradigmatic figure of black masculinity: the jazz musician.

> Jazz musicians also get a screwed-up sex life. . . . When the musician goes out and plays for the public on a bandstand, ninety percent of his audience in the nightclub is sexually oriented. . . . So therefore it ain't music, it's sexual attraction. . . . You don't know how many times I've come off the bandstand and had girls

come up to me and hand me a note with their address on it. . . . Sometimes I say to myself, 'Well, shit, if this is what it's all about, we should all be standing up there with hard-ons, and everybody should come to the club naked, and the musicians should be standing up there naked. Then there wouldn't be any confusion about what's supposed to happen, and people wouldn't say they came to hear the music' (Spellman, 1967, p. 139).

Clarke's decision to end with the question of Coleman's relationship to masculinity is not coincidental, given that the challenge that he posed in 1950s jazz circles was not limited to his music. As David Ake (1998) has argued, he represented a new concept of masculinity that ran against the dominant performance of jazz masculinity as a hyper-heterosexual masculinity — take for example Miles Davis or Red Garland and their representation of 'jazz-musician-as-boxer masculinity' (Ake, 1998, p. 34). This critique of the traditional jazz masculinity that Ornette presented with his long straight hair, thin body, long beard, homemade clothes, gentle demeanor and vegetarianism was no small thing. Since its (somewhat mythical) origins in Storyville, the red-light district in New Orleans, jazz has not only been a predominantly male space, 'creat[ing] and recreat[ing] notions of manhood' (Ake, 1998, p. 27), it has also always been intimately connected with sex. Of course this is the result of a particular 'race-zon[ing] by the white supremacist state' that rezoned New Orleans' sex district 'smack dab in the middle of a black working class neighbourhood, revealing the state's construction of 'blackness [as] hypersexual' (Tucker, 2008, p. 5). Ornette had no doubt about it, 'the jazz scene hasn't really changed that much since it left the New Orleans whorehouses. The nightclub is still built on the same two things: whiskey and fucking' (Spellman, 1967, p. 139). So it wasn't only the music that he was questioning and turning on its head, he was also posing the question as to what it meant to be a man in jazz, 'it was not simply a matter of not knowing what to play, but who to *be*' (Ake, 1998, p. 40).

One of the spaces where this hyper-heteromasculine performance was honed was in the jazz jams, or cutting contests, where musicians competed in terms of virtuosic performance and mastery of their instrument. Coleman, despite the difficulty inherent in achieving the particular sound he does from the saxophone, consciously avoided engaging in the virtuosic style of playing which was the norm in the post-bebop period. At one point in *Made in America*, the jazz critic Martin Williams recounts how one night at the Five Spot Cafe he heard Coleman play the blues like Charlie Parker, he says, 'and I have never heard anyone else other than Charlie Parker do that that way', but as the rest of the film clearly shows, Coleman's focus was not on individual proficiency but on the interaction and communication between the different instruments, the whole ensemble. He spoke of his own musicianship with an astounding humility, as is revealed during one scene in the film, when he is talking to a grown-up Denardo about his playing and says: 'I'll tell you the truth, I think you do it much better than I do.' His choice of instrument was also revelatory, a white plastic saxophone, again eschewing the fetishisation of the instrument and its mastery typical of jazz performance at the time. He was clearly claiming a different form of masculinity for himself — 'I'd rather be a man' — away from the dominant hypersexual masculinity with which jazz musicians identified and which Coleman recognized as being produced by the racist context of US society, 'made in America'.

Ornette: Made in America was Clarke's final film. Three years after its release, she started to show symptoms of Alzheimer's disease, and died ten years later in 1997. The film epitomises Clarke's lifelong engagement with filmmaking: it offers both a critical reflection on the nature of the documentary image, something which was a concern of hers throughout her career, as well as a portrait of an idiosyncratic and radically experimental artist, Ornette Coleman, and through him, Clarke herself. It manages not only to convey the freedom in Coleman's approach to improvisation, and to reflect the heterogeneous and disjunctive quality of his music, it also replicates the self-reflexive nature of Coleman's music and character, revealing along the way Coleman's rejection of the limitations imposed on him by a racist American society and his self-fashioning against its constrictions. If his music creates the space for freedom, which Jones alludes to in the opening citation of this text, Clarke's film addresses the question of how this freedom can be 'made in America' by a man like Ornette Coleman.

Bibliography

Ake, D. (1998). Re-masculating jazz: Ornette Coleman, 'Lonely Woman', and the New York jazz scene in the late 1950s. *American Music, 16*(1), 25 – 44.

Auerbach, M. (1998). Film notes: a collection of stunning classics and originals. *LA Weekly*, April 2 – 8, 82.

Baldwin, J. (1985). *The price of the ticket: collected non-fiction*. London: Michael Joseph.

Bogle, D. (2003). *Toms, Coons, Mulattoes, Mammies, & Bucks: an interpretative history of blacks in American film*. New York: Continuum. 4th edition.

Breitrose, H. (1960). Films of Shirley Clarke. *Film Quarterly, 13*(4), 57 – 58.

Capper, B. (2013). Ultimate participation video: Shirley Clarke's Tee Pee Video Space Troupe. *Art Journal, 72*(1), 43 – 63.

Cohen, T. F. (2012a). *Playing to the camera: musicians and musical performance in documentary*. London: Wallflower Press.

Cohen, T. F. (2012b). After the New American Cinema: Shirley Clarke's video work as performance and document. *Journal of Film and Video, 64*(1 – 2), 57 – 64.

Green, J. F. (2006), This reality which is not one: Flaherty, Buñuel and the irrealism of documentary cinema, In G. D. Rhodes and J. P. Springer (eds), *Docufictions: Essays on the intersection of documentary and fictional filmmaking*. Jefferson and London: McFarland & Company, 64 – 86.

Gurian, A. (2004). Thoughts on Shirley Clarke and the TP Videospace Troupe. *Millennium Film Journal, 42*.

Jones, L. R. (1969). *Black music*. London: MacGibbon & Kee.

Litweiler, J. (1984). *The freedom principle: jazz after 1958*. Poole: Blandford.

Litweiler, J. (1992). *Ornette Coleman: a harmolodic life*. New York: W. Morrow.

Mandel, H. (2008). *Miles, Ornette, Cecil: jazz beyond jazz*. Abingdon, Oxon: Routledge.

Milestone Film and Video (2014). *Kathelin Hoffman Gray reminisces about Ornette and Shirley*.

Murphy, T. S. (2004). The Other's language: Jacques Derrida interviews Ornette Coleman, 23 June 1997. *Genre, 37*(2), 319 – 329.

Nilsen, S. (2011). *Projecting America, 1958: film and cultural diplomacy at the Brussels World's Fair*. Jefferson, NC: McFarland & Company.

Rabinovitz, L. (2003). *Points of resistance: women, power & politics in the New York avant-garde cinema, 1943 – 71*, 2nd ed. Urbana: University of Illinois Press.

Rice, S. (1972), Shirley Clarke: image and images. *Take One*, 07/02/1972, 22.

Ryan, P. (1988). A genealogy of video. *Leonardo, 21*(1), 39 – 44.

Snowden, D. (1986, January 21). Jazz portrait 'Ornette' 20 years in the making. *Los Angeles Times*. Retrieved from http://articles.latimes.com/1986-01-22/entertainment/ca-31685_1_ornette-coleman

Spellman, A. B. (1967). *Four lives in the bebop business (Cecil Taylor, Ornette Coleman, Herbie Nichols, Jackie McLean)*. London: MacGibbon & Kee.

Tucker, S. (2008). When did jazz go straight? A queer question for Jazz Studies. *Critical Studies in Improvisation/Études critiques en improvisation* DOI 10.21083/csieci.v4i2.850

Wilmer, V. (1977). *As serious as your life: the story of the new jazz*. London: Allison & Busby.

CHAPTER 6

Progress Music

James Bulley

Thanks go to Goldsmiths Special Collections, The Daphne Oram Trust, The Hugh Davies Collection, The BBC Written Archives, The British Film Institute Special Collections, Tom Richards, Dave Charlesworth (South Kiosk), Philip Zavier Serfaty (South Kiosk), Netta Pelota (South Kiosk), Daniel Jones, Ben James (Jotta), and Andrew Lister & Matthew Stuart (Bricks from the Kiln).

This chapter existed in an earlier incarnation as writing commissioned for *Bricks from the Kiln #2*. (Lister & Stuart, 2017)

> In the Golden Age, progress music was heard in the
> background by nearly everybody.
> The first phone, the first car, the first house,
> the first summer holiday, the first TV — all to progress music.
> Then the arrival of sexual intercourse, in 1966,
> and the full ascendancy of the children of the Golden Age
> > Martin Amis, The Pregnant Widow, 2010

This project explores a speculative era of 'Progress Music', unfolding narratives written from and through the archive. Here, form is found first as textual historical analysis, and then in the documentation of a multi-channel sound-film artwork, *Progress Music I*. This is a document of a time in 1960s Britain where the rapid rise of industry, communications and air travel was teamed with a spirit of idealistic public- information- film commissioning to inspire patternings of rhythmic, experimental, and incisive industrial documentary film. It is illustrated here by the collaborative work of British filmmaker Geoffrey Jones, and the composer and co-founder of the BBC Radiophonic Workshop Daphne Oram, on the British Petroleum (BP) documentary film *Trinidad and Tobago* (1964).[1] This inquiry began in 2012, stemming from research in the Daphne Oram collection, hosted at Goldsmiths, University of London, where I became curious about *Trinidad and Tobago*. In February of 1964, during the development of the 19-minute short film, Oram travelled to Trinidad to make field recordings and visit the yearly Carnival. On her return to her studio at Tower Folly in Kent, Oram composed a bombastic, electronically-effected concrète set of tape pieces, utilising pioneering sampling and tape manipulation techniques. For the final edit of the film, Jones then used Oram's soundscape works to create a highly detailed and rhythmic 'visual' graphic score that precisely defined his editing and shot selection (Jones, 2004).

'Progress Music,' as both text and installation work, is a project that maps alternate pathways through a speculative era, delineating a shifting, indeterminate relation to the archive, exploring stories as ever-changing, unstable, authored in the contemporary. Through this mechanism, the project seeks to highlight a vital but oft-overlooked time in experimental film and sound practice in Britain, refracted through the lens of two of its most underrepresented actors, Jones and Oram.

Archive

At first, the barren practicality of the housing of the Daphne Oram collection is chastening the modern archive is delimited by principles of preservation, classification and inter-relation. Light and temperature-controlled environs induce sterility — a context-free capsule frozen in time. Gone are the nostalgic days of dust, of Jules Michelet's feverish breathing and Walter Benjamin's card systems. Contemporary archives swim in a networked stream, perpetual and dematerialised. Surrogacy ghosts them from their shelves, away from the concerned purview of the archon.[2] Digital reformation unfetters the information in lines of data and meta-data — searchable, browsable, zoomable. Tactile encounters in the place of origination have become distant and rarefied. The material remains untouched, structured and conserved from the chaotic environment outside, liberated by digital avatars from institution and hierarchy. These surrogate fragments are summoned at will, activated and mediated by technology. In a visual-internet age, archival material shifts like ink on blotting paper – no sooner is it posted than it pixelates, reappearing cropped from context, reformulated, reanimated, a digital *I'm Sitting In a Room*.[3] The scale and form of the originating stuff is made skeletal in myriad transformations. But archival material does not only emanate outwards. Each archive has an inversion – that which is not there – excluded by choice, flippancy and chance. As the historian Carolyn Steedman has adroitly observed, 'there is history because there is absence' (Steedman, 2001, p. 146): writing history is the stuff of non-presence — stories are framed by what exists and refracted by the space between.

Sounds Index

The following index details the provenance of the sound fragments referenced throughout this writing.[4]

The sound excerpts referenced throughout this writing can be accessed by appointment with Special Collections & Archives at Goldsmiths, University of London.

Sound 1. 'Tuesday at Carnival' (February 1964) (excerpt from ORAM/11/DO283).

Sound 2. 'Flute and steel drum manipulation' (April 1964) (excerpt from ORAM/11/DO019a).

Sound 3. 'The Eyes Have It' and 'Come Leh We Go' sung by Mighty Sparrow (February 1964) (excerpt from ORAM/11/DO286).

Sound 4. 'Carnival' (February 1964) (excerpt from ORAM/11/DO285).

Sound 5. 'Drumming at Hindu wedding ceremony from distance' (February 1964) (excerpt from ORAM/11/DO284).

Sound 6. 'Drumming at Hindu wedding ceremony close' (February 1964) (excerpt from ORAM/11/DO284).

Sound 7. 'Bongo and Shango manipulations' (February 1964) (excerpt from ORAM/11/DO284).
Sound 8. 'Cocoa Songs' (February 1964) (ORAM/11/DO03).
Sound 9. 'Kiskadee' (February 1964) (excerpt from ORAM/11/DO284).
Sound 10. 'Traffic in Trinidad' (February 1964) (excerpt from ORAM/11/DO089).
Sound 11. 'Abide With Me' (February 1964) (excerpt from ORAM/11/DO089).
Sound 12. 'Steel drum manipulation' (April 1964) (excerpt from ORAM/11/DO019a).

Image Index

See Figure 1
Plate 1 'Flight to Trinidad and Tobago' (ORAM/7/8/001).
Plate 2 'Arrival in Trinidad and Tobago' (ORAM/7/8/003).
Plate 3 'Palm cutting' (ORAM/7/8/004).
Plate 4 'Car in palms' (ORAM/7/8/016).
Plate 5 'Family at harvest' (ORAM/7/8/038).
Plate 6 'Outside the wedding ceremony' (ORAM/7/8/013).
Plate 7 'Wedding ceremony' (ORAM/7/8/048).
Plate 8 'Steel-pan workshop' (ORAM/7/8/014).
Plate 9 'Daphne Oram and turtle' (ORAM/7/8/047).
Plate 10 'Drumming group' (ORAM/7/8/017).

See Figure 2
Plate 11 'Steel-pan band at Trinidad Carnival' (ORAM/7/8/024).
Plate 12 'Carnival man' [ORAM/7/8/019].
Plate 13 'Carnival costumes' (ORAM/7/8/020).
Plate 14 'Carnival costumes' (ORAM/7/8/021).
Plate 15 'Carnival man and police man' (ORAM/7/8/025).
Plate 16 'Carnival costumes' (ORAM/7/8/037).
Plate 17 'Carnival devil' (ORAM/7/8/027).
Plate 18 'Daphne Oram on Maracas beach' (ORAM/7/8/066).
Plate 19 'New York City view' (ORAM/7/8/064).
Plate 20 'View from the plane' (ORAM/7/8/068).

Figure 1 © The Daphne Oram Trust.

Figure 2 © The Daphne Oram Trust.

Beginnings

One Saturday morning in 2012 I hunched over a desk in the reading room of Goldsmiths Special Collections, digitising one of the last boxes of slide photographs in the Daphne Oram collection. The slides were dirty and scratched, and the scans came up on screen in blocks. Decades of deterioration had rendered ruin on the set of holiday photographs. A dusted narrative unfolded from aeroplane window, palm-lined shore and road, traversing city streets and continuing out into fields of sugar cane, cocoa and spice. Amongst the Caribbean landscapes were two washed-out shots of the British composer Daphne Oram, seated on a beach. In the first she looks away, inspecting the undercarriage of a turtle (Plate 9); in the second, one of the last of the sequence, she sits alone on a beach, centred, smiling at the camera (Plate 18). Curious, I moved through to the reading room adjoining the closed stacks where the collection is preserved and leafed through a grey series box containing a half-catalogued stack of papers that I thought might provide context. I came across Oram's notes regarding the film soundtracks she had worked on in the early 1960s, and found amongst them a handful of thin airmail paper and a thick dark green notebook. The papers were a four-page typed treatment for a film entitled 'Trinidad and Tobago.' Their heading denoted their sender:

GEOFFREY JONES (FILMS) LIMITED
28 HAMILTON TERRACE, N.W.8.   CUN. 4276

Figure 3: Excerpt from 'Trinidad and Tobago Treatment' (Oram, 1964). © The Daphne Oram Trust.

Geoffrey Jones's work seems known now only to the most inveterate British film enthusiasts, his fate cast in a post-war industrial era, shadowed in the glow of the documentary masterpieces of John Grierson, Humphrey Jennings and Paul Rotha. His was a uniquely 'pure' documentary art form (Russell and Taylor, 2010, p. 7), a self-contained genre centred on dynamic rhythmic editing, free from commentary, closely synchronised to music. His work teems with a musicality born from childhood trips to the cinemas of North West London where, accompanied by his mother, Jones watched a wide range of British, German and Russian films, including early shorts by Norman McLaren and Len Lye, and the epoch defining silent film *Man With A Movie Camera* (1929) by Russian filmmaker Dziga Vertov. Vertov's film had an indelible influence on the young Jones, and it became a driving force in the pursuit of his own visual language.[5] In the 1930s, Vertov had proved a divisive figure for pre-war British documentary makers, his rapid editing and playful camera technique generally regarded as either lacking in substance and overtly exoticised (Roberts, 2000, p. 99) or ingenious and virtuosic (Grierson, 1966, p. 129). British documentary filmmakers of the time sought to explore a very different focus, emphasizing the dignity and stature of working people and the nation: a portraiture of empire, of industry and its propagators. This so-called 'Golden-Age' of documentary in Britain eclipsed the quality of drama produced at the time, which often paled in the big-budget shine of the American releases that populated the British cinemas. Crucial to the resonance of this documentary era was the film maker John Grierson who headed up the Empire Marketing Board (EMB) creating informational documentaries that were sent out across the British Empire before World War Two. At the EMB, and in his following position as the head of the General Post Office (GPO) film unit, Grierson was responsible for nurturing the early careers of numerous now well-known artists and filmmakers, including the Scottish animator Norman McLaren, and the New Zealand artist Len Lye.

In the 1930s, sound and music in British documentary filmmaking was often functional, romantic and derivative. But there were notable exceptions: the 1936 GPO production *Night Mail*, directed by Harry Watt and Basil Wright, introduced an innovative visual-sound narrative, tracking the journey of a Postal Special train from Glasgow to London. The film showcases the compositional dexterity of Benjamin Britten, whose music develops to a surreal staccato underlay for the rapped rhythmic verse of W. H. Auden's extraordinary 'beat' coda.[6] *Night Mail* heralded the potential of a novel film-sound combination, and in its evocative imagery portrayed the towering industrial landscapes of the British North as a sleeping giant, ready to awake:

> Towards the fields of apparatus, the furnaces,
> Set on the dark plain like gigantic chessmen. (Auden, 2002, p. 2)

Whilst the arrival of the Second World War necessitated a shift in focus towards national propaganda, the experimentalism of the British film and music industries endured. Humphrey Jennings' documentary *Listen to Britain* (1942) showcased a stark lack of spoken narration, informed by his work with the *Mass-Observation* organisation.[7] In predominantly utilising music and diegetic sound, Jennings cast ambiguity on his intention, allowing the viewer space to understand the film from their own perspective.

The early 1940s saw rapid technological advances in the broadcasting of film and sound in Britain. In October 1943, a 17-year-old Daphne Oram arrived in London to take up a position at the BBC.[8] Oram worked in the music department at the Royal

Albert Hall, exploring novel microphone techniques for radio broadcast of instrumental performance, and studying composition privately with the composer Ivor Walsworth. As bombs fell over London, Oram and her colleagues broadcast concerts from a balcony high up under the domed glass roof of the hall, tracking audio gain against the dynamics of the score, ensuring that a 78rpm disc recording of the same piece was cued up, so if the hall were to be evacuated, the concert broadcast could appear to continue as normal:

> *From standby gram records (to fool the Germans!)*
> *Doodle bugs — Proms left London.*

Figure 4: Excerpt from 'Handwritten biographical interview transcript by Daphne Oram' (c.1988) © The Daphne Oram Trust.

Just a mile away on Southampton Row, Jones had begun studying at the Central School of Art and Crafts, where he encountered the work of Italian film-director Luciano Emmer[9] whose narrative films probed the internal rhythm of the still image. Jones was captivated by Emmer's work *Goya* (1951), in which a tightly choreographed topographical dance amongst Francisco Goya's 33 series of prints *Bullfighting* plays a precise duet to the interlocking rapidity of Andrés Segovia's flamenco guitar. At Central, Jones organised screenings of the graphic sound experiments of Len Lye and Norman McLaren who had been experimenting with 'Visual Music' — drawing directly onto the optical soundtrack of film. What was seen and heard became one and the same.[10] Jones also screened Dutch filmmaker Bert Haanstra's *Glas* (1958), a hypnotic feat of editing that illustrated the precocious potential of non-verbal sound-film. *Glas* is a film of process whose focus is not strict narrative or dramatis personae, but the systems and mechanics of glass making — the rhythmic music of manufacture.

Whilst working at the BBC, Oram studied the technological advances taking place in the film industry. In 1950, she distributed a paper to colleagues entitled *The Broadcasting of Music* in which she proposed that, rather than paying attention to the work of Stockhausen, Schaeffer and the serialists, the BBC should look for inspiration to the nascent film art being produced in Britain at the time.

> My contention is that a great opportunity has been missed b not looking on the microphone as a camera. Although for 25 years we have been using it only as a reproduction instrument in serious music to eavesdrop on the concert hall or opera house, is it too late to explore its real potentialities?

Figure 5: Excerpt from 'Broadcasting of Music paper' (Oram, 1950) © The Daphne Oram Trust.

Oram's interest in the relationship between film and music grew in her time at the BBC. Personal correspondence from 1957 details her plans to create a drawn sound machine, through which a new landscape for sound composition could be explored.[11] She researched the work of experimental filmmakers, including Norman McLaren,[12] and, as part of the newly established Radiophonic Workshop[13] was sent in October 1958 with three colleagues on a fact-finding mission to the *Journées Internationales de Musique Expérimentale* at the Brussels World Trade Fair. There, as well as witnessing Edgard Varèse demonstrate his *Poème* Électronique, Oram met the pioneering American visual-sound artist Jordan Belson, who at the time was organising a series of audiovisual shows with musician Henry Jacobs known as the 'Vortex Concerts' at the planetarium in San Francisco.[14] On her return to London, Oram resigned from the Radiophonic Workshop (only six months after it had opened), on 1 November 1958, frustrated by its lack of ambition, and anxious to pursue her own ideas. Oram left London and moved to an old Oast House in Kent named 'Tower Folly,' where she set about gathering the equipment she required to start her own electronic music studio.

Meanwhile, by the early 1950s, Jones had completed his studies at the Central School of Arts and Crafts. Influenced by Emmer's illustrative films, he created his own hand-drawn animations, which earned him a job with an advertising agency. Jones then took up a role as supervisory director for animation at the Shell Film Unit where he made his first documentary *Shell Panorama* (1959), his only film with spoken commentary. When the in-house animation department at Shell was closed in 1961, Jones formed his own company, 'Geoffrey Jones (Films)' and was re-contracted as a freelancer. The result was the giddy rhythmic journey of *Shell Spirit* (1962). In the early 1960s at Tower Folly, Daphne Oram focused on the creation of her drawn sound machine, a project she titled *Oramics*. The composer would draw onto a synchronised set of 10 35mm film strips, overlaid on light sensitive components that generated electrical charges to control amplitude, timbre, frequency and duration of sound. In early 1960 she was awarded a grant from the Gulbenkian foundation to develop the 'Oramics Machine'.[15] To support her work Oram took on a series of commissions, including composing animation soundtracks for the drinks company Horlicks, composing the anthology *Electronic Sound Patterns* for EMI records, and designing electronic sound effects for Jack Clayton's 1961 film *The Innocents*.

Snow

In September 1962, the head of the British Transport Film Unit[16] Edgar Anstey invited Jones to begin work on a new commission to explore the forthcoming electrification of the railways. Jones agreed and set off across the British Isles, filming the length and breadth of the rail network. As he travelled, Jones became acutely aware of the juxtaposition between the comfortable well-heeled passengers and the hostile conditions faced by the railwaymen working in all weathers to keep the trains running. In January 1963, Anstey met Jones for an update on the film's progress. Jones described to him an idea for a different short film, focusing on the railway in winter and documenting the reality for the workers pitted against the inclement conditions. With a sharp eye for an excellent filmic subject, and aware of the rapidly changing weather, Anstey commissioned *Snow* (1963) the next morning.

In *Snow*, the hypnotic tension of its cascading soundtrack is the linchpin of the film. Initially, Jones had wished to use the hit song *Teen Beat* by the American drummer Sandy Nelson, but was unable to obtain a licence. Hearing of Oram's work at the BBC Radiophonic Workshop, Jones asked her to rework Nelson's song, employing British musician Jonny Hawksworth to record a new arrangement, expanding it to twice its length and filtering and effecting the result. Oram finished the sound score in February 1963. The resultant film was edited by Jones in tight counterpoint to Oram's tape manipulations. It is a staccato masterpiece, a virtuosic interplay of rhythmic film editing and clattered electronic manipulation that embodies the passenger train's progress, made possible by untold human endeavour.[17] After Jones had finished shooting *Snow*, further work on the railway electrification project was put on hold as it became apparent that work across the rail network had not progressed sufficiently at that time. In the autumn of 1963, Jones was then approached by a film officer for British Petroleum (BP) to create a documentary about their operations in Trinidad and Tobago. With his railway project on hold, Jones agreed. In the winter of 1963, he flew out to the islands with his friend and director of photography Wolfgang Suschitzky[18] to spend five weeks filming for the documentary. Buoyed by his experience working with Oram on *Snow*, Jones asked her to join them. He posted her a four-page brief for the film, typewritten on wafer thin airmail paper (Oram, 1964). Jones proposed that Oram should create a location sound score that could act as the foundation for a rhythmic, narration-free documentary. Jones planned to use a graphic scoring technique, allowing him to compose and edit his filmed material precisely to the timbral and rhythmic character of the sounds produced by Oram:

> Method... To compose a framework in sound that throughout the film will be evocative of the subject, and to make the action of the individual pictures, and, or, the action of the transition from picture to picture, relate to the rhythm, textural instrumentation, and where used, the melody in the composition.

Figure 6: Excerpt from 'Trinidad and Tobago Treatment' (Oram, 1964) © The Daphne Oram Trust.

The film, titled *Trinidad and Tobago*, was to be structured into four sections — history, landscape, work and play. Under each heading Jones added his impressions as to the film and sound materials required:

> Work. Visual.
> The emphasis here is on manual labour, skill and dexterity. Sequences will also contain portraits illustrating the multi-racial composition of society, and details of crops unfamiliar to audiences outside the tropics. Special attention will be given to team work, and the interrelation of actions in cutting.

Figure 7: Excerpt from 'Trinidad and Tobago Treatment' (Oram, 1964) © The Daphne Oram Trust.

> Mama Dis Is Mas!
>
> —Lord Kitchener, 1964[19]

Mas

Oram joined Jones and Suschitzky in the last week of January 1964, taking photographs as she flew in over the Caribbean with a Kodak Bantam camera loaned by her mother (Plates 1 & 2). The islands of Trinidad and Tobago had gained independence from Britain in 1962, just one year after BP had begun operating off their eastern coast. Trinidad was famous for its yearly Carnival, a celebration that Jones planned to make the centrepiece of his film. In the late eighteenth century, 'Mas' traditions had started in Trinidad, when French plantation owners held masquerade parties to mark the beginning of fasting for Lent. In response, the slaves working on the plantations formed their own parallel celebration, 'Canboulay' (from the French *'cannes brulées'*, meaning burnt cane). Canboulay featured stick fighting, and a call-and-response protest music called 'Cariso'. Cariso music was a form of vocal protest for the enslaved population, and its verses carried oral traditions from their ancestral homes. During Canboulay, torches of burning sugar cane were carried in procession as symbols of resistance. After the abolition of slavery

Progress Music

in 1834, Canboulay merged with Mas, becoming Carnival, a celebration of freedom, multiculturalism and defiance. From 1845, large influxes of indentured immigrants from India, Syria and Africa dramatically changed the ethnic composition of Trinidad and Tobago, adding new folk musics into the existing Creole mix. In February 1881, stick fighting, torch burning and percussion music were banned in response to the Canboulay riots where descendants of freed slaves protested against attempts by British police to crack down on the celebrations.[20] It wasn't until the mid-1930s that the traditions began to reappear, transformed amongst large orchestras of tuned inverted oil drums. These steel pans were forged in the industrialisation of the time — a processual by-product of the swelling petroleum industry, sculpted as a melodic percussion instrument, a unique 'rolling' of history in a physical sounding vessel.

From the documents and photographs amongst the papers of the Oram collection, it was clear that over her three weeks in Trinidad, Oram travelled widely (Plates 3 & 4) — her notebooks refer to around 20 1/4" tapes of sound recordings made during the trip. I spent days listening to a stack of uncatalogued tapes that seemed to relate to her work on the film, eventually confirming at least six of the tapes as being from the trip.[21] As I sat listening, I pieced together how Oram's soundtrack was recorded and composed. One tape was particularly curious. Unlabelled except for a small sticker on its reel simply denoting 'Birthday Message,' it seemed unlikely to relate at first. As the tape crackled and began, the crisply modulated tones of Oram's Received Pronunciation came to life through the loudspeakers. What followed was a 20-minute message recorded from her Hilton hotel room in Port of Spain and sent to her father back in Wiltshire – an oral birthday card that described in detail her time spent recording in Trinidad (Sound 1). 1964 was a defining moment for Carnival in Trinidad, marking not only the advent of the first official steel pan 'panorama' competition, but also the moment that Trinidad's Carnival reached across the globe, inspiring communities in London to launch a now famous offshoot in Notting Hill. Oram was enthralled by the music of carnival, and on her arrival immediately began meeting and recording the local musicians who were taking part. She visited a steel pan yard to learn the mechanics of how the instruments were made (Plate 8) and set up a recording room in a small theatre near her hotel in the capital, Port of Spain. In the theatre, she recorded sessions of Shango spiritual music with a local percussion–flute duo (Sound 2), and taped a cappella performances of *The Eyes Have It* and *Come Leh We Go!*[22] (Sound 3) with the calypsonian, Mighty Endeavour. She also recorded some of the most well-known steel bands of the time, taping performances by Mighty Sparrow, Lord Kitchener and Lord ('Warlord') Blakie. Unfortunately, these latter recordings do not survive, and the only reference to the sessions having taken place are Oram's cursory notes and accountings (Oram 1964b).

On the first day of carnival Oram woke early to walk down Frederick Street in the centre of Port of Spain. She watched thousands of revellers dressed in the surreal attire of striped robbers, horned devils and African warriors spill out of bars and alleyways into the morning light, the aftermath of all-night jump-up calypso parties across the district (Plates 12 & 13). She spent the second day of carnival in Savannah Park, viewing proceedings from a large photographer's platform that provided a perfect centre point for the Carnival parades. She watched enthralled as carnival-goers dressed as Vikings, bronze–helmeted Goths swathed in fur, and children wearing oriental carpets as robes danced to vast steel bands numbering as many as 4000 players (Plate 11). In the intense heat of the day, Oram found a cool spot, ducking underneath the viewing platform to sit and watch proceedings through the dangling legs of the people sitting on its edge. Every now and then she dashed out with her Nagra tape recorder and microphones to record the bands as they passed (Sound 4). She took numerous photos of carnival-goers in the park throughout the day, marvelling at their barely describable costumes (Plates 14–16). After Carnival, Oram spent days back at the hotel collating and listening through the tapes she had recorded. On the Sunday, her driver invited her to attend his niece's Hindu wedding ceremony (Plates 6 – 7). At the wedding, Oram captured a recording of the traditional stick drum battle outside of the venue (Sounds 5 & 6).

Trinidad and Tobago

Trinidad and Tobago[23] begins with Jones and Suschitzky's serene vistas of coastal landscapes and mangrove swamps, ancient and untouched by human hand. Footage of birds duets with flute, floating atop undulating waves of echo-effected Shango drums (Sound 7). The drums and flute increase in pace, propelling a visual multicultural exposition, a journey through architecture, iconography and people at work and play. We jump to footage of Cocoa bean workers, their circular stamping of beans ground to dust[24] cut incisively against the gestural sounds of their work song (Sound 8).[25] After the historical landscape sequence, Jones unfurls a dynamic encounter with the mechanics of progress. Oram's manipulated drum loops and steel pan recordings scatter percussive counterpoint to footage of manual and mechanical labour. Sweeping footage of blazing sugar cane,[26] accompanied by a slowed tattoo of low sonorous drumming (a fleeting evocation of Canboulay) is immediately overrun by oil lines, pylons and transportation. The echoing drums are subsumed by the rapid back-and-forth of high frequency bongo patterns, an industrial rattle that speeds up and slows down in mimicry of the machinery. As we watch an oil drill burrow down into the ocean floor, the patterns spiral into a clattering steel pan introduction, heralding the climactic carnival sequence (Sound 4). The recordings that Oram, Jones and Suschitzky captured of Carnival are the main feature of *Trinidad and Tobago*. Indeed, in an interview late in his life, Jones commented that the combination of sound and film was deemed so effective that audiences were convinced that they must have been recorded simultaneously (something, he notes, that would have been nigh impossible at the time).[27] The carnival sequence in *Trinidad and Tobago* is bizarre, joyous and fantastic. Cultures merge and entwine — parodies of British colonials with huge papier mâché heads dance with Trinidadians, dressed in US navy uniforms, who stumble cartoon walks to triumphant discordant brass music, pipes in one hand, fake guns in the other. A giant red and black devil toots a paper clarinet (Plate 17), glaring menacingly as geisha women sway amongst crowds of Western tourists dressed as scarecrows. At the end of the sequence, just before the end credits of the film, we see a tiny flash of Wolf Suschitzky in amongst the multitude, Jones' self-referential nod to his hero Dziga Vertov.

Tuning

The changing soundscape of Trinidad fascinated Oram. The arrival of BP and other oil companies had brought a wave of imported machinery and vehicles to the island. As the number of cars grew, so did the background noise of traffic, and Oram's notes are littered with lost battles against the noise, including numerous attempts to capture clean recordings of the song of the local onomatopoeic kiskadee bird (Sound 9):

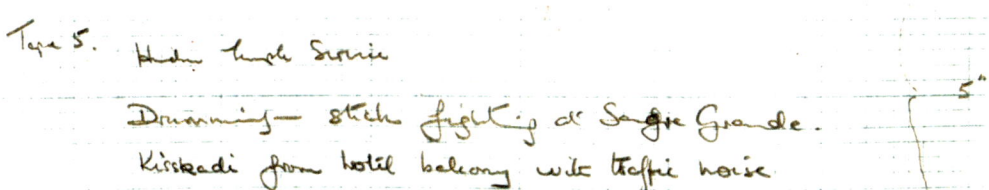

Figure 8: Excerpt from 'Trinidad and Tobago Notebook' (Oram, 1964b).

When Oram discussed the problem of traffic noise with Jones, he asked her to record separate tapes of the sound, so that she might thread the interruptive car horns and throbbing engines into musical rhythm for him in sections of the film. Oram went out into Port of Spain the following morning and recorded over 20 minutes of traffic sounds for Jones (Sound 10). A roadside meeting with a family, their horse and cart laden with the day's harvest (Plate 5)[5] led to Oram being invited to visit a sugar cane farm, where she recorded the burning of the cane and the slashing and cutting of the resultant crop. The following day she organised a visit to hear a police brass band, where she recorded a bombastic militarised version of *Abide With Me*. In retrospect, the triumphalist brass fanfares and distant gun salutes of her recordings evoke a faded afterglow of colonialism, slipping away in the dawn of Trinidad's independence (Sound 11).

As her trip drew to a close, Oram spent a few days swimming and relaxing on Maracas beach to the north of the island, renowned as one of the most beautiful on Trinidad. She flew back to England at the weekend, waiting an extra day longer than planned in order to fly via New York (Plate 19) with Jones and Suschitzky. On her return to Tower Folly she immediately set to work, reviewing, editing and composing the tapes from Trinidad. She spent February creating the composition for the film; looping, splicing and adding effects to the tape recordings to structure and compose the otherworldly soundtrack, providing Jones with what he later called the 'matrix' of the film (Jones, 2004).

Return

Jones' *Trinidad and Tobago* documents an age when progress was celebrated in the industrialised world, a time when mechanisation was teamed with prosperity, spiriting things forward, a progression against the odds. In Oram's deftly manipulated soundtrack, the steel pan drum acts in counterpoint to this progression, a tuned inversion of an industrial by-product whose rhythms celebrate human expression and ingenuity. Listening to Oram's raw tape recordings provides a uniquely unmediated document of a pivotal time in the island's culture. In the early 1960s the country was changing rapidly; old manual industry was being replaced by mechanisation, and the newly independent nation was celebrating its freedom from colonial rule. This was a time of self-determination, and it is clear from both the working notes and the final film that Oram and Jones sought to capture this vibrancy, replete in contradictory ebullience. *Trinidad and Tobago* represents a forgotten impressionistic form of what a public information film could be. It is indicative of a mostly unrecognised spectrum of rhythmic, artistic documentary sound-films that stretches from Vertov's *Man With A Movie Camera* through Grierson's *Night Mail* and Haanstra's *Glas*, to the morose environmental coda of Derek Williams' 1970 documentary *The Shadow of Progress*. *Trinidad and Tobago*, alongside these films, portrays an era of 'Progress Music', employing radical 'synchretic' techniques[28] to combine sound, music and film to create novel combinatory meanings.

In the five years following *Trinidad and Tobago*, a surfeit of visual material born from the ubiquity of television caused hyperactive short-form advertising to become the industry standard, and for Jones, the commissions dried up. The days of open briefs and forward-thinking commissioning came to an end. Oram and Jones worked on only two other films together: *Rail* (1967) saw the completion of Jones' railway electrification project with Anstey, for which Oram provided additional sound effects on top of Wilfred Joseph's score, and *This Is Shell* (1970), for which Oram provided additional sound effects as counterpart to Donald Fraser's music.[29] Oram's experiences working with Jones on *Trinidad and Tobago* had a profound impact on her compositional practice, enabling her to master highly intricate tape manipulation techniques and furthering her work with sound-visual narrative. Following the completion of the soundtrack she remained fascinated by the timbral characteristics of the steel pan (Sound 12). Two years later, in her composition *Episode Metallic* (April 1965) she became the first electronic musician to manipulate the steel-drum, adding effects and splicing her recordings from Trinidad with other *concrète* acoustic material to form the sound element of the futuristic sculpture *Nucleus* by Andrew Bobrowski. *Nucleus*, an early example of electronic interactive art, was exhibited alongside Barbara Hepworth's *Theme on Electronics* in December 1965 at the Mullard Electronics Centre in London. In the sounding sculpture, the concrete rhythmic music of Trinidadian progress became the raw material for the ethereal electronic music of a new atomic era.

> Knowledge that is organised in slips and scraps knows no hierarchy.
> — Esther Leslie, *Walter Benjamin's Archive*, 2015

Progress Music I

Progress Music I is the first in a series of film-sound installations by the author, originally commissioned by South Kiosk[30] for a solo gallery exhibition in October 2014 (Figs. 9 & 10). Taking as its provocation the fragment of writing by Martin Amis that prefaces this chapter, it is a generative non-linear film-sound installation that seeks an alternate, non-textual extrapolation of a speculative era of 'Progress Music' through an autonomous film archive, developing and mapping pathways through its corpus. *Progress Music I* is composed entirely from hundreds of fragments of 1960s British industrial documentary

Figure 9: *Progress Music I* installation view, South Kiosk, London 3–25 October 2014.
Photograph: Ben James

Figure 10: *Progress Music I* installation view, South Kiosk, London 3–25 October 2014.
Photograph: Ben James

films and their soundtracks, collected by the author. As such, the work is an example of 'plunderphonics,' what Chris Cutler has defined as a practice that 'radically undermines three of the central pillars of the art music paradigm: originality (it deals only in copies), individuality (it speaks only with the voice of others), and copyright (the breaching of which is a condition of its very existence)' (Cutler, 2015, p. 143). By employing a plunderous methodology, the piece communicates only from the material it is comprised of.

Progress Music I is structured by three distinct movements; I. Landscape, II. Machines and III. Progress, with each movement exploring different sound-film synchronicities relating to its categorisation. Human actors are removed from the source material by editing, echoing the 'pure documentary' style of Jones and other filmmakers, enhancing focus on the mechanics, landscapes and industry of the era. The installation runs on a 12-minute loop, with each four-minute movement unfolding different patternings of synchretic sound and film at each play through. Each movement of *Progress Music I* generates new combinations of film-sound material in

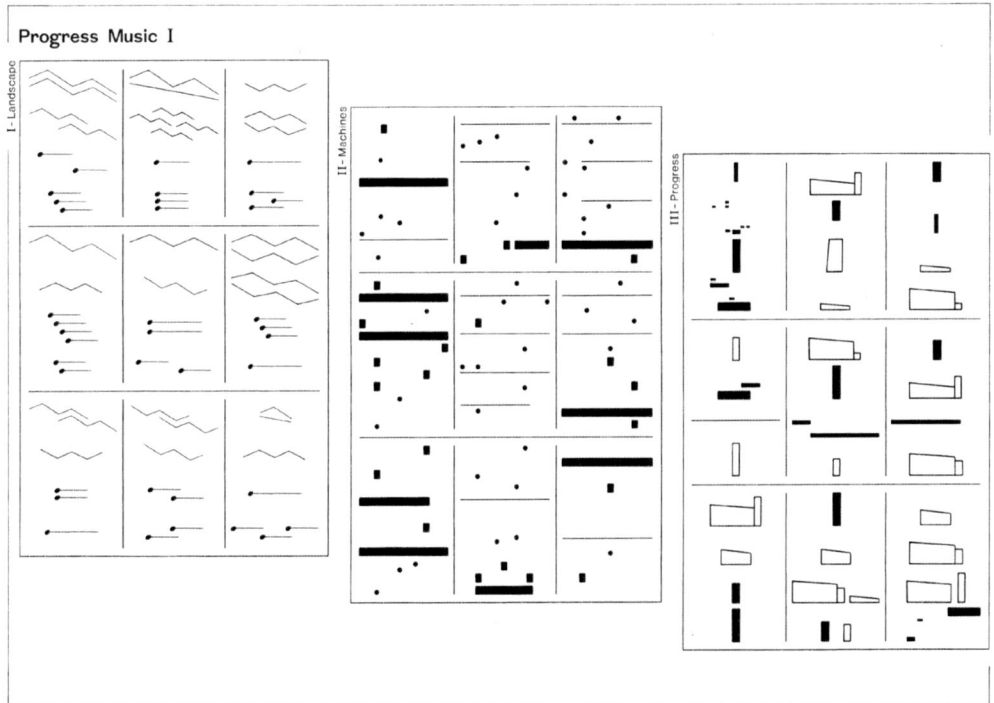

Figure 11: *Progress Music I* instruction score.
October 2014

real-time using chance and procedural techniques, rendered in custom software. This software also spatialises the material over nine CRT cube monitors with loud speakers attached to them. The rhythmic, contrapuntal composition of *Progress Music I* is defined by an overarching instruction score (Figure 11), which draws inspiration from the compositional methodologies of Geoffrey Jones and Daphne Oram's collaborative work on *Trinidad and Tobago* (1964). The resultant spatialised nine-channel film-sound composition excises and portrays 'Progress Music' in its core tenets, combining and recombining rhythmic fragments of sound and film in real-time to spatially explore the power of synchretic rhythmic editing to portray the rise and documentary vitality of the 1960s industrial complex. The *Progress Music* installation series is what Hal Foster has called an 'archival art,' a setting somehow successive to site-specific art that aims 'to make historical information, often out or displaced, physically present' (Foster, 2004, p. 4). In *Progress Music I*, history is presented as live composition, a complex combinatory patterning, altering in each telling, rendering its material visible, audible and malleable in the present.

Conclusion

As both textual analysis and film-sound installation, 'Progress Music' activates the historic material it is drawn from. As Wolfgang Ernst has noted, 'it is the energy of utilisation which activates the archive' (Ernst, 2005, p. 101). Within 'Progress Music' archival material is activated by re-composition, provoking speculative narratives and untold histories to unfold. In this practice-research project explorations are made into a vital and underrepresented era of industrial short film in Britain. The traces of material that form the corpus of the research are necessarily reordered, decontextualised and reclassified, freed from their originating archives and fragmented in the spaces of book and exhibition. Writing between and amongst them is not intended as fiction — it is a conversation engendered where there wasn't one, connections made that now might become apparent. The era of 'Progress Music' that I have defined here merits further detailed and discursive examination. Its commercial commissioning processes, ties to industrialised processes now recognised as environmentally detrimental, and relatively sporadic and lesser-known practitioners may have caused it to fall under-the-radar. It is clear however that in its tenets of audiovisual synchronisation, what Holly Rogers has described as 'the use of music and sound to determine the pace and structure of a narrative' (Rogers, 2014, p. 83), and in its vibrant portrayals of the mechanics of industrialisation it provides an important insight into the pre-atomic industrialised period and demarcates a genre of documentary film that is often overlooked. Its core techniques draw rich inspiration from the 'visual music' techniques that occurred in animation in the 1950s and 'Progress Music' can be seen as a natural successor to the experimental documentaries of the post-war period. Furthermore, in the rapid fusion of sound and film that underlays 'Progress Music' we can speculate an important precedent for music video[31] which at its core has markedly similar stylistic and technical audiovisual synchretic methodologies. 'Progress Music' might then be understood not only as an important witness to a bygone era, but also as a key point in the development of audiovisual culture.

Endnotes

1 Daphne Oram was one of Britain's earliest and most innovative composers of electronic music. She died in 2003 and left behind a wealth of compositions, writings and recordings. Her archive is a history written in life, a biographical template teeming with reflections and addenda.

2 In Jacques Derrida's Archive Fever, Derrida describes the archon as "first of all the documents' guardians. They do not only ensure the physical security of what is deposited and the substrate. They are also accorded the hermeneutic right and competence. They gave the power to interpret the archives." (Derrida, 1995, p. 10)

3 Alvin Lucier's 1969 piece I Am Sitting in a Room involves Lucier recording himself narrating a text, and then repetitively playing back and re-recording the fragment until the words become unintelligible, and only the resonant frequency of the room remains.

4 These sound media and image plates 1 – 20 in Figures 1 and 2 have been included with the kind permission of the Daphne Oram Trust and were digitised with the assistance of Goldsmiths Special Collections, Tom Richards and Goldsmiths Electronic Music Studios.

5 Jones discusses his early years and the formative influences on his work at 02:40 in the DVD extras for the BFI release 'Geoffrey Jones: Rhythm of Film' released in 2004.

6 The original score manuscript for Night Mail by Benjamin Britten (1936) is preserved in the British Library as part of the Benjamin Britten Archive (MS 60621). W. H. Auden's verses for Night Mail also provide the core fragmentary sample for a track uploaded by anonymous 'user18081971' to the music hosting website 'Soundcloud' in February 2015. The track is one of nearly 300 tracks that have reputedly been uploaded by the musician Richard D. James (also known as Aphex Twin) since January 2015.

7 The Mass-Observation social research organisation was co-founded by Jennings in 1937. The organisation sought to use anthropological methods to gather records of the everyday lives of the people of Britain.

8 See: 'A letter from P. A. Florence, Engineering Establishment Officer,' where Oram is offered a post as 'Technical Assistant (Class II) on the unestablished staff of the Engineering division in Programme Engineering based in London at a weekly wage of £2.15.0d' (ORAM/3/1/109).

9   For a detailed account of the work of Luciano Emmer, see: Jacobs, S. (2011). *Framing Pictures: Film and the Visual Arts*. Edinburgh University Press.

10 Experiments in visual and electronic music had begun in Russia decades before this. See Andrey Smirnov's book *Sound in Z* (2013) for detailed information about the many pioneering figures in Russian film and music of the early 20th century.

11 See: 'Pen and pencil notes detailing plans for the Oramics technique'. [ORAM/1/1/008]. Copies sent to Mr Porter and Mr Garrard at the BBC on 4 April 1957.

12 See 'Radiophonic Workshop Log Book 2', notes by Daphne Oram and Alec Nisbett in the BBC Written Archives (1957) (R97/23/1).

13 For further information about the founding of the BBC Radiophonic Workshop and its legacy, see Louis Niebur's *Special Sound: The Creation and Legacy of the BBC Radiophonic Workshop* (2010).

14 See: 'Radiophonic Effects Committee and Electronic Composition Workshop 1956-68' in the BBC Written Archives (R97/9/1).

15 For full details of the Oramics machine, see: sub-fonds ORAM/1 in the Daphne Oram Collection. Also see: Richards, T. (2017). *Oramics: Precedents, Technology and Influence*.

16 In the aftermath of the Second World War, the British prime minister Clement Atlee had created the British Transport Commission (BTC), a vision of integrated, publicly owned transport, whose aim was to inspire the British population with a feeling of progress into the future. Within the commission was British Transport Film (BTF), which aimed to use the innovative short-film form to communicate to the public and its own employees the technological progress being made as transport networks were upgraded across the country. At this time, the BTF was headed by Edgar Anstey, a filmmaker who had learnt his craft under John Grierson.

17 *Snow* went on to gain an Oscar nomination in 1965 and received over 14 other major awards at film festivals.

18 Wolfgang Suschitzky is perhaps best known for his collaborations with Paul Rotha in the 1940s, and his work on Mike Hodges' 1971 film *Get Carter*. Suschitzky is also a successful photographer whose photographs have been exhibited at the National Gallery, London.

19 Lord Kitchener's *Mama Dis Is Mas* was the calypso hit of the steel band panorama competition in 1964.

20 For an overview of the history of Carnival, see *Carnival: Culture in Action - The Trinidad Experience* (2004) edited by Milla Cozart Riggio.

21 The tape section in the Daphne Oram collection consists of over 500 tapes, about half of which are catalogued and digitised at this time. It includes full compositions, field recordings, audio letters and process tapes relating to around 100 different works and projects.

22 *Come Leh We Go!* was a calypso originally written in the early 1960s by the Guyanan singer King Fighter.

23 *Trinidad and Tobago* was released as part of a British Film Institute DVD collection entitled 'Geoffrey Jones: The Rhythm of Film'. The collection also features a unique interview with Jones, filmed in the last few months of his life, where he discusses *Trinidad and Tobago* and his collaborations with Daphne Oram.

24 Cocoa production had been affected by a severe drought in Trinidad (1957 – 1962) and the film captures a rare moment of optimistic recovery before the industry changed beyond recognition with the mechanisation of the late 1960s.

25 *Cocoa Songs* can be heard at 04:18 in Jones' final *Trinidad and Tobago* film.

26 Sugar cane is burned before harvesting to remove the leaves and insects from the crop.

27 Jones discusses this audience reaction to the carnival sequence of *Trinidad and Tobago* at 20:24 in an interview included in the DVD extras for the BFI release 'Geoffrey Jones: Rhythm of Film' released in 2004.

28 The film-sound theorist Michel Chion has described 'synchresis' as a simultaneity of disparate sound and image, deriving new meaning and form in each recombination (Chion, 2009, p. 214).

29 Both films can be seen on the DVD *'Geoffrey Jones: The Rhythm of Film'* published by the BFI in 2004.

30 For more about *South Kiosk* gallery, please see their website: http://www.southkiosk.com/ [accessed: 2018-01-24].

31 In fact later in life Geoffrey Jones used his virtuostic editing technique on a number of uncredited music videos where he worked as editor.

Bibliography

Amis, M. (2010). *The pregnant widow*. London: Random House.

Auden, W. H., Britten, B., & Kildea, P. F. (2002). *Night mail: for speaker and small ensemble*. Chester Music.

BBC Written Archives. (1956 – 68). 'Radiophonic Effects Committee and Electronic Composition Workshop 1956-68'. R97/9/1. BBC Written Archives, Reading.

BBC Written Archives. (1958). Notes by Daphne Oram and Alec Nisbett in 'Radiophonic Workshop Log Book 2'. R97/23/1. BBC Written Archives, Reading.

Bulley, J. (2017). Progress Music. In A. Lister & M. Stuart (Eds.) *Bricks from the kiln #2* (pp. 5 – 22). London: Tenderbooks

Chion, M. (2009). *Film, a sound art*. (C. Gorbman, Trans.). New York: Columbia University Press.

Cutler, C. (2015). Plunderphonia. In C. Cox & D. Warner (Eds.), *Audio culture: readings in modern music* (pp. 138 – 156). London: Bloomsbury.

Derrida, J., & Prenowitz, E. (1995). Archive fever: a Freudian impression. *Diacritics*, 25(2), 9 – 63. http://doi.org/10.2307/465144

Ernst, W. (2005). Art of the archive. In H. Adkins (Ed.), *Kunstler.archivneue werke zu historichen Bestanden*. Koln: Walter Konig.

Foster, H. (2004). An archival impulse. *October*, (110), 3 – 22.

Grierson, J. (1966). *Grierson on documentary*. Berkeley, California: University of California Press.

Jacobs, S. (2011). *Framing pictures: film and the visual arts*. Edinburgh University Press.

Jones, G. (2004). *Geoffrey Jones: the rhythm of film*. London: BFI. Retrieved from http://www.bfi.org.uk/blu-rays-dvds/rhythm-film

Leslie, E., & Benjamin, W. (2015). *Walter Benjamin's archive*. London; New York: Verso.

Niebur, L. (2010). *Special sound: the creation and legacy of the BBC Radiophonic Workshop*. Oxford: Oxford University Press.

Oram, D. (1950). 'Broadcasting of Music'. ORAM/3/2/025/001. Daphne Oram Collection, Special Collections and Archives, Goldsmiths, University of London.

Oram, D. (1957) 'Pen and pencil notes detailing plans for the Oramics technique'. ORAM/1/1/008. Daphne Oram Collection, Special Collections and Archives, Goldsmiths, University of London.

Oram, D. (1957). *'Devizes girl constructs new type of music for the BBC'*. ORAM/3/1/002. Daphne Oram Collection, Special Collections and Archives, Goldsmiths, University of London.

Oram, D. (1964). *'Trinidad and Tobago Treatment'*. ORAM/8/35/001. Daphne Oram Collection, Special Collections and Archives, Goldsmiths, University of London.

Oram, D. (1964b). *'Trinidad and Tobago Notebook'*. ORAM/8/35/003. Daphne Oram Collection, Special Collections and Archives, Goldsmiths, University of London.

Oram, D (c.1988). *'Handwritten biographical interview transcript by Daphne Oram'*. ORAM/9/6/001/006. Daphne Oram Collection, Special Collections and Archives, Goldsmiths, University of London.

Richards, T. (2017). *Oramics: precedents, technology and influence*. Goldsmiths, University of London.

Riggio, M. C. (2004). *Carnival: culture in action: the Trinidad experience*. London: Routledge.

Roberts, G. (2000). *The man with the movie camera: the film companion*. London: I. B. Tauris.

Rogers, H. (2014). The musical script: Norman McLaren, animated sound and audiovisuality. *Animation Journal, 22*, 68 – 84.

Russell, P., & Taylor, J. P. (2010). *Shadows of progress*. London: BFI.

Smirnov, A. (2013). *Sound in Z: experiments in sound and electronic music in early 20th century Russia*. London: Koenig.

Steedman, C. (2001). *Dust*. Manchester: Manchester University Press.

Creative use of voice in non-fiction narrative film: an examination of the work of Peter Mettler

Lars Koens and Demelza Kooij

Before film, before writing, storytelling was spoken word: the sharing of an experience, legend, poem, or song. Thus storytelling has traditionally been associated with the voice of a narrator or singer, either as part of the story or as the person delivering and performing the story. With some exceptions, notably live narration in Japan's Benshi tradition and the *'bonimenteur'*, early cinema was voiceless for many years. But it did often contain a written voice: elaborately decorated text boxes communicated what actors silently mouthed. With the invention of synchronised sound, these mute and written voices were exchanged for the speech of the sound film.

In documentary film, voice is usually contained in the form of speech as uttered by a presenter, interviews with subjects, or included as voice-over. In particular, 'voice of God' narration is commonly understood as a key trait of documentary. Yet, the inclusion of voice-over in documentary film has been criticised for being pressingly didactic, anti-democratic, and is by some regarded as a sign of an inept filmmaker: 'Voice-over is the unnecessary evil of documentary, the resort of the unimaginative and incompetent' (Bruzzi, 2006, p. 48), and 'Narration is what you do when you fail' (Drew, 1983, In: Ibid, p. 48.). Bruzzi (2006) suggests that the source of this criticism is rooted in the relation between sound and image: voice-over is often extra-diegetic (p. 47). Thus voice is often a mere added sound layer, without a connection to the diegetic film space.

To highlight the creative potential of voice in documentary film, especially in unison and juxtaposition with imagery and sound design, we provide a discussion of the creative use of voice in three films by the Swiss-Canadian filmmaker Peter Mettler: *Picture of Light (1994)*, *Gambling, Gods and LSD (2002)*, and *Petropolis: Aerial Perspectives on the Alberta Tar Sands (2009)*. Mettler holds a prominent place in contemporary cinema, exemplified by many prizes and awards at prestigious festivals across continents. His work embodies and acknowledges the fact that cinema is a constructed illusion. Indeed, his film practice has been described as rigorously dedicated to connections between form and content (White, 2007, p. 50), as pushing cinematic boundaries thematically and stylistically (McSorley, 2005, p. 43), and as having tremendous integrity (Gill, 2006 in White, p. 60). He has directed fiction and documentary films, and has provided cinematography for numerous films, including the documentary *Manufactured Landscapes* (Baichwal, 2006).

As practitioners in various forms of audiovisual media, we emphasize techniques, intentionality and other creative and authorial issues, more so than the cultural or social implications of audiovisual constructions. Authorial intent in relation to documentary filmmaking lags behind the assessment of aesthetics and decision-making in fiction film. Here we want to demonstrate creative potential and skilfulness in the use of voice in non-fiction narrative film. Where possible, we use vocabulary by the composer, filmmaker and theoretician Michel Chion, who is regarded as the most important writer on the complex relationship between sound and image in audiovisual media. As typically seen in film theory, Michel Chion's analyses are concerned predominantly with fiction film. However, most of his findings have relevance to both fiction and documentary filmmaking. Here we apply some of his vocabulary to the experimental documentary films of Mettler.

The films of Mettler contain various uses of voice: dialogue between subjects; dialogue between Mettler (off-screen) and on-screen subjects; disembodied voice such as radio conversations; crowds of people talking, chanting; and his own voice delivered as a scripted voice-over. A Chion term we will frequently refer to is *acousmêtre* (Chion, 1999), a specific type of film character whose body, or at least its speaking part, remains hidden, while having influence on the on-screen action. *Acousmêtre* is a telescoping of the words acousmatic (of a sound when its source or cause is hidden) and the French être (being). According to Chion, voice-over is too external to the on-screen action in order for it to qualify as an *acousmêtre*. We argue that Peter Mettler's voice In *Picture of Light* and *Gambling, Gods and LSD* does exhibit acousmêtric qualities, for example by letting characters briefly lip sync to his words.

Mettler's voice-over sounds warm. It is low-pitched, monotonous, fairly slow, and meditative, but not boring or unpleasant. The delivery of content is dry. He does not entertain. He simply speaks. It is a pleasant voice that is simply there, without forcing an emotion or rigid opinion on to the listener. He is always mindful and open — even on the rare occasions when he presents facts. The quality of Mettler's voice has led him to perform narration for several films, such as the documentary *The Sound of Insects: Record of a Mummy* (Liechti, 2009). Rather than addressing every instance where voice is used creatively, we discuss a few moments where voice, sound, and image intersect in exciting ways. We have chosen parts from *Picture of Light*, *Gambling, Gods and LSD*, and *Petropolis: Aerial Perspectives on the Alberta Tar Sands*. We hope this serves to reveal some of the eloquence of Mettler's practice at large.

Picture of Light

'We live in a time where things do not seem to exist if they are not contained as an image', proclaims Mettler as the voice-over in *Picture of Light*, about 15 minutes into the film. Since the release of the film in 1992, our day-to-day use of screens and interfaces has increased and, accordingly, this statement has grown in significance. The film is a pursuit of the Aurora Borealis, an enigmatic natural phenomenon that leaves an impression, which cannot be contained as an image. The ungraspable, untranslatable is what underlies Mettler's filmmaking. *Picture of Light* was recorded during two trips to Churchill, a small town in the North of Canada. The film starts in an artificial cooler where the film crew is testing their recording equipment to see whether the (then) new technology is able to cope with Arctic temperatures. The film maintains this reflexive mode throughout. Mettler explains in an interview for offscreen.com: 'It is not necessarily about the Aurora Borealis, rather it's about what we believe in and how we relate to each other' (Stefik, 2002). The film demonstrates that perception and experience are mediated by the technology of the camera, sound equipment, television screens, the human eye, and as dictated by cultural dispositions. As White explains (2007, p. 26), what lies at the heart of *Picture of Light* is the imperfect translation from lived experience to aesthetic experience.

Practitioners of Magic

Early on in *Picture of Light*, paired with slow-paced imagery of the film crew on a nightly train journey, we hear:

> Practitioners of magic do not like electricity. It confuses magic just as it confuses people. I once took a bus tour where the guide said certain things twice, for emphasis, for rhythm, to fill the quiet space.

After a short pause, with the words still resonating in our minds, the voice-over returns with striking effect: 'Practitioners of magic do not like electricity. It confuses magic, just as it confuses people, he would say twice.' The delivery of the repeated words is essentially the same as the first — monotonous, emotionless, and slow-paced. It would seem that Mettler places himself in the position of tour guide by saying the line twice, and the audience in the position of tourists on a trip to Churchill. Or perhaps the images suggest a different interpretation. Immediately after the first rendition the film cuts to the train operator (though this may also be the sound recordist) slowly turning an intercom microphone away from his face. The quality of the voice-over foretells that it is closely recorded in a quiet studio, evidently not spoken into the microphone shown on screen. It would have sounded vastly different; the type of microphone, reverb, and train movements would have affected the delivery. Is this perhaps an example of the type of confusion ('it confuses magic just as it confuses people') that is alluded to in the voice-over and may apply to the current scene? Is he teasing the audience? To address this, we need to place the scene in a wider context.

The opening voice-over ends with the sentence: 'As the night closed we agreed to share a path we had in common, the pursuit of wonder'. After 'pursuit of wonder' the film cuts to an unclear view from the back of a train when it departs of a dark, foggy train station with lights barely reaching through the wall of snowy mist. This visual play is aesthetically pleasing, but not extraordinarily beautiful. Mettler is not showing a particular kind of pursuit of wonder. In relation to cinema more generally, Chion notes there are many occurrences in film where the image is modified or chosen to respect the more general nature of the spoken words (Chion, 1994, p. 172). In the case of this scene in *Picture of Light*, the words remain applicable to a greater possibility of wondrous images, as opposed to referring to the particular image on screen.

With 'pursuit of wonder' still in our minds, when 'Practitioners of magic . . .' comes in, it is tempting to draw the following parallels:

– Who are the *practitioners*? Does he refer to the film crew or is the audience practising magic by watching the film?
– What is the *magic* he refers to? Is it wonderment at the Northern Lights, the electricity of film equipment, film itself?

During the second rendition of 'Practitioners of magic do not like electricity . . .' we see a flashing light, a reference to electricity, filmed from a train window. If Mettler clearly wanted to put the audience in the position of tourists (and himself as tour guide), would he not have shown the passing of landscape from a train window?

With the allegory of Mettler as the practitioner of magic, the scene would seem to address technology as an uncertainty ('Mettler does not like electricity'). The status of technology is a theme throughout the film and is the main theme in the opening scene. In the cold chamber the characters have to talk loudly in order to be heard over the noise from the cooler. The volume of their voices is a measurement for the level of technology involved. The louder they have to shout the greater is the presence of the cooler. Chion lists other examples of raised voices due to loud ambient noise that give a sense of the severity of its source such as a storm or ocean waves (Chion, 2009, p. 346). The uncertainty is also felt just before the 'practitioners of magic' scene, when Mettler's voice-over says: 'We were escaping the electrical world with 50 pounds of batteries in our bags', which underlines the dependency on electricity and technological innovation.

Chion discusses repetition in film speech in the context of the genesis of language, ascribing a 'particular resonance' to repeated words (Chion, 2009, p. 329). He explains that the words we normally hear in life-action scenes come from a selection of many takes, but we only get to hear one of the takes. He also refers to the infamous 'Are you talking to me?' scene in *Taxi Driver* (Scorsese, 1976) where the viewer enjoys a certain intimacy with the character because we are in the room with him as he rehearses these words. We hypothesise that the 'resonance' effect is due to how in real life, witnessing rehearsal is only for the privileged, the people close to the rehearser. Hence, the repetition in *Taxi Driver* and voice-over of *Picture of Light* establish an intimacy between the film and the spectators. Interestingly, in *Taxi Driver* the main character asks 'Are you talking to me?', whereas Mettler indirectly says 'I am talking to you'.

The power of the Practitioners of Magic scene is that it embraces both 'not knowing' and technological uncertainty. The words, sounds, and images merely hint at being logically connected, not least because of the logical construction in repeating the voice-over. But it carefully denies exact interpretation with subtle devices, keeping us in a state of not knowing, which follows the narrative curve of the film.

Train operator or sound recordist? © Grimthorpe Film Inc.

Creative use of voice

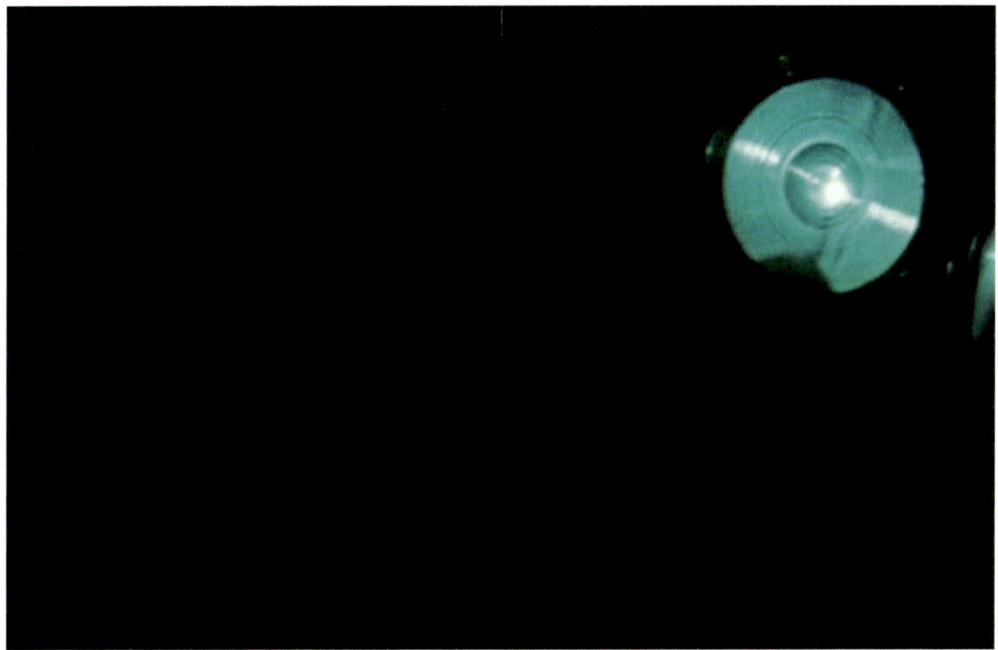

Flashing light. © Grimthorpe Film Inc.

Mettler as Puppeteer

In *Picture of Light*, as well as in *Gambling, Gods and LSD*, Mettler occasionally pays a visit to the diegetic space, appearing onscreen without speaking or off-screen behind the camera interviewing on-screen characters. There are long shots of him in both films where we see him filming himself as a reflection in a mirror or a window. In *Picture of Light*, this is accompanied by a voice-over, disconnecting his body and voice and emphasizing the material organisation of the film medium. We never see him speak. Or using Chion's terminology, the voice is never completely de-acousmatized, but the possibility is hinted at. For example, a train passenger is edited so that it seems as though he partly lip syncs Mettler's voice-over (interestingly, with the word 'surrogate'). Mettler's voice-over and bodily appearances can be related to what Chion calls a semi-*acousmêtre*, or partial de-acousmatization, where the 'voice retains an aural of invulnerability and magical power' (Chion, 1999, p. 28). Similar powers are ascribed to the *acousmêtre* (voice without a body) as to the body without a voice (Chion, 1999, p. 97; 2009, p. 327).

Chion notes that due to the nature of the film medium, a talking person on the screen is a combination of two separate recordings — of voice and of body (1999, p.

125). In early sound film this construct was hidden because it was thought that body and voice were only separate due to the methods of recording, not by nature, which it aimed to depict. Chion argues, referring repeatedly to the ancient art of puppetry that predates cinema, that one of the great assets of sound film is this voice-body dichotomy, giving numerous examples from fiction films where the body houses a different voice (Chion, 1999, p. 171). Here we note a scene in *Picture of Light* where Mettler masters the art of puppetry brilliantly.

Approximately a third into the film and after a few minutes of talking head interviews with locals about seeing the Northern Lights, a puppet show commences. Resident of Churchill, Father Verspeek, explains about the mysteries of experiencing the lights, and, as his voice continues, the image briefly cuts to a different person, thus de-synchronising the source of the voice and the body that we see onscreen. The film cuts to an Aboriginal and his translator, but the Father's voice is heard. Still visually with the Aboriginal and his translator, the voice of Father Verspeek is taken over by another off-screen person, to which the film then cuts, bringing voice and body back together to normal screen speech, though in a different person. We then see other characters making gestures over his voice until the sequence ends with a shot panning up into the sky. The result is comical, but also shows the unity in the people and the similarity in their relation to the Northern Lights. The timing of body gestures and voices is carefully executed, with the characters appearing to occasionally lip-sync the voice they cannot hear and did not speak, making gestures that correspond to it.

In this scene, the gestures become more pronounced than the content of what is said. Arguably, it is the voice that is used to emphasize bodily movement and gestures, similar to what Chion calls 'Mickeymousing' (Chion, 1994, p. 121). We hypothesise that this emphasis on body derides the meaning of the words, since the voice has taken the role of sound effect, at least in part. The way the interviewees use their arms and hands to illustrate their words (that we cannot hear) shows us that if we could hear what they are saying, it would most likely be about the Northern Lights because their gestures perfectly follow the movements and shapes of electric drawings in the sky. The emphasis on gestures emphasizes the problem involved with describing in words the natural phenomenon. The film is like the gestures, an impossible attempt to capture and show an authentic experience of the Aurora Borealis.

Creative use of voice

Mouthing the word 'surrogate'. © Grimthorpe Film Inc.

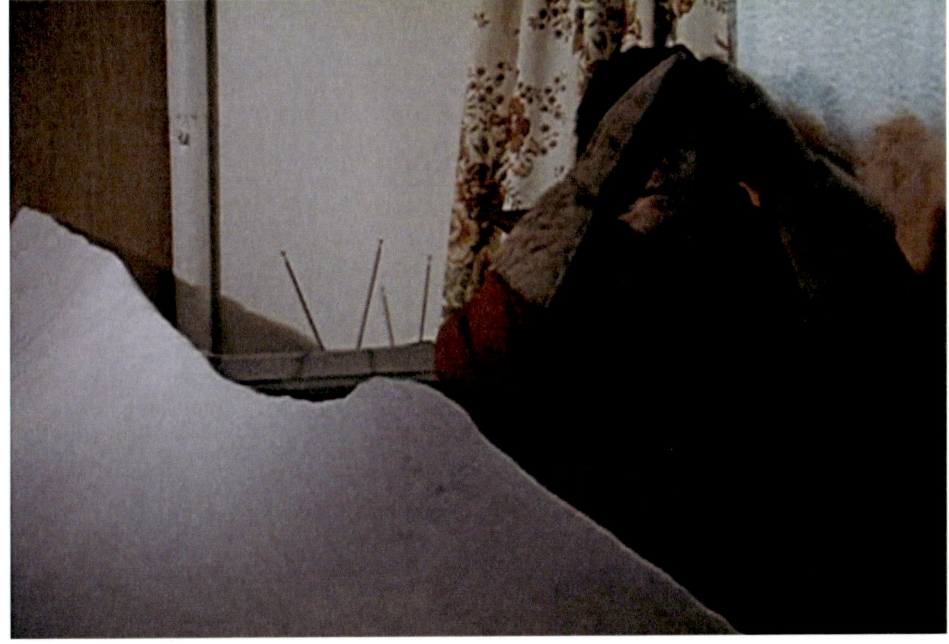

Gesturing 'edges'. © Grimthorpe Film Inc.

Land and Language: Empathetic Music

Most of *Picture of Light* is shot in Churchill, a small town in the North of Canada. More than half of the population is Aboriginal, of which the Inuit make up a small part. The Old Inuit, as Mettler calls him, speaks a language most of us do not understand. He is neither translated nor dubbed. Instead, we listen to the texture of his voice, its metre, the melody of the language. Then the image cuts to a vista of a white landscape where sheets of ice stand upright, trails of snow blow over the surface, his voice continues and subtitles remain absent. As a result, land and language form a striking audiovisual contract. The two sing together for approximately 25 seconds. The voice stops while the camera pans over the landscape, finding nothing but snow and ice in different formations. With the voice gone, the terrain feels distant; we would need a translator to understand it.

Although the act is simple, an audiovisual analysis is not straightforward. First, consider the chronology of the sequence:

Sound	Sight
1. (31s) Breathing (17s), Inuit's voice (14s)	Old Inuit (talking head), sync sound
2. (27s) Wind, Inuit's voice	Snow/ice terrain, snow blowing in wind
3. (33s) Wind	Snow/ice terrain, snow blowing in wind

Visually, the talking head forms a stark contrast with the terrain. Yet, we perceive the sequence as a smooth transition. The rhythm and textures of the voice seem to correspond with the rhythm and textures of the landscape. In harmonic counterpoint, the landscape articulates the voice and vice versa, a case of what Chion calls *prosopopeia* (Chion, 2009, p. 339), giving the inanimate landscape a voice.

The sound of the voice acts first as speech and then as a kind of music. Speech, because we may expect it to be translated within the scene; this happens earlier in a talking heads scene where a character speaks a language we do not know. To be precise, the Inuit's voice is translated, but not until much later when Mettler's voice-over explains 'The Old Inuit said that most of all he liked to hunt'. A kind of music, because we cannot understand its semantic meaning, shifting our hearing to the changing of rhythms and textures in the voice, which structure time and how the image is perceived. Hence, we are considering the voice here as 'empathetic music' (Chion, 1994, p. 8; Chion, 2009, p. 430), since it is a sort of 'added value' (Chion, 1994, p. 5). Chion defined his concept of 'added value' as the value of what we see in the image

Creative use of voice

'Old Inuit'. © Grimthorpe Film Inc.

Language Terrain. © Grimthorpe Film Inc.

from the sound that we hear and vice versa. Here, it works both ways. However, the fact that we cannot understand the words does not mean the semantic listening mode is completely switched off (for listening modes, see, 1994, p. 25). We keep searching for meaning, and all we see is harsh terrain.

The land and language scene is clearly powerful as an audiovisual construct in its own right, regardless of its relation to the film as a whole. However, the contrast with an earlier scene is worth pointing out. It is similar in its use of voice-over and landscape, but with the important differences that the voice-over is Mettler's, and the landscape is filmed at night as a long point-of-view shot lit by a torch. The voice-over starts self-consciously with 'You've probably heard that the Inuit have 17 words for ice, but in truth it is much closer to 170'. He then lists the Inuit words with English translations while the camera pans over the terrain. He never gets anywhere near 170. The search is hopeless. Nothing is found by translating the Inuit's language. The camera halts when the voice-over stops and we see a character with a torch searching the dark landscape. The scene reads as a critique of semantic meaning in the voice-over, especially when analysed in relation to the Old Inuit's land and language scene.

Gambling, Gods and LSD

In a similar fashion to *Picture of Light*, *Gambling, Gods and LSD* engages with themes of technology and experience. The film is shot on four locations: Mettler's hometown Toronto, Las Vegas including parts of the surrounding dessert, Switzerland, and India. The focus of the film is the ecstatic in different forms, such as sexual, religious, and drug-infused. The local/global relation also forms a central theme throughout the film, perhaps best exemplified by a scene of the shooting of a Bollywood film in his local Switzerland. In the same way as experiencing the Aurora Borealis in *Picture of Light*, Mettler points out the impossibility of translating the ecstatic to cinema, but this challenge is turned into a highly regarded cinematic experience with similar, though different, moments of ecstasy.

The Problem of the Radio Acousmêtre

In *Gambling, Gods and LSD* the radio features as a bridging device between characters and places. Conversations and general radio noise appear and fade of their own accord, often without a visual cue. This takes on different forms: airport control tower conversations; police walkie-talkies; and security staff communicating through radio devices. Sometimes Mettler's camera takes the position of security cameras,

Creative use of voice

Control tower. © Grimthorpe Film Inc.

Church security watch. © Grimthorpe Film Inc.

and parallels have been drawn between the control room and the editing suite (Russell, 2006). The radio frequencies signal connectivity, travelling, or the global — or combinations of these. Although we can treat them as a single sonic entity, they do not have a single physical body (and therefore no singular visual reference). Furthermore, it has by nature an off-screen element. Hence, de-acousmatization occurs only insofar as we see people and instruments, presumably responsible for a part of the sound's source. It is problematic to denote this sonic theme an *acousmêtre* because (1) complete de-acousmatization is impossible and (2) it consists of an unknown number of people and devices.

Before the scene at the Toronto Airport Christian Fellowship Church, there are some shots from within the air traffic control tower. The radio voice is switched on briefly when we look at the back of someone's head, just enough to reminds us of the first occurrence of this sound at the start of the film. However, the dominating voice around these control tower shots is that of the leader of the church, to which the film cuts subsequently. Still in the control room (visually), whilst the voice addresses an audience asking where everyone is from (audio only), we see airplanes landing and departing, watched by the control tower. We note that the source of the radio voices remains hidden, even though we see an on-screen set that could be it. There is still tension.

In the subsequent church scene, the ecstatic state of bodies and voices builds up, accentuated by an eerie musical soundscape at the end, which is mixed with singing and crying voices to which the sound of a ticking watch provides a reference. Before we revisit the airport control tower, the film cuts to electricity pylons — giant, cold bodies in stark contrast with the previous emotional wilderness. The concept of technology forms an overarching narrative in the church scene, with security cameras and screens, reminiscent of the control tower looking at the world from a distance. Back in the control tower, the radio voices are finally, though partly, de-acousmatized. It signals the end of this chapter of the film.

With the distance between body (instruments and people) and voice (instrumental noises and radio voices) cleared, the scene comes to its end, in a manner reminiscent of Chion's discussion of the *acousmêtre* in *Wizard of Oz* (1939), (Chion, 1999, p. 28). However, the radio *acousmêtre* can never be fully at rest, since the noises we hear refer to off-screen sources. Indeed, the shot from within the control tower room, with diegetic sound, merely marks the end of a scene, while the film travels to the next location, possibly where the sound is coming from.

Creative use of voice

Petroglyphs. © Grimthorpe Film Inc.

'It is the morning of shot day . . . '. © Grimthorpe Film Inc.

The Radio Suspension

A different type of radio texture comes in over petroglyphs in the Nevada desert. We see human figures carved out in the rocks hundreds, if not thousands, of years ago, while we hear radio voices referring to the present. As with the Land and Language scene in *Picture of Light*, prosopopeia comes to mind, but a dissonant one given the huge vertical time gap in the audiovisual relation. The sound refers to the present, while the visuals refer to ancient history. Chion discusses vertical and horizontal time (Chion, 1994, p. 35), but not in the sense where they are vertically out of sync, as here.

Several shots of the desert follow. We see an old car upside down with bullet holes. The rust on the car and around the holes tells us this is not a recent crime scene. Hence, the vertical time gap remains, but is smaller. Then, the camera takes the position of this new radio *acousmêtre*, becoming its body, when we hear it asking over the radio 'Are you there?', looking at a house. The film cuts to another house and the radio voice repeats the question. We see policemen walking, some of whom may be hearing the radio voices that the camera apparently speaks out to them. The joining of camera and radio is reminiscent of the shots of and from surveillance cameras in the church scene. While the voice continues we see shots of the Nevada desert from a police car, noting that this perspective is probably also a constructed illusion.

During a panning shot of a red desert slope the radio voice suddenly disappears. It leaves the spectator alone in the desert. In the preceding shots Mettler established a connection between radio, the landscape, and the camera. Suspension is the effect associated with the disappearance of an ambient sound, although the source is still felt in the image (Chion, 1994, p. 131). The wind takes over where the radio stopped. A similar occurrence of this technique is in a later scene taking place at a nuclear missile silo in New Mexico. We hear a countdown to detonation in a radio-type voice, possibly recorded by Mettler's crew at the nearby information centre. At the same time we see a barren desert terrain, giving the impression there is something about to happen here. The explosion features in the film neither audibly nor visually; we only see the landscape and hear some light wind, which then picks up as we see a cloud moving over the landscape.

Petropolis: Aerial Perspectives on the Alberta Tar Sands

In *Petropolis: Aerial Perspectives on the Alberta Tar Sands* the camera sweeps over industrial devastation. The film is shot exclusively from a helicopter with a camera attached to its body that records colossal machines causing the environmental

Creative use of voice

Trucks as seen from a helicopter. © Grimthorpe Film Inc.

In the year . . . © Grimthorpe Film Inc.

catastrophe below. Throughout the film the movement of changing camera positions is emphasized, visually and also by sound. For 35 minutes the film contains no voice, but when the film is slowly coming to its end, the voice-over enters as a wake-up call.

Mettler's voice starts with a story of a historical hot air balloon flight 'In the year we call 1783, two brothers named Montgolfier flew the first passengers suspended in a hot air balloon: a sheep, a rooster, and a duck . . . '. It contrasts with the extremely modern feel of the entire film, a striking dissonance that can be interpreted as another example of a vertical time gap that we also observed in the previous section. Furthermore, suspension is at work here. As Chion notes, suspension may function according to conventions in audiovisual relations, giving the example 'sun-dappled woods = birdsongs' (Chion, 1994, p. 133). The absence of birdsong generates strangeness, because it is contrary to how we normally experience sun-dappled woods. Similarly, the absence of voice-over narration in a Greenpeace funded activist film, also generates strangeness, as is the case in *Petropolis*.

The voice-over continues after the short story of the hot air balloon: 'Today, in the summer of 2008, we fly a machine, powered by the combustion of petroleum . . .'. Herewith, Mettler makes the film, and thereby the audience, part of the presented problem. The film lets the spectator marvel at the beautifully shot images, before making them aware that these perspectives are dependent on the destructive factors framed.

Conclusion

The voice takes on a variety of forms in Mettler's films. Instead of going through Chion's vocabulary and attaching new examples for the phenomena he describes, we used Chion for context, showing that his vocabulary aids discussions of Mettler's often complex treatment of documentary form. We described parts from *Picture of Light*, *Gambling, Gods and LSD*, and *Petropolis: Aerial Perspectives on the Alberta Tar Sands* that we found especially exciting for their use of voice.

It should be noted that creative uses of voice are also present in Mettler's more recent documentary *The End of Time* (2012). To give one beautiful example, consider the scene of a Hindu funeral ceremony. Mettler finds an opportunity here to address both the subject of time and the artificiality of film. The survivors of the deceased repeatedly sing a phrase out loud while they carry the body to the sea shore. Over one of the cuts their voices have drastically changed in both rhythm and tone, the amount of which is a measure for the amount of time passed. A deliberate piece of discontinuity editing, it is reflexive also to the film's subject of time.

Creative use of voice

It was not our aim to find coherence in Mettler's use of voice, however we did find some. For example, the body and voice are often kept separate, with almost every character entering the film as an *acousmêtre*. And when the body enters the screen, Mettler often hesitates to connect the two. For example, the preacher in the airport church scene at the start of *Gambling, Gods and LSD* is first filmed from the back. The voice of the former prisoner, also in *Gambling, Gods and LSD*: is heard for a long time before we finally see his face, which is first shown with lips sealed, while his voice continues. The voice of Albert Hofmann, the inventor of LSD, first starts inaudibly from a television set over a repeated panning shot. At the second visual repetition his words are intelligible, but when we see him as a television personality in diegetic space Mettler first shows the reflections of the television lights on what appears to be the ceiling, retaining the aura of the *acousmêtre* just a little longer. And there are also more such examples in *The End of Time*.

Mettler's treatment of characters as dissolving *acousmêtres* is one example of his use of horizontal relations between audio and visuals, meaning that a sound heard at some point connects to an image that is shown at some other time. Sometimes Mettler treats non-vocal sounds similarly, such as the rain on a car roof in *Gambling, Gods and LSD*, which is heard long before its source is shown. In *Picture of Light* another example of a large gap in horizontal time is between Mettler's voice-over about the famous Lumière brothers' film of an arriving train *L'arrivée d'un train à La Ciotat* (1895), and the scene more than half an hour later when Mettler shows an approaching train in a very similar way. We have also observed the use of vertical time differences, both in *Petropolis* and in *Gambling, Gods and LSD*. In both cases the gap seemed to refer to technological advancement in relation to landscape.

As a further indication of coherence, radio-type voices are abundant in all the films discussed here. We have already analysed radio occurrences in parts of *Gambling, Gods and LSD*. Radio features occasionally in *Petropolis* and heavily in *Picture or Light* and *The End of Time*. It refers both to the local (such as the petroglyphs discussed) or the global (such as the air traffic control room). In *Petropolis* it gains in volume when we fly over a residential area, as if the voices are coming from the houses we see, casting a technological shadow on the people who live there.

Language forms an integral part of Mettler's filmmaking process, exemplified by the diverse use of voice. In *Gambling, Gods and LSD* he shows a large array of Post-it Notes with words and short sentences referring to the film we are watching, such as his thoughts on film, events, and places. His personal notes and files featured in an exhibition about the project (White, p. 39).

He prefers to reveal the limits and artificiality of language, as opposed to reading out facts. For example, the voice-over in *The End of Time* starts with what could be regarded as a Nietzschean claim: 'Things don't have names, we made them all up' (comparable with Nietzsche in *Human, All Too Human*, 1878, about *aeternae veritates*, p. 16). Film provides an excellent ground for such philosophical explorations, only to find new boundaries of course — those of the film medium itself. In the cinema, we cannot authentically experience the Northern Lights nor feel the effects of LSD. The translation from lived to cinema experience is fundamental to Mettler's reflexive style. It is suffused with numerous inventive constructions of audiovisual relations, which we hope to have illustrated by focussing on his diverse use of voice.

Bibliography

Bruzzi, S. (2006) *New documentary*. (2nd ed.). Abingdon, Oxon: Routledge.

Chion, M. (1994). *Audio-vision: sound on screen*. New York: Columbia University Press.

Chion, M. (1999) *The voice in cinema*. New York: Columbia University Press.

Chion, M. (2009). *Film, a sound art*. (C. Gorbman, Trans.). New York: Columbia University Press.

McSorley, T. (2005). Paradox and wonder: the cinema of Peter Mettler. *Take One: Film & Television in Canada, 14*(50).

Mettler, P. (Director). (1994) *Picture of light* [Motion picture]. Canada, Switzerland: Grimthorpe Films

Mettler, P. (Director). (2002) *Gambling, Gods and LSD* [Motion picture]. Canada, Switzerland: Odeon Films

Mettler, P. (Director). (2009) *Petropolis: aerial perspectives on the Alberta Tar Sands* [Motion picture]. Canada: Greenpeace Canada

Mettler, P. (Director). (2012) *The end of time* [Motion picture]. Canada, Switzerland: National Film Board of Canada

Nietzsche, F. (1878/1996). *Human, all too human: A book for free spirits*. (R.J. Hollingdale. Trans.) (7th ed.). Cambridge: Cambridge University Press.

Russell, C. (2006) *Cinephilia and the travel film: gambling, gods and LSD*. Jump Cut: A Review of Contemporary Media, No. 48

Stefik, D. (2002) An Interview with Peter Mettler. Retrieved from http://offscreen.com/view/mettler

White, J. (2007). *Of this place and elsewhere: the films and photography of Peter Mettler*. Bloomington, Indian: Indiana Univ Pr.

CHAPTER 8

Documentary film as a backdrop for active thinking

Ana Berkenhoff

Film Still: View of London City. © Ana Berkenhoff and Ethan Folk

This chapter is about a short film and some thoughts relating to it. The film is *Cormorant*. It is by Ana Berkenhoff and Ethan Folk and its running time is 7′ 33″. It was shot in the City of London and looks for an interaction between a documentary setting and an artistic approach, a conversation between imagination and reality. The film focuses on the thoughts of pleasure and interruption when confronted with the everyday life of the City. *Cormorant* is a movement and perspective study that questions the life of human beings in their financial centres. The body is placed like an unusual object in everyday places. The dance is the city life that exists around us.

A Note on Screenings

Cormorant debuted at *Unit 61: Movable hosts* in London, April 2015 and was shown as part of the offical selection for *Festival Internacional de Videodanza de Chile* (sociedad contemporanea), November, 2015. Official selection at *Plano Lisboa*, Alternative Worlds programme, Lisbon, 2015. Official selection at *Premios Latino del Cine e Musica*, Marbella, May, 2016

Sound& Music in Documentary Film Symposium Huddersfield, February 2017. Konzert der Generationen, *Evimus*, 4 Saarbrücker Tage für elektro-akustische und visuelle Musik, Saarbrücken, November 2017.

The Making of *Cormorant*

The film was shot in one day and finished in three. The consecutive filming, and the direct recording and composing of the voice-over and music, helped to create both the specification and the magic invoked by the film. It is a collaboration between a first time visitor to London (Ethan Folk) and a resident (Ana Berkenhoff). We decided that we would shoot at a few specific places in London that take me aback or that I find striking. These include Richard Rogers' Lloyd's building, the glass elevator of the Heron tower, a square hole in a building site, the birch trees in front of the Tate Modern, and the view from a tower which served as artist studios in Hackney but is now empty as a result of gentrification. We were looking for places that mirror feelings of claustrophobia, endlessness and isolation and emphasize our role as observers. We wanted to document these places and our reactions towards them.

The film starts in silence. People are looking up towards something, clapping their hands. Then the music starts. The camera is running down from the open sky, along a building, into a street in the City of London. A voice is talking from outside the picture. You see people dressed for business, typical red double-decker buses, the life on the street: a simple urban reality. In opposition to the business life, one performer places herself in unusual places, silently looking straight into the camera. The picture of dramatic clouds above the skyline keeps reappearing during the film. The floating camera creates a sense of ease in the spectator. The voice reflects on the environment, offering audible guidance as well as points of confusion throughout the film.

I was inspired by the approach to performing and speaking in the film *Wings of Desire*, made in 1987 as a collaboration between the director Wim Wenders and the authors Peter Handke and Richard Reitinger. The original title was *Der Himmel über Berlin* (*The Heavens Over Berlin*). Two male angels observe people in Berlin, their isolation and hopes. They are visible and their thoughts are audible, they even communicate through thinking. I wanted to make a simple experiment with documentary filming and a sound and voice added from outside. I am experienced at working in public spaces, choreographing people without them knowing it, and combining fiction within documentary filming. The approach to voice in *Wings of Desire* made me curious as to how the technique could be expanded. I was looking for pictures that were as simple as possible and a voice sounding as personal as possible. No fiction, only the added music as a carrier of emotional possibilities. Can the simple friction created by the co-existence of performers and non-performers form a base with which to stimulate the audience's imagination?

Wenders: 'And that's really the only thing I have to say about stories: they are one huge, impossible paradox! I totally reject stories, because for me they only bring out lies, nothing but lies, and the biggest lie is that they show coherence where there is none. Then again, our need for these lies is so consuming that it's completely pointless to fight them and to put together a sequence of images without a story — without the lie of a story. Stories are impossible, but it's impossible to live without them' (Wenders 1988/1991).

Cormorant was made in a constant dialogue between the two artists, sharing observations and interviewing each other. This produced the voice-over. Although filming in a documentary style means that many things can't be planned, a big advantage is the resulting flexibility that allows you to focus on your intention. Not taking sound on scene made a small mobile team possible. Shooting in a public space without being recognized as a film crew was crucial. The mode of observation in *Wings of Desire* led me to the idea of confronting documentary scenes and non-performing people with the still and direct gaze of a performer, looking directly into the camera. The intention was to create a kind of feedback-loop of gazes and thoughts that become vivid in the viewer: documentary film as a backdrop for active thinking.

I focused on the fluidity of the process, especially using the shift between documentary and storytelling in the use of sound and voice. I did not want to implement a view, but to open a timeframe (the film) for many personal views. Documentary film uses the art of storytelling. It is never the pure documentation of a reality because it is always involves choice, an excerpt of reality. But it tends to work from a particular stance, one that does not draw the audience in but privileges the observing position.

Being a performer in the midst of non-performers can produce interesting tensions in a picture, even without anything happening. It can also be a means to emphasize the relationship with the people around. I use reality in film to show the open gap between real life and fiction, seen through a lens. Reality is the place where you start to develop a fantasy, a utopia, a question. I want to open the space of questioning for the audience and give back possibilities. Experiencing the strange, uninviting space of a financial city centre called us to action. The City of London is a place where people work, represent work and seem isolated. What has led to the people's isolation? Martin Heidegger writes in his essay 'What Are Poets For?' (1971) that living merely as a productive consciousness establishes life on goal-oriented strategies. This leaves the subject feeling fragmented from those around him and thus suspended over an abyss where little meaning remains: 'What threatens man in his very nature is . . . the uniformity of production, . . . [which] from the outset destroys the realm from which any rank and recognition could possibly arise' (Heidegger, 1971).

When watching and directing films I prefer an independent sound. I like the clash of the dramatic and everyday life. In *Cormorant* I used non-diegetic sound, sound whose source is neither visible on the screen, nor has been implied to be present in the action. There is a very slow time flow in the music, while the pictures are (apart from the time-lapse in the clouds) at their original speed. The sound is a long continuous, sometimes wavering, tone, the heartbeat of a city. You can hear many overtones, slowly developing over the length of the film. The slow-moving music focuses the view on the pictures and their content. The music ebbs and flows and swells with little development over time, it adds breath and life. The sound, image and voice differ, constantly shifting the perception from inside the picture to the outside. It questions whether the picture and words correlate.

The speaker's voice is husky, with an accent, sometimes close to breaking. She voices a stream-of-consciousness poem, describing for example a bush, a human, a future. The voice goes beyond the scene, connecting to the moment the film was shot. Her words connect to the feelings and relationship the authors experienced towards the film. As a documentary, the sound takes a rather classical approach in creating

Film Still: Thinking. © Ana Berkenhoff and Ethan Folk

tension and expectations (ones that will not be met). The calm pictures of the cityscape provide a counterpoint to the slight weirdness of the voice.

The music is continuous and establishes a flow: a visual, acoustic and sensorial environment that implements a varying imagetic dramaturgy. Although the film is open to the viewer's interpretation in its structure, the voice offers an imaginative world of thought that actively engages the listener leading towards an interpretation.

> Wenders: 'Images are acutely sensitive; like snails they shrink back when you touch their horns. They don't have it in them to be carthorses: carrying and transporting messages or significance or intention or a moral. But that's precisely what a story wants from them' (Wenders, 1988/1991).

The voice, with its ambiguity, its secrets and suggestions as to what the film and the sound could be about, says:

While you thought that it has this form and it's concrete and it's there and it's the truth, suddenly it can move. We can't control it. Every sound you hear, that sound, the other one is a mixture of all the sounds. It's laughter and crying and screaming and silence, all at once.

It is just a *draft* of being. The subject is immediately drawn into larger connections than it existed in before. Is this the space of the heart or the interior space of the productive consciousness? For Heidegger, who thinks about what good poets are for, the space of the heart is 'beyond the arithmetic of calculation' and can 'overflow into the unbounded whole of the Open' This 'open' is what I aim for in my music and in the mix of available filmic tools. Without big effects in picture and sound, the mere combination can have enough friction to make a call to action on the most profound level.

Ekphrasis is a Greek concept, a skill that enabled the audience to visualise scenes, places and historical events, it was a strategy for constructing speeches that would suggest, establish, and awaken images 'before the very eyes' of the audience. Ekphrasis leads us to a dynamic and complex play between the presence and absence of for example a bush, an animal, an idea.

Enargeia, the quality that makes an ekphrasis and distinguishes it from a plain report of the facts, is a paradoxical phenomenon. It is able to arouse emotions through immaterial semblances of scenes that are not present to the listener and may never take place. For what lies behind vivid speech, is the gallery of mental images, impressed by sensations in the speaker's mind.

The ability to signify absence in presence allows the artist to call new realms of meaning into existence, creating new worlds that call the dominance of the present

Documentary film

life into question. What can make us attempt to see our situation more clearly? Can we attempt to become aware of *options* rather than *solutions* in a traditional sense?

Always trying to be crystalline with a desire to engage in a possible transformation, and not be static. Always being in a state of genesis or development, of de-centring and re-centring the senses, with a willingness to reach out of the film and enter the dialogue with the world. Wenders: 'I prefer movies that ask me to see' (Wenders 1988/1991). This voice says:

'Listen!'

'This must be the other side.'

'I see, I see, now I know where we are, we are in that kind of space!'

The music stays, even after the last image.

Suggested viewing, reading and listening

Cormorant is available at https://anaberkenhoff.com/cormorant/

Peter Handke's radio play *Hörspiel Nr.2* which takes place in the streets of Berlin where taxi drivers form a group of actors meandering through the city.

The work of Roland Barthes. *S/Z: An essay* is a useful reference for processes involving agency and interaction.

Film Still: Helicopters over the City. © Ana Berkenhoff and Ethan Folk

The transformative power of performance: a new aesthetics by Erika Fischer-Lichte is a useful reference for sound, rhythm, atmospheres and meanings in performance

All pictures are from the film Cormorant by Ana Berkenhoff & Ethan Folk

Ethan Folk is a Berlin-based artist, filmmaker and fisherman from Seattle/ Canada. He has exhibited in Canada, Italy, Spain and wider Europe and is engaged in several artist collectives. His latest work *Vernae* is an experimental dance film based on *The Rite of Spring*, Igor Stravinsky's masterpiece of 1913, which has gained much attention because of its unconventional approach to dance, landscape and ritual.

Bibliography

Barthes, R. (1974) *S/Z: An essay.* (R. Miller, Trans.). New York: Farrar, Straus and Giroux. (Original work published 1970)

Heidegger, M. (1971) 'What is Poetry For?' In *Poetry, language, thought.* (A. Hofstadter, Trans.) New York: Harper and Row.

Fischer-Lichte, E. (2008) *The transformative power of performance: a new aesthetics* (S. I. Jain, Trans). London: Routledge.

Wenders, W. (1991) 'Impossible Stories'. In *The logic of images: essays and conversations* Frankfurt: Verlag der Autoren, 1988 (M. Hofmann, Trans.). London: Faber and Faber Limited (Original work published 1988, Frankfurt: Verlag der Autoren)

Film Still: People Clapping. © Ana Berkenhoff and Ethan Folk

CENTREPIECE

The Unwanted Sound of Everything We Think We Want

Andrew Kötting

Imagine a vinyl record playing throughout
FRONT LINE - VIRGIN COMPILATION

Apparently Kötting hopes to dig into himself like an archaeologist in a hopeless attempt to explain the sounds that abound therein.

Ps Every documentary film, even the least self-referential, demonstrates in every frame that an artist's chief material is himself.
It is an excavation of oneself.
It is an ego trip.

DUB REGGAE - I ROY - U ROY - AUGUSTUS PABLO - DR ALIMANTADO PRINCE FAR I and ADRIAN SHERWOOD

THE WOLFGANG PRESS - WIRE - YOUNG MARBLE GIANTS and PUBLIC IMAGE LIMITED

STELLA CHIWESHA - NUSRAT FATEH ALI KHAN - JALI MUSA JAWARA
and SALIF KEITA

MEREDITH MONK – MORTON FELDMAN and LAURIE ANDERSON's *OH SUPERMAN*

Music for me was always about atmosphere.
Something that might surround you
Enter into you and invariably eat at you
It was about the not-knowing, the non-existent, the non-narrative.
It wasn't about clever structure – middle eights – harmonies and guitar breaks.
It was about being spooky and exotic.
Confused and erotic.
Dreamy and quixotic.

John Cage gave a lecture once at the Seattle Arts Society, in which he suggested that the noun *'music'* should be replaced by a more meaningful term: **The organisation of sound.**
But that was then.
This is now.
It's always difficult to separate what happened from what seemed to happen.

Memory is the past rewritten in the direction of feeling and anything processed by memory *is* fiction.

Therefore our memories **are** fictions.
Memory loves to go hunting – especially in the dark.
And the dark is VERY atmospheric.
The dark is last week or a few months back – the further back you go the hazier it gets.

Or does it?

I'm interested in the generic edge – the thin membrane between what might be called fiction and non-fiction.
The foggy no-man's land between what *is* and what *isn't*.
I draw from the real in order to make an 'unreal' or 'ethereal'.
And the work involves the organisation of both *sound* and image.

And the soundscapes that I create attempt to dig into the clouds of consciousness.

When I first started filming other people MY head would be full of questions;
What does it mean to set another person in front of the camera?
Am I not trying to extract something from their soul?

When am I exploiting?
When am I exploring?

When am I adoring?
Or is it all just one and the same?
Perhaps that is the truth of all human relationships?

So I'd fabricate my own responses.
Let non-sequiturs be the order of the day I thought.
Let the tangential take hold:

Close your eyes, prick up your ears, and from the softest sound to the wildest noise, from the simplest tone to the highest harmony, from the most violent, passionate scream to the gentlest words of sweet reason, it is invariably Nature that speaks to us.

She reveals her *being*, her *power*, her *life*, and her relatedness - so that maybe even a blind person, to whom the infinitely visible world is denied, can grasp the endless vitality in what can be heard.

No monotheistic belief systems explaining divine interventions or man myths – just pure unadulterated Nature.

It's as loud as it gets – it's as loud as it needs to be....
Nature is both Landscape and Cityscape.

I'd like you to watch a film I made way back before I had the learning
HOI POLLOI
It's both document and documentary.
Both Fact and Fiction.
A portrait of a life led in the French Pyrenees in the late 80's.
A portrait of a disabled daughter.
My daughter.
Eden.
She was born with a rare neurological dis-order, Joubert Syndrome.
She was missing a bit of her brain.

The vermis.

An important part of the cerebellum.
And it was this loss that provoked in me a sense of loss.
An imminent loss:

The voice of authority with its clinical prognosis - Gleaned from Senate House Library, University College London, whilst I was a student at The Slade – still rings in the ears:
'Life-expectancy is not good and few if any sufferers live into adulthood'.....

The words had an impact on me
I was overcome by an urgency.
I began to document her life.
Our life together.
But never the morbidity - I wanted it to be a celebration – a celebration of lives lived within a Landscape – our Pyrenean Landscape
A Nature fantasy – make believe and fact.
And the **hoi-polloi** of the title represents the voices inside Eden's head
The voices inside my head.
The voices outside in the forest – resplendent in their phantomic animistic presence.
I made them up or cobbled them together.

Cabin doors to manual.

HOI POLLOI - https://vimeo.com/55218526

Eden as both cipher and Sybil – a flesh radio that we tune into …

With the look-back from today the film seems strangely cathartic yet deeply darker than I had imagined – perhaps a subliminal Freudian understanding in my desire at such a young age to be rid of the responsibility that was Eden.
And yet ironically - she has grown into my liberator - inspirator and facilitator but more on that later.

The poet **Gerard Manley-Hopkins** used the terms **inscape** and **instress**.

These were words, which always had a hold on me; they beguiled me and confused me.

Did he mean that *mindscape* that we carry around with us from day to day and moment to moment, that safe haven behind your eyes that is looking out at the world - your inspace - the place that works as an antidote to the great-out-of-doors?

Did he mean Herzog's *ecstatic truth-space*, Beckett's *cerebral hinterland*, Tarkovsky's *zone*, Sinclair's *thinkspace* or John Clare's *headtalk*?

Perhaps by *inscape* he meant the unified whole of the things that give consciousness its uniqueness and that makes each thing different from all other things.

Perhaps by *instress* he meant either the force-of-being which holds that inscape together or the unfathomable-thing from that inscape which sticks to the minds of others.

Did he mean glue?
Whatever Manley Hopkins meant, for me *inscape* is the metaphysical manifest.

The interior *noisescape*, the inside sent out or the outside brought in.

I believe in the arts as a type of knowledge.
I believe in science AS a quest for knowledge.
I believe in religion as superstition and myth or at best a Friday night Morris Dancing Session.
Some truths we NEED
Some *truths* are myths.

The Pre-bronze-ageist **Aristotle** mooted that music was character forming and that it should be introduced into the education of the young.

Now there was a *proper* thinker.

When one listens to music our souls undergo a change he said - a transformation - it arouses moral qualities - but he also went on to say that it must be the 'right sort of music'.

The wrong sort of music - particularly that of the flute might prove too exciting or too tempting for both children and slaves - which was just too 'vulgarizing'.

Plato of course thought that The Arts just made people worse - unlike Reason and Science.

The Arts he suggested were way off the mark when it came to the TRUTH.
At best they were only a form of sport or mucking about.
And besides the fact that they encouraged the passions flew in the face of the principles of the SOUL.

And
When arranging human SOULS into nine grades - **Plato** put philosophers at the top - tyrants at the bottom and artists at number six - just above artisans and farmers. He does however make an exception for musicians (provided that the music they make is virtuous and not intended for children and slaves) in which case they come in at number five.
I'm forever looking backwards
Gathering up fragments and re-using them
Re-assessing them
The memories
The difficulties
The probabilities and the possibilities
They balm me and soothe me and hurt me
I enjoy the pain of the revisit
I receive the memory as punctum.
Palpable and potent.
The past is the one thing we are.

Sound is ubiquitous, immersive and unstoppable.
The agency through which music is absorbed and spoken language is understood.
Sound works quietly with the other senses in an attempt to scan the environment - to

The Unwanted Sound

define orientation within a place and to register the feeling that we might describe as *atmosphere*.

All Sound is music.
OR IS IT?

Some quotes:
Goethe - *Blowing is not playing music – you have to make use of your fingers*

Beethoven - *I am inclined to think that a hunt for folk songs is better than a hunt for heroes who are so highly extolled*

Anonymous - *It is easier to understand a nation by listening to its music than by learning its language*

Anne Carson – *Every sound we make is a bit of autobiography*

David Toop - *Visual work has boundaries; a position that is fixed, if only from moment to moment; a capacity to express specific ideas. Sound, on the other hand, may come and go; be perceived at all points in a space, even behind the listener's head or out of sight; be resistant to verbal interpretation, or attachment to any kind of meaning other than the way it alters an environment.*

Andrew Kötting - *Your eyes have eye lids but your ears don't*

Sound can be fun.

I'd like you to watch **Jaunt**.
A television commission and a running time set-in-stone.
But a commission nevertheless, in which I was left alone - to document trips up and down the River Thames – from Southend-on-Sea to The Houses of Parliament.
Eversuchalongtimeago.

JAUNT - https://vimeo.com/55220005

There are waypoints, markers, buoys and signifiers in all the work I make.
They come about through something I've seen or heard or smelt or remembered.
Something I might even have tasted.
However it is the sound that informs the picture.
The memory the significance.
The companionship of shooting - the tradition – the process.

Meanwhile
Collaboration undermines the authority of control.
And I'm glad of it.
It let's you Letgo
It helps to dilute the ego.

Thus I'm ever hopeful that something else 'might' happen.
BUT in the edit suite or on the paper that I write this, begins the real work.
The job of **reverse engineering**.
Coaxing out of the various parts - a structure and possibly *meaning*.

The latter invariably something that I might not even 'recognise' until months or years later.
If at all.

Paradoxically it is the subjective space
The personal space
The autobiographical space
The MySpace
That helps me to understand The BIGGER PICTURE

So today - I'm corralling ideas from the page and out into the auditorium in pretty much the same way that I collage sound and image into the film work.
Confabulation and improvisation is often my compass
As well as:
Randomness
Openness to accident
Assemblage
Anthropological autobiography
Appropriation
Collage
Discontinuous
Emotional urgency
Impetuousness
Non-linear
Plasticity of form
Risk

Criticism
Self-criticism
Serendipity
Self-reflexivity
Stupidity
Self-ethnography
Spontaneity
Self-evident
The blurring
(Sometimes to the point of wanton invisibility)
Happenstance
The psyche and its geography….

Psychogeography
Psychogeography as an approach to geography that emphasises playfulness and drift.
Psychogeography as jaunt.
Psychogeography as the study of the precise laws and specific effects of the environment, consciously or not, on the emotions and behavior of individuals.
Psychogeography as box of tricks or a bucket of eels. Playful and inventive with its' exploration of the landscape.
Psychogeography as anything that takes us away from our pre-determined trajectories and jolts us into a new awareness of the world.

Let the **not-knowing** OR the **trying-to** be my motor.
Let absurdity of ill-fitting configuration be my titilator.
Let the taking from the 'real' and collaging into a coherent but fluid disorder be my meter.
Let serendipity be my map.
Italy - Sicily - France and Spain
All round the coast of Britain with Gladys and Eden
And back again.

GALLIVANT - https://www.youtube.com/watch?v=gilKsrTlRal

To **gallivant**, is, according to a dictionary definition 'to wander about, seeking pleasure or diversion; to gad about with members of the opposite sex'

Perhaps we were mapping the atmospheric pressures that the process of travelling together produces.
Perhaps some satisfaction was gleaned through the process of making public the intimacies of autobiography and serendipity.
The letting-in of others.

A film that one critic demanded 'should have been drowned at birth like the runt of a litter…'
Perfect for the poster.

Atmosphere as the layer of hot air that surrounds the work ….

And **Collage** as pieces of 'other' things.
Collage as a demonstration of the many becoming the one, with the *one* never fully understanding what became of the many that informed it in the first place.
Collage as fragmented materials, often mis-aligned and even out of context.
Collage as an accentuated act of editing, picking through options and presenting a new configuration, albeit one that is never smooth and complete within the 'traditional' sense.
Collage as **key** to the post-modern predicament.
Collage as a contender to the present-day non-binary norm!
Perhaps another purpose of my work is to impart the sensation of things as they are perceived and not as they are known.
Which is why collaborating with **Eden** has brought us both into our own.

She reminds me all the time that Art exists in order that we might recover the sensation of life.
It exists in order that we might *feel* things.
It helps make the sound better heard and also helps make the pictures better seen.

Maybe all art aspires towards the condition of music?

Who you talk with alters the mind, the soul, the opinion.
Who you walk with alters the view, the vista, the vision.
None of us are **autodidacts**.
None of us learn alone.

We live in a manufactured and artificial state in which we yearn for the real, or at least a semblance of the real.

I want to pose something non-fictional against all the fabrication.
I want to indulge autobiographical frissons.
Those framed or filmed or captured moments.
And in their seeming rawness I want them to possess at least the possibility of breaking through the clutter.

What a beautiful picture.

The mimetic function in art hasn't so much declined as mutated.
The tools of metaphor have expanded and as the culture becomes more saturated by different media, artists can use larger and larger chunks of culture to communicate.

All of culture thus becomes fair game for appropriation.

But perhaps a lot of this is just repetition?
I love repetition.
Repetition changes nothing in the object repeated, but it does change something in the mind, which contemplates it.

The looping of rhythm
The rhythms of looping:
Philip Glass - Steve Reich and Michael Nyman
Gavin Bryars - John Tavener and La Monte Young
Terry Riley - Arvo Part and Kim Jong-Un

Just as letters in a language are metaphors for specific sounds, and words are metaphors for specific ideas, shards from all cultures now form a kind of language that we will never know how to speak.

It doesn't need to be spelt out.
It's quicker and easier to go to the existing material – film footage, vinyl records, radio recordings, old cassettes, newspapers ….
It's the artist's job to breathe new life into the selected material.
To generate new footage - to fill in the gaps
This is what we do.

This is what I do.
And like Eden in **Hoi Polloi** - I've become a *flesh radio*
There is nothing new in what I do.
Re-configurations through new re-gurgitations

ORIGINAL is nothing but a collection of previous cultural moments.
God is Dead.
No Supermans – No Ubermensches
Not even Geniuses.

But Brian Eno suggests there might well be **Sceniuses**
David Bowie was a Scenius
Eno moots that **Scenius** is the intelligence of a fluxus or group of people.

He wants us to forget the idea of 'genius and think about the whole ecology of ideas that give rise to good new thoughts and good new work.
Individuals rising like a phoenix from the ash trays.
They suck in heavy from the dandruff of the shoulders of bygone GIANTS:
Leonardo
Giotto
Picasso
Caravaggio
Risotto
Oxo
Botticelli
Lorenzo de Medici
Leon Battista Alberti
Lamborghini
Maserati
Bucati
Linguini
Spaghetti ….

And with cognition comes THEORY OF MIND – the ability to think oneself into another's position – to empathise, sympathise or even despise.
To worry the work into existence.
The theory of mind.

And **Women** have more THEORY OF MIND than men - which is why men have always been so frightened and threatened by them - which is why they were burnt at the stake, dunked in rivers or nowadays just stoned.

Out of sight out of mind.

To think with any seriousness is to doubt.
Thought is indistinguishable from doubt.
To be alive is to be uncertain.
The essayist should be at war with herself.
The essayist should argue with the reader.
The essayist should enact doubt as a genre.
The keynote speaker should be a non-believer.

When we are not sure we are truly alive.
Apparently the world holds two classes of men - intelligent men without religion, and religious men without intelligence.

Eden reminds me every day of her inability – her inadequacy – her dependency – from dressing her - to toileting her – to trying to understand her.
We work together – dig into life together and now for an excerpt from something we made together:

THIS ILLUMINATED WORLD IS FULL OF STUPID MEN - https://vimeo.com/90691946

The final 'product' should always and necessarily remain unfinished or open-ended, no full stops, no new paragraphs only commas and semi-colons …

In a world full of noise silence is like saffron

SO
I'm going to leave you with a consideration followed by an important list.
***Postmodernism**, the (my) school of 'thought"' that proclaimed 'There are no truths, only interpretations' has largely played itself out into absurdity, but it has left behind a generation of academics in the humanities disabled by their distrust of the very idea of truth and their disrespect for evidence, settling for 'conversations' or 'dialogues' in which nobody is wrong and nothing can be confirmed, only asserted with whatever style you can muster ….*

Professor Daniel Dennett

And the list:

NOISE – A HUMAN HISTORY by Professor David Hendy – with chapter headings such as: **echoes in the dark – the singing wilderness – the ritual soundscape and the roaring crowd**

Spoken word as atmosphere by Robert Ashley
Anna Homler (better known as BREADWOMAN)
Tim Hecker
Christain Marclay
Dial H-I-S-T-O-R-Y by Johan Grimonprez
David Toop's Ocean of Sound and his SONIC BOOM exhibition at the Hayward Gallery
Melvyn Bragg's Routes of English
Jem Finer's LONGPLAYER
Anything by **Iain Sinclair**
Pierre Bastien
Chris Watson
Anselm Kiefer
Joan of Arc
Joseph Beuys
Egyptian mummies
Shrunken heads
Stelarc
Jack-in-the Green
Samuel Beckett
Mummers plays
Emile Cioran
Theatre de Complicité
Margaret Atwood
John Clare
Kathy Acker
Morton Feldman
Meredith Monk
Andy Stott

And **Alison Streeter – The Queen of the channel** – 34 hours 40 minutes – 1990 swimming from England to France – France to England and then England back to France again
And of course **William the Conqueror**

ALSO as a footnote:

DEEPITY – a term somewhat redefined by Professor Daniel Dennett but originally coined by Miriam Weizenbaum.

Dennett uses "**deepity**" as a definition of a statement that at first seems profound, but is actually trivial on one level and meaningless on another.

Generally, a **deepity** has two (or more) meanings: one that is true but trivial, and another that sounds profound and would be important if true, but is actually false or meaningless.

Examples MIGHT BE
Que sera sera!
Beauty is only skin deep!
The power of intention can transform your life!
Or
THE UNWANTED SOUND OF EVERYTHING WE THINK WE WANT

The talk culminated in a collaborative performance with Claudia Barton and inspired by Kötting's most recent work about **Edith Swan Neck**:

NB: Thereafter **EDITH digital pinhole timeline** runs and Claudia Barton and myself perform – A CUP – THE ARROW AND THE SONG – GONE WITH THE WIND IS MY LOVE – THE RIVER IS FLOWING – spreading the sounds throughout the auditorium as best we can….

Production photographs from *EDITH WALKS* (2016). © Andrew Kötting

Part 3:
Nationhood and Conflict

# CHAPTER 9

The 'Appassionata' Sonata in *A Diary for Timothy*

Tsung-Han Tsai

The opening of the 'Appassionata' Sonata is almost inaudible in Humphrey Jennings' *A Diary for Timothy* (1946). Often regarded by critics as one of the key works in Jennings' wartime documentaries (Anderson, 1961 – 2; Hodgkinson & Sheratsky, 1982; Jackson, 2004; Beattie, 2010; Logan, 2011), *A Diary for Timothy*, filmed between 1944 and 1945, records 'images of Britain at home and at war' for a new-born baby; it depicts 'a nation on the brink of victory, but uncertain of its postwar objectives', thus offering 'British cinema's most self-conscious engagement with the process of readjustment demanded by war's end' (Plain, 2013, p. 214). About 10 minutes into the film, the camera shows a man listening to a radio report on the British force's struggle in Arnhem, where an airborne force has been surrounded by the German army. Behind the voice of the newsreader comes, almost eerily, the first few notes of Beethoven's Piano Sonata in F minor, Op. 57, or, more commonly known, the 'Appassionata'. The music only becomes clearer towards the end of its first theme. When the theme moves to G flat major with the camera cutting to a close-up of two hands gliding over a Steinway & Sons grand piano, what originally seemed to be background music turns out to be somebody's actual performance. It slowly zooms out — as the steady beat of repeated low D flat and low C sets up the second motif — and we recognize Dame Myra Hess at the piano, dressed completely in black, playing the sonata. It zooms out further and shows a stage surrounded by the audience. In bar 20, the camera zooms in and focuses on Hess's expression: frowning slightly, she follows the juxtaposition of *fortissimo* and *piano* by lifting her eyebrows every now and then. When the steady beat re-emerges in E flat in bar 24, a shot of the concert poster shows that this performance is one of the National Gallery concerts during the Second World War. The billing is '5th Birthday Concert, Myra Hess'; the date is Tuesday, 10th October 1944, with Elena Gerhardt's recital to take place the next day. Before long, we are led back into the gallery, not towards the stage but into the audience. The camera pans across the rows of listeners, male and female, old and young, military and civilian. Eventually it stays on an attentive young woman just when the A flat major second theme unfolds its warm lyricism. Yet it does not last long: as the minor mode is reimposed in bar 42, the camera goes back to the pianist and then her hands. No sooner does Hess start the three trills in bars 44 – 46 than the same newsreader's voice floats in, reiterating the endurance of the soldiers in Arnhem: 'For the last three days', his voice has a certain mechanical clarity against the music's downward passage at its *pianissimo*, 'they have had no water, very little but small arms and ammunition, and rations were cut to one sixth. Luckily or unluckily, it rained, and they caught the water in their capes and drank that.' The end of his sentence is interrupted by the A flat minor explosion in bar 51, with the image cut to a street corner in London: a hose, a small pool of water, a bus, a pedestrian walking by, and incessant rain. Other shots of the city follow — houses in rubble, a man on the rooftop relaying the slates, another group of men busy with more repairs. 'It's the middle of October now', the voice of the commentary suddenly emerges, 'and the war certainly won't be over by Christmas, and the weather doesn't suit us. And one third of our houses have been damaged by enemy action.' His voice is low, his pace slow. He starts to comment on the music: 'They do like the music that the lady was playing; some of us think it's the greatest music ever.' The semiquavers of the high treble and the slowly descending bass eventually end on A flat in the *pianissimo* bar 65. 'It is German music', the commentator continues as the main theme, this time in E major, recurs, 'and we are fighting against the Germans.' At this moment, there is a montage sequence, during which the shot of urban rubble is overlaid with Hess's hands on the piano. The commentator announces: 'There is something you have to think over later on.' The end of his sentence overlaps with the silence in the latter part of bar 70. When the music shortly resumes, it cuts to a shot of heavy rain, the volume of which seems to be turned up a level and almost obscures the music. The commentary continues: 'Rain, too much rain, and it's even wetter under the earth.' The camera follows accordingly, showing coal mines, accompanied by the E major cadence in bars 73 – 75, though less and less clear. Just before it can resolve into an E major triad, the sound of drilling bursts out.

To read this two-and-a-half-minute passage of the 'Appassionata' Sonata as a recording of Myra Hess's performance accompanying a montage of images would be to obtain only a fraction of its meaning. The interweaving of Beethoven's music with speech and sound creates a listening experience that is literally and ideologically polyvocal. This chapter aims to tease out its nuances. Examining how the BBC report, the sounds of rain and mining, the commentary, and Hess's performance of the 'Appassionata' overlap and become juxtaposed against one another, the chapter analyses the clashes of ideas crystallized in this auditory complex. Instead of regarding the other auditory elements as subordinate to Hess's Beethoven, it reads them all as contributors to a dialogue between multiple parties across national, class, and generational boundaries. In so doing, it argues that the components in the 'Appassionata' passage are mutually interrogative, producing a self-consciously ambiguous and multivalent narrative. If scholars are more familiar with the ways in which Jennings' works use images to document and explore the complexity of twentieth-century Britain (Jones & Searle, 2013), the chapter reveals how the 'Appassionata' passage achieves this through a variety of sounds.

This chapter therefore scrutinizes a passage of the film frequently cited but not yet extensively examined by critics. It argues that it is both more experimental and complicated than previously thought, countering Alessandra Marzola's interpretation of the scene as a moment of 'hypnotized listening'. Reading the images of the audience as a depiction of people's 'subjugation to the frozen version of history fed by patriotic discourses', Marzola misreads the mood of the passage as sheer 'melancholy' and fails to acknowledge the interplay of various sounds (2013, p. 134 and p. 135). By analysing how the overlap of sound, music, and speech generates meanings contingent on different wartime experiences, the chapter also gives another example of Jennings' experiment with the auditory suggestiveness of a documentary. While *Listen to Britain* is often noted for its portrayal of the nation by representing its discrete soundscapes (Corner, 2002, pp. 359 – 61), the 'Appassionata' passage in *A Diary for Timothy* provides a no less innovative exploration of the creative possibilities opened up by sound and music. In many ways, as the chapter aims to demonstrate, the auditory experimentation of the 'Appassionata' passage suggests an awareness of differences across various demarcations in British society. It thus differs from the sense of communal bonding, created by what Lara Feigel calls 'across-class montage', employed in *Listen to Britain* (2010, p. 105). Although it would be simplistic to conclude that the confrontation of different identities is better evoked by sounds than by sights, what the chapter intends to highlight is that Hess's playing of the 'Appassionata', rather than being simply affective and non-referential, makes an ideological intervention in contemporary debates about Britain's future.

Additionally, the chapter addresses issues relevant to historical musicology. In her recent review article, Kate Guthrie (2013) asks how it might be possible to write a musical history that investigates the contentious relations between music and ideology in the Second World War, without reiterating the myth of the democratization of art music during the war, or subscribing to the characterization of wartime musical activities as extraordinarily distinct from those in peacetime. This is not to say that the chapter is using the 'Appassionata' passage as a representative model to show how art music was being performed and consumed at the time. Instead, by acknowledging that the documentary has both propagandist and anti-propagandist dimensions, the chapter perceives the passage as a specific musical moment produced by the contributions of many. That is to say, the chapter assesses this part of the documentary as an epitome of contemporary collaboration between artists. These include not only Jennings and Hess, but also the actor Michael Redgrave, the writer E. M. Forster, the producer Basil Wright, the cutter Jenny Hutt (interestingly, not Jennings' long-term collaborator the editor Stewart McAllister), plus the documentary's composer Richard Addinsell and many others in the Crown Film Unit and in the Ministry of Information. In so doing, it explores how the end result does not simply delineate Jennings' vision, but represents all these individuals' negotiation with the politicization of music and aesthetics, thus offering a case study of a unique form of wartime engagement with music.

This was not the first time when a concert of Beethoven's music had been extensively featured in Jennings' films; nor was it the first time the director included Hess's performance in his work. As such, the 'Appassionata' passage echoes previous musical moments in Jennings' *The Heart of Britain* (1941) and *Listen to Britain* (1942), reflecting his perception of music as a form of art particularly expressive of human emotions during the war. In 1941, when working with McAllister on what later became *Listen to Britain*, Jennings' working notes reveal his belief that, as 'war involves everyone', the 'hearts' of British people

> need music. All kinds of music — classical music, popular music, the nostalgic music of a particular region and just plain martial music to march and work to. For music in Britain today is far from being just another escape: it probes into emotions of war itself — love of country, love of liberty, love of living, and the exhilaration of fighting for them. Listen (cited in Logan, 2011).

The passage projects a patriotic vision of the diversity of musical activities in wartime Britain, partially redressing the cliché that England is a 'land without music'. It extends people's love of music beyond leisure by underlining the proximity between music and public morale. Celebrating a sense of democracy in people's choices of music, the passage presents music as a spirited expression of humanity and suggests a perception of the nation in accordance with the official narrative as the stronghold of civilization. This illustrates Jennings' championing of music's communal value of being testament to wartime living experiences. For example, in his notes on the London Symphony Orchestra for an unmade film in 1948, a performance of *A London Symphony*, conducted by the composer Ralph Vaughan Williams, led Jennings to write that the music 'is of us, written for us, written about us'; it 'says' how 'we as Londoners had all been through' (1961 – 2, p. 18). While this is an observation on the specific musical work by Vaughan Williams and its significance for Londoners, Jennings' words also articulate an interest in capturing, during a rehearsal or a performance, 'moments' of 'the emotional and cathartic effect' of music on audiences and musicians (1961 – 2, p. 17). Such an emphasis on music's expressivity of individuals' shared experiences within a community is both in line with and more nuanced than the administrative view on music's role in documentary-making at the time. According to Muir Mathieson, then the Music Director of the Crown Film Unit, music provides 'entertainment' as well as 'help[s] to humanize the subject', 'mak[ing] the film less intellectual and more emotional' (1948, p. 323). Jennings' repeated thematizations of music in his documentaries thus express a more personal concern for and engagement with music.

The 'Appassionata' passage in *A Diary for Timothy* exemplifies Jennings' belief in music's expressivity, but the intervention of human speech also self-consciously tests it. A comparison with the Mozart concert in *Listen to Britain* reveals how *A Diary for Timothy* here is more experimental in exploring and problematizing the expressivity of music and sound. Similarities are many and obvious. The sequence of shots (of performers, audiences, and poster) through which the concert's specificity is established and the performance is unfolded is almost the same; although the mood evoked by Mozart's Piano Concerto K.453 is different from that of the 'Appassionata', how music subsequently turns to accompany images of the London city and how music is cut by harsh industrial sounds in the end are similar. Yet the BBC report about Arnhem, and the film's commentary written by Forster, give the 'Appassionata' passage more layers. That is, Hess's performance of the sonata, when listened to as a non-verbal narrative in relation to the verbal narratives provided by the two human voices, becomes interactive with them. The meanings of its music are modulated by and responsive to the overlaid words. In this respect, in the 'Appassionata' passage, it is not merely sound that comments on image; words participate in this interplay, complicating the scene's emotional appeal and ideological positioning.

It is worth emphasizing here that the 'Appassionata' passage is an edited segment. In 1945, the film of Hess's complete performance of the first movement of the sonata was released by Crown. Although moving to the front to capture Hess's expression occasionally, the camera stays mostly behind her from the audience's side, zooming in every now and then on her hands to showcase her virtuosity; there is no shot of the audience. The version of her performance in *A Diary for Timothy* features shots of Hess from different angles; images of the wider stage, the poster, and the audience give the music its time and location. Yet these details do not just mark a moment in the war: the BBC report helps to situate the concert within *the* specific context of the withdrawal in Arnhem, thus highlighting the chronology of the events. The way that the first few bars of the sonata emerge behind the report creates an impression that the music is extra-diegetic, serving as an accompaniment to the voice of the newsreader. As the newsreader informs Timothy, his family, and all other characters, about the British force's struggle in Arnhem, the half-veiled entrance of the sonata heightens the tension of the fighting. The sombre F minor suggests that this moment in October in 1944 was a frustrating setback for Britain from the almost foreseeable route to victory. The beginning of the movement, according to Barbara R. Barry, creates a 'discourse of conflict' that hinges on the Neapolitan pitch — the supertonic G-flat — as it is the 'most powerful agent for engendering tension and deflecting tonal direction' in the sonata's opening phrase (1992, p. 207). The following compression of the phrase, plus the four-note motif insistently repeated in the bass, creates an urgency. In many ways, then, the 'Appassionata' plays an emotive role when it first appears in the documentary. Accompanying and taking up the narrative of the BBC report, the music augments the tension described in the news, reflects the anxieties of those listening to it in the documentary, characterizes the war in late 1944 as conflict unresolved, and conveys to the viewers the tumult of ongoing fighting at the front.

However, if the music evokes struggle, it also encodes heroism. Critics have interrogated the alignment of Beethoven and his music with the concept of heroism and its political resonances, analysing how the 'Appassionata' and the other works from Beethoven's middle period have been repeatedly used as illustrative of the paragon of the heroic (Burnham, 1995; Dennis, 1996; Pederson, 2000; Head, 2006). The emotive power of the sonata when it first appears in the documentary after the BBC report is thus steeped in tragic heroism; the news about how soldiers, who were 'men of no ordinary calibre', resolutely and defiantly withstood enemy attack, strict rationing, and poor conditions in Arnhem becomes the music's programme. The part of the report about how rain saved these 'tough' soldiers reappears in the middle of Hess's performance, thus framing the music as a celebration of British endurance and resilience. Compared to the film's theme (composed by Richard Addinsell) a short ascending phrase of F-sharp – G – B – C-sharp – E played by a solo violin, whose dissonance and irresolution conjure up a haunting sense of uncertainty, the 'Appassionata' manifests a spirit of tenacity and virility. The relationship between the BBC report and the 'Appassionata' is therefore one where the latter accompanies, extends, and glorifies the former. From the announcement of the withdrawal in Arnhem, to the music that builds up conflict and releases energy, the sonata, though entering the scene secretly, amplifies the volume of the struggle but also characterizes it as heroic.

The fact that this 'virile' Beethoven is played by Myra Hess is significant. While Beethoven's work was a staple in Hess's repertoire, an anecdote told by the broadcaster John Amis is revealing: he recalled how Howard Ferguson once heard Hess's performance of the sonata and 'mutter[ed] in awe', 'What the devil has got into the old girl' (1990, p. 85). Even if said jokingly between friends, Ferguson's words suggest a perception of women playing Beethoven as transgressive. By presenting her confident mastering of the sonata on stage in the absence of men, the documentary portrays Hess as a potent symbol of resistance. Hess, in her black dress, calm and steadfast, not only becomes associated with the characteristics of the soldiers in Arnhem, but also stands as a figure of authority, around which the stability of the Home Front pivots. The minimalistic aesthetics of Hess alone at her piano in *A Diary for Timothy* signals an independence. This sends out a message distinct from her sharing the stage with an orchestra in *Listen to Britain*. As well as it simply being a different spatial arrangement because it is a piano recital, it is the mental fortitude of the individual that the 'Appassionata' passage implies, whereas the concert scene in *Listen to Britain* puts more focus on the community and its adjustments of peacetime conventions to the condition of war. It is also noteworthy how, compared to the shots of cracked windows, of sandbags and fire buckets, and of the Queen in *Listen to Britain*, here, in *A Diary for Timothy*, Hess singlehandedly embodies endurance, with a disciplined audience under her control, as if the fight — implicit too in the music — required a final effort from everyone. What is particularly conspicuous is how the camera follows the narrative of the music to construct a contrast between gendered characteristics: it is exactly at the unfolding of the warm lyricism of the second theme when the camera introduces to the viewers the attentive young woman. Though both are static, Hess is self-assuredly commanding in her 'public' role whereas the young woman is understandably docile in her 'private' listening to the music. If, as Susan McClary has argued, 'the conventional schemata of tonality and sonata' prescribes the 'triumph' of the 'masculine' and the 'resolution' or 'containment' of the 'feminine' Other (1993, p. 332), the shot of the young woman is destined to be brief before the camera returns to the theme of struggle and resistance, either embodied by Hess herself or presented through images of a shattered city being gradually rebuilt.

Jennings' portrayal of women has been called 'passive' (Thomson, 1993, p. 59), but what we have seen in Hess's performance is a woman prominently undertaking social responsibility. It is possible to suggest that the documentary reflects women's contribution to war and their rising social status; one might also note that the young woman in the audience is shown later in the film making a tracing of a housing plan, thus being represented as one who actively contributes to the reconstruction of Britain. More importantly, the war was as much between nations as between ideologies. The documentary is using Hess's performance to present Britain as a sanctuary of art, where she, a Jewish woman, and Elena Gerhardt (who relocated from Germany in the 1930s) could continue their lustrous musical careers. This propagandist characterization of the war as a battle between continuation and annihilation of 'culture' was common among liberal intellectuals at the time. In a radio broadcast to India in 1943, Forster said that 'in the heart of a war and close to destruction, great music is being upheld.' For him, 'great' music is German music: 'They ban German music, we don't' (2008, p. 218). Forster is building on, as well as moving away from, the widely circulating notion about Germany's musical supremacy and the perception of the German national character as musically intelligent and aesthetically sophisticated. Similarly, Hess's performance of the 'Appassionata' forcefully displaces Germany from its musical traditions and instead centralizes Britain as the place where 'great' music still burgeons in wartime Europe.

Beethoven becomes the point of contention: if his music could be perceived as a shared expression of heroic confrontation against predicaments, it was also recognized as explicitly German. Following this logic, the intrusion of the commentary is unsurprising, but, read alongside what precedes its appearance, it produces unease. The commentary first takes up where the BBC report ended: there is still more fighting as the war does not seem to approach its end as previously predicted, and many of 'our' houses have been damaged by 'enemy action'. This reference to the 'enemy' seems to galvanize the commentary to contemplate Anglo-German antagonism, prompting the interrogation: 'They do like the music that the lady was playing; some of us think it's the greatest music ever. Yet it is German music, and we are fighting against the Germans. There's something you'll have to think over later on.' Although this comment does not undermine the rationale and righteousness of the British war effort, it is anti-propagandist in a way as it disputes the perception of Germany (rather than the Third Reich) as an adversary. Up to this point, the 'Appassionata' passage seems to encourage heroism against hardship and looks forward to victory in the near future over the 'enemy'. The commentary problematizes aspects of this position by refusing to indulge in the glorification of endurance and exposing the difficulty in future reconciliation between the two countries. More importantly, it voices hesitation and gestures towards, if not explicit pacifism, at least a degree of dilemma, thus problematizing the call for violence when the BBC newsreader closes his report by saying 'All right, water and rations didn't matter. Give them some Germans to kill.' The commentary therefore questions heroism: although not pacifist, it highlights the German identity of the music to challenge the simplification of the war as a conflict between national cultures and to force a self-reflexive examination of nationalism and patriotism.

Intriguingly, what seems to have polarized critical opinions is less the message the commentary wants to convey and more the tone and accent of the commentator: from condemnation of the commentary as suggestive of 'smugness, insensitivity and unwitting class arrogance' (Jackson, 2004, p. 305) to derision of the role of the commentator as 'a mealy-mouthed schoolmaster' (Thomson, 1993, p. 59); from some mild bemusement about the commentary's 'kindly' 'condescension' (Hunter, 2010, p. 90) to an interpretation of its 'dominant tone' as 'ruminative, reflective and questioning' (Beattie, 2010, p. 110). While the functions of accent, dialect, and language in constructing identity and demarcating boundaries between communities in wartime films have recently attracted critical attention (Fox, 2006), what the various responses to Michael Redgrave's voicing of the commentary demonstrates is the irreducible mediation of subjectivity in a viewing and listening experience. In the end, it is one's own background — and the way in which one perceives the historical moment within which the film is placed — that determines how he or she will perceive Redgrave's voice. A question pertinent to our discussion of the 'Appassionata' passage, and one that critics have so far not asked, is whether we can really regard Redgrave as the commentator. Reading a script written by Forster and addressing Timothy the infant in an avuncular manner, there is a performative quality in Redgrave's voice. Philip C. Logan's description that Redgrave 'intones' and speaks 'with theatrical inflection' reveals how it is more than plausible to read Redgrave as impersonating Forster (2010, p. 267 and p. 266). In this case, he is not commentating, or simply narrating a script, but acting a part.

This allows us to have a better understanding of the documentary as a 'dialogue' between generations. Given that Redgrave, alongside Jennings and the producer Basil Wright, were in their late thirties at the end of the war, the commentary's message that the upcoming years would be the time when 'we' step back and 'you', Timothy and other babies, take charge, seems, if not irresponsible, at least unnecessarily resigned. If the collective 'we' refers to the generation of Forster, who was 66 at the time, it seems possible, then, to interpret the didacticism and condescension of the commentary as symptomatic of the rhetoric of the seniority. On the one hand, it is not explicitly interventionist because questions are raised for 'you' to ruminate on in the future, but not answered. On the other hand, for all its reticence, some of its messages are prescriptive as they articulate clear value judgments, such as the remark, 'some of us think it's the greatest music ever'. However, to read it autobiographically also risks reducing the commentary to Forster's personal advice. It is to neglect its echo with Forster's 1910 novel, *Howards End*, in the sentence, 'It will be generally admitted that Beethoven's Fifth Symphony is the most sublime noise that has ever penetrated into the ear of man' (1997, p. 25). I am not suggesting that the documentary's commentary achieves the same level of ambiguity as the novel's narrator does. Rather, as the narrator in *Howards End* is often read semi-satirically, we perhaps need to take cautiously the commentary's championing of Beethoven. That not all but only 'some' of 'us' worship Beethoven's work reveals, not just differences in taste, but, in the context of the documentary's overarching concern with issues of class, the privileged access to 'culture'.

In the frequently quoted letter from Forster to Wright, written after the former viewed the rough copy, Forster critiqued the implications of choosing a middle-class baby as the protagonist of the film: 'the film comes out with a social slant' (1985, p. 212). We do not know, as many have acknowledged, how Forster's letter might have prompted any revisions of the film, but there are traces in the final result that suggest an attempt to redress the 'slant'. That the commentary makes it clear in the beginning that Timothy is among the 'lucky ones' can be read as one of Forster's strategies of foregrounding the discrepancy between the 'haves' and the 'have nots'. The paralleled wartime experiences of the miner, the engine driver, the gentleman farmer, and the pilot also suggest that the documentary results from a wariness of the pitfall of making Timothy as the representative (Eley, 2001, pp. 835 – 6). The 'Appassionata' passage, though seemingly preoccupied purely with Anglo-German antagonism, makes class conflict conspicuous at the end by cutting the sonata to the harsh sounds of mining. This particular sequence deserves a close reading. First, a shot of a man and a horse walking past a rainy street is accompanied by amplified sounds of rain, the commentary's words 'Rain, too much rain', and the music. The commentary changes into a matter-of-fact tone, 'look at the place where Goronwy has to cut coal', when the camera moves underground. As the drilling silences the music, the camera cuts to a shot of Tim in his cot, who is told by the commentary that he is kept warm indoors by the fire. There is a challenge here, in both words and images, suggesting that though the rain seems everywhere, baby Tim does not, and cannot, become as wet as Goronwy, or indeed as the man on street. The issue is not so much failed sympathy or empathy as difference in physical environments, which encodes different social strata, and which entails different experiences. What underlies the demarcation of classes, the commentary and the images seem to suggest, is the material limitations of one's circumstances.

It is evident, then, that this limit is also auditorily dramatized by the editing of sounds, voices, and music. Rain serves as an important motif here. As if the words of the commentary were not sufficiently evocative, the heightened sound effect augments the sense that the rain percolates down into every pore of the earth. However, not only do images and words inform us that it is not a shared experience, both the voices of the BBC report and of the commentary also exemplify how, even if experienced, the natural phenomenon produces different significations. For the soldiers in Arnhem, as the BBC report informs us without sounding unnecessarily rousing, the rain perhaps signifies luck. The commentary at first laments the bad weather that has disappointed our wish for a quick end to the war, and later becomes elegiac before ushering in the shots of the mines. What seems common and natural — after all, it is simply rain — becomes conditioned by local specificities and endowed with individual feelings. That the 'Appassionata' is cut short by the drilling and remains unresolved can thus be read as an awareness of the exclusivity of Beethoven's music during the war. For all its professed openness to war-stricken Londoners, many did not have the opportunities to attend the National Gallery concerts in person, let alone show appreciation of Beethoven's sonata as 'some of us' do. This leads us to recognize that the documentary's politicization of the 'Appassionata' is the result of the contemplation of a cultured minority. The frisson of shock created by the contrast between the piano music and the mining sound suggests an alertness to 'the outside': beyond the makeshift but nevertheless sheltered space of the National Gallery, there are many who hear other sorts of sounds during the war.

The 'Appassionata' passage thus produces a moment where the lesson offered by the sagacious 'us' to the innocent 'you' is haunted by an awareness of the existence of others. This is not to gloss over the commentary's didacticism, or to pretend that Redgrave's tone is not condescending to some. What needs to be emphasized here is that each of the auditory elements in the passage appears to undercut one another, refusing to sustain a grand narrative. The BBC report's urge to use violence is restrained by the commentary's challenge to nationalism; the music's glorification of heroic endurance turns into a state of elegiac resignation after the incessant rain; the heightened sense of virility becomes in discordance with the general uncertainty evoked by Addinsell's scores; and the way the drilling overwhelms the sonata offers an allegory of social differentiation. The interweaving of speech, music, and sound in the 'Appassionata' passage places conflicting viewpoints alongside, and against, each other. The result is a constellation of ideas, irreconciled and problematic, resisting homogenization and demanding investigation. In this respect, what 'we' offer is simply one of the voices within the polyvocality of the passage. The commentary may be most audible in one's viewing experience, but, as our discussion of the 'Appassionata' passage has shown, words do not always yoke images; nor do they silence the repercussions and resonances created by the other sounds.

This understanding of the 'Appassionata' passage provides us with a new perspective on the message conveyed by the documentary as a whole. There is an eagerness to impart to the young the values 'we' believe, but at the same time there is an alertness, not only to the limit of 'our' own outlook but also to circulating ideas and opinions. As such, the documentary seems to hover between two attitudes, exemplified, incidentally or not, by two of the collaborators on the 'Appassionata' passage. On the one hand, its attempt to illustrate ways to contemplate and tackle postwar problems can be traced back to an educational ideal similar to what underpins Hess's organization of the National Gallery concerts. According to Sir Kenneth Clarke, the Concerts were meant '[t]o maintain [a] sense of quality . . . that there are standards which must survive all disasters' (1944, p. 6). If not unreflectively self-entitled, the concerts, as well as the documentary, at least reveal a belief that there are values deemed by an elite minority as worthy to be disseminated to a wider public or preserved for the future generations. The 'Appassionata' passage can thus be regarded as consecrating the cultural status of Beethoven's music: despite, or because of, the existence of all the other sounds and voices, Hess's playing of the sonata is still given a stage, recorded, viewed, and remembered. On the other hand, that the documentary notices difficulties and unveils contradictions, registering how one vision can be at odds with another and how one's experience can be far detached from someone else's, delivers something akin to Forster's notion of 'tolerance'. Regarded as a 'quality which will be most needed after the war', Forster in 1941 proposed 'tolerance' as 'a makeshift, suitable for an overcrowded and overheated planet'; as a replacement of 'love', which 'is a great force in private life' but 'in public affair does not work', 'tolerance', though 'dull', is 'wanted above all between classes, races and nations' because 'it is very easy to see fanaticism in other people, but difficult to spot in oneself' (1972, pp. 44 – 46). Through its presentation of parallel experiences, juxtaposition of scenes at home and at the front, and allusions to lives beyond the lens, the documentary is a self-conscious examination of identity politics, testing the boundary between self and others, and thus proposing an attitude that accommodates differences. The 'Appassionata' passage sends out a similar message through the interweaving of sound, music, and speech. It does not just re-create the historical presence of sounds once heard; it also suggests an ideological openness attuned to the coexistence and intersection of diverse forms of human relationship.

Bibliography

Amis, J. (1990). Dame Myra Hess remembered. *The Musical Times, 131*(1764), 85.

Anderson, L. (1961 – 2). Only connect: some aspects of the work of Humphrey Jennings. *Film Quarterly, 15*(2), 5 – 12.

Barry, B. R. (1992). Pitch interpretation and cyclical procedures in middle-period Beethoven. *The Musical Quarterly, 76*(2), 184 – 215.

Beattie, K. (2010). *Humphrey Jennings*. Manchester: Manchester University Press.

Beethoven, L. (1806) *Piano Sonata No. 23 in F minor, Op.57 'Appassionata'* London: Edition Peters

Burnham, S. (1995). *Beethoven hero*. Princeton: Princeton University Press.

Clarke, K. (1944). From the National Gallery. In *National Gallery Concerts: In aid of the Musicians' Benevolent Fund 10th October 1939 — 10th October 1944* (pp. 5 – 6). London: Printed for the Trustees.

Corner, J. (2002). Music and documentary. *Popular Music: Music and Television, 21*(3), 357 – 66.

Dennis, D. B. (1996). *Beethoven in German politics, 1870-1989*. New Haven: Yale University Press.

Eley, G. (2001). Finding the people's war: film, British collective memory, and World War II. *The American Historical Review, 106*(3), 818 – 38.

Feigel, L. (2010). *Literature, cinema, politics 1930-45. Reading between the frames*. Edinburgh: Edinburgh University Press.

Forster, E. M., M. Lago, L. K. Hughes, & E. M. Walls (Eds.) (2008). *The BBC talks of E. M. Forster 1929 – 1960*. Columbia: University of Missouri Press.

Forster, E. M., P. B. Armstrong (Ed.). (1997). *Howards End*. New York: Norton.

Forster, E. M, M. Lago & P. N. Furbank (Eds.). (1983 – 5). *Selected letters of E. M. Forster*. London: Collins.

Forster, E. M., Oliver Stallybrass (Ed.). (1972). *Two cheers for democracy*. London: Edward Arnold.

Fox, J. (2006). Millions like us? Accented language and the 'ordinary' in British films of the Second World War. *Journal of British Studies, 45*(4), 819 – 45.

Guthrie, K. (2013). Soundtracks to the 'People's War'. *Music and Letters, 94*(2), 324 – 33.

Head, M. (2006). Beethoven heroine: a female allegory of music and authorship. In *Egmont. 19th-Century Music, 30*(2), 97 – 132.

Hodgkinson, A. W., & Sheratsky, R. E. (1982). *Humphrey Jennings: more than a maker of films.* Lebanon, New Hampshire: University Press of New England.

Hunter, J. (2010). *English filming, English writing.* Bloomington: Indiana University Press.

Jackson, K. (2004). *Humphrey Jennings.* London: Picador.

Jennings, H. (Director). (1941). *The heart of Britain* [Motion Picture]: United Kingdom: Crown Film Unit.

Jennings, H. (Director). (1942). *Listen to Britain* [Motion Picture]: United Kingdom: Crown Film Unit.

Jennings, H. (Director). (1945). *Myra Hess* [Motion Picture]: United Kingdom: Crown Film Unit.

Jennings, H. (Director). (1946). *A diary for Timothy* [Motion Picture]: United Kingdom: Crown Film Unit.

Jennings, H. (1961 – 2). Working sketches of an orchestra. *Film Quarterly, 15*(2), 12 – 18.

Jones, B., & Searle, R. (2013). Humphrey Jennings, the Left and the Experience of Modernity in mid twentieth-century Britain. *History Workshop Journal, 75,* 190 – 212.

Logan, P. C. (2011). *Humphrey Jennings and British documentary film: a reassessment.* Abingdon: Routledge.

McClary, S. (1993). Narrative agendas in 'Absolute' music: identity and difference in Brahms's Third Symphony. In R. A. Solie (Ed.), *Musicology and difference: gender and sexuality in music scholarship* (pp. 326 – 44). Berkeley: University of California Press.

Marzola, A. (2013). Negotiating the memory of the 'People's War': *Hamlet* and the ghosts of welfare in *A Diary for Timothy* by Humphrey Jennings (1944 – 45). In C. Dente & S. Soncini (Eds.), *Shakespeare and conflict: a European perspective* (pp. 132 – 44). Houndmills: Palgrave Macmillan.

Mathieson, M. (1948). Music for Crown. *Hollywood Quarterly, 3*(3), 323 – 6.

Pederson, S. (2000). Beethoven and masculinity. In S. Burnham & M. P. Steinberg (Eds.), *Beethoven and his world* (pp. 313 – 31). Princeton: Princeton University Press.

Plain, G. (2013). *Literature of the 1940s: war, postwar and 'Peace'.* Edinburgh: Edinburgh University Press.

Thomson, D. (1993). A sight for sore eyes. *Film Comment, 29*(2), 54 – 59.

A 'Symphony of Britain at War' or the 'Rhythm of Workaday Britain'? Len Lye's *When the Pie Was Opened* (1941) and the musicalisation of warfare.

Anita Jorge

Introduction

> 'Do you think that modern war has no music? That mechanisation has banished harmony, and that because her life is for the moment so grim Britain no longer thinks of singing? What an error' (Jennings, 1942, p. 1).

These words, taken from Humphrey Jennings's treatment of his 'sonic documentary' *Listen to Britain*, made in 1942 and sponsored by the British Ministry of Information, are emblematic of the wartime official discourse that postulated the intrinsic musicality of the sounds of warfare.

Official discourses on sound were not new: they had started to develop in the inter-war period in reaction to the emergence of new kinds of noise that came to be associated with the advent of 'modern civilisation'. As extensively shown by James Mansell (2016), during the war, the debate broadened out to become a matter of national well-being, and above all, social cohesion. Positing that a discrete collection of sounds possessed an intrinsic musicality was part and parcel of the official propaganda discourse aimed at rationalizing the unknown and controlling the fears of civilians. It implied that something as chaotic and unfathomable as the sounds of warfare was actually driven by a sense of purpose and harmony, and that Britons were 'pulling together' in the war effort to the sound of a 'national symphony' across social and geographical divides. It was also a way of reassuring the people by maintaining the illusion that there existed an organised and systematic retaliation to enemy attacks. As a result, such phrases as the 'symphony of war', the 'melody' of the guns, the 'tones' of the cannons, or the 'score' played by bombers were commonplace in government-sponsored documentaries. The most famous example of this idea is Humphrey Jennings's *Listen to Britain,* produced in 1942 by the Crown Film Unit under the aegis of the Ministry of Information. It is built around a collage of ordinary sounds made by the people of Great Britain at the height of the Blitz, which, 'blended together in one great symphony'[1], emerge above the sounds of the enemy. The film was even built with an ear to the symphonic form — a device that was imitated by several of his contemporaries.

A substantial number of documentary films sponsored by the government during the war concurred in suggesting that, diverse though the sounds of the nation at war were, they formed a coherent whole, an organised work of art, which was the manifestation of the people's unity.

A 'Symphony of Britain at War'

Certain documentaries, however, were also a field for formal sonic experimentation, and, due to the intrinsic polysemy of sound, appeared as a conduit for criticism against political power. This was especially true in the case of expatriate artists — a majority of whom were German or Hungarian refugees — whose ideas about the musical properties of sound were highly influenced by the Soviet school. This paper will focus on one such documentary, *When the Pie Was Opened*, made in 1941 by New Zealand-born filmmaker Len Lye, under the sponsorship of the Ministry of Information.

When the Pie Was Opened: a 'symphony of Britain at war'?[2]

After moving from New Zealand to London in 1926, where he had become a member of the London Film Society and an artist associated with the Seven and Five Group, Leonard Charles Huia Lye, also known as Len Lye, began making commercial spots for the GPO Film Unit. This gave him the financial and technical means to perfect his technique of the hand-painted film.[3] When the war broke out, Len Lye went on to produce several documentaries for the Crown Film Unit, as the GPO was renamed after it was transferred to the Films Division of the Ministry of Information. *When the Pie Was Opened* was the third of seven films that Lye made for the Ministry of Information,[4] and the first that he directed in collaboration with sound recordist Ernst Meyer, a German refugee whose leftist political allegiances (he belonged to the German Communist Party) led to his activities being monitored by MI5 throughout the war.

The subject matter of *When the Pie Was Opened* is rather simple: the film deals with wartime rationing, and how to make a vegetable pie in the absence of meat. It is set in a country house and features what appears to be a middle-class family, composed of a little girl, bored and longing for 'blackbird pie' (from the famous nursery rhyme 'Sing a Song of Sixpence', on which most of the film's imagery and script are based[5]), her mother (set on making a vegetable pie, whose recipe she reads from a newspaper clipping) and her father. It was commissioned by the Ministry of Food and produced by the Realist Film Unit, an offshoot of the Crown Film Unit, which mainly produced instructional films, and for which Len Lye had gained several jobs during the war. All the actors are non-professional, as was the case in many GPO documentaries made during the war. The film corresponds to Grierson's definition of documentary as the 'creative treatment of actuality' (1933, pp. 7 – 9) — actuality being in this case the shortage of food during wartime, and the creative aspect of its treatment being the scripted and 'story' aspect of it.

But despite the austerity of its subject matter, the film is extravagantly surreal and experimental, mainly due to its audacious sound effects. The whole documentary works according to the principle of asynchronicity and aural counterpoint — as theorized by Russian filmmakers Eisenstein, Pudovkin, and Alexandrov in their 1928 joint manifesto (Eisenstein, Pudovkin, & Alexandrov, 1928). The sequence that is most emblematic of this aesthetic is the pie-baking sequence. Indeed, it is built around a collage of sound effects, including the clank of factory machinery as well as the cackling of farmyard birds as the mother chops the vegetables, the lapping of waves and the cry of seagulls as the water boils, the sounds of sawing wood and hammering as the pie crust is indented, that of a train puffing as the mother brings the pie to the table, and the sound of marching orders and stomping feet as she collects the vegetables. Moreover, the sequence is characterized by the recurring voice of a woman reading the recipe aloud and giving the mother cooking instructions — or rather orders — to the accompaniment of a series of military drum rolls, and whose mouth surrealistically emerges from the newspaper clipping on which the recipe is written[6] (Figures 1 & 2). This contrapuntal sound collage epitomises the aesthetics of the origins of the word symphony,[7] that sounding together of all people across social classes, all contributing in their own way to the war effort. That the baking and serving of a pie by a civilian at home should be accompanied by marching orders, soldiers parading, drum rolls and bugle calls (especially the famous 'mess call', traditionally signalling mealtime to soldiers, played on the bugle when the pie is cooked and the table is laid[8]), could be seen as a direct illustration of the 'pulling together' principle. Keeping in line with propaganda principles, the feminine voice giving 'marching orders' to the mother in the kitchen could be that of Britannia herself, guiding her people throughout the ordeals of wartime.

The distant rumble of war

Surprisingly enough, the war itself is never directly mentioned or heard in the film — it is only hinted at through visual or aural symbols, including trivial sounds that seem strangely ominous. This is not an altogether unusual device in wartime films — several of Humphrey Jennings's films made for the Ministry of Information, such as *Listen to Britain* (1942) and *The Silent Village* (1943), do not overtly show civilians under direct enemy assault. Moreover, the enemy is neither seen nor heard in the former, and merely heard in the latter. But war is nevertheless omnipresent: we see RAF airplanes streaking the sky; armoured cars careering down the streets; and soldiers on leave at the ballroom, in the case of *Listen to Britain*.

A 'Symphony of Britain at War'   223

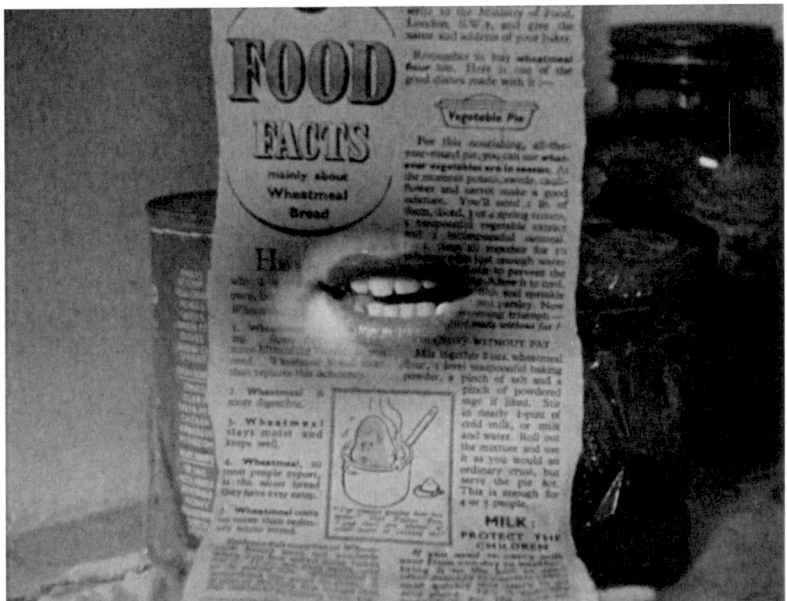

Figure 1: 'Take the season's vegetables . . . ' *When the Pie Was Opened* (Lye, 1941), 04:09 © British Film Institute

Figure 2: 'About one pound in all . . . ' *When the Pie Was Opened* (Lye, 1941), 04:32 © British Film Institute

But war does not directly feature in *When the Pie Was Opened*. The film opens with a trumpet melody on the radio (which is later revealed to be the opening to the song 'Solitude' composed by Duke Ellington and sung by Louis Armstrong), played against the background of a sky seen through a dotted curtain, as though ridden with bombs, which recalls the wail of an air raid siren — typically heard in contemporary instructional shorts. In a later sequence, the little girl's father, sitting at a table with a crown on his head, drops a plate containing a slice of pie. The plate crashes down to the ground and breaks into pieces with a sound that would no doubt have been associated by audiences with that of a bomb. As well as being shown at traditional theatre screenings, instructional films were channeled through non-theatrical distribution, organised by the GPO's mobile units, in factory canteens, social clubs, and village halls, and financed by the Ministry of Information. By 1941, people across the country were well aware of what an air raid typically sounded like, even if they were not direct eye (or ear) witnesses of the conflict. They would no doubt have been conscious of the similarities between the sound effects used in the film and their real-life counterparts. As explained by Roger Horrocks (2017), Len Lye's own family did not live in the city. In 1941, his wife and two children had been transferred to a cottage near Leigh, in Kent, so that they would be safer from German bombs than in their London home. Kent adjoined the Strait of Dover, the narrowest part of the English Channel and the most likely landing site for a German invasion. The sky was regularly streaked with German bombers and Spitfires passing over the farm on their way to London, their rumbling formed part of the regular soundscape of the area. Although Kent was not directly touched by the war at the time, the fear of German invasion was pervasive hence its indirect evocation in the film. Conversely, the natural sounds of daily life in rural Britain — the cackling of farmyard birds, the sound of a running stream, birdsong, and the cry of seagulls, the lapping of waves — are to be heard throughout the film as the aural foil to those ominous aural cues. They stand out and resound as the symbols of the nation's beauty and peacefulness, to be preserved at all costs. The survival of the natural sounds of the nation, in spite of the enemy's aural invasion, is a staple of wartime documentaries of which *Listen to Britain* is probably the most famous example.

These two types of sounds — alien and domestic — are not merely pitted against each other. Just as in a certain number of documentaries made during the war, there seems to be a conflation of domestic sounds and the sounds of warfare connoting the progressive assimilation of the war effort. The idea that everybody could contribute to winning the war — not just the soldiers on the front, but also simple civilians — is

A 'Symphony of Britain at War'

illustrated by the sound collage in the pie-making sequence early on in the film.

The rationale behind this pervasive evocation of the war and the unifying sound collage is to be found in Len Lye's own political beliefs and theoretical writings. In the early months of 1941, Len Lye and his friend the poet and novelist Robert Graves, started to work on a pamphlet entitled 'Individual Happiness Now' or 'A Definition of Common Purpose'. Their aim was to produce a statement of values that could function as an alternative to Nazi propaganda. In the statement, Lye maintained that, since the beginning of the war, the shortage of amenities allowed people to concentrate more on the simple pleasures of life:

> It may seem cynical to speak of 'Individual Happiness Now' in so cruel a year as this. Yet despite destructive air bombardment, separation of families, sinking ships, shortage of food, loss of amenities, it would be untrue to say that there has been less individual happiness since the Germans reached the Channel ports. It might even be maintained that there is more: because the emergencies and trials of the time have brought out individuality which was previously smothered in dead-alive routine, and people have a new sense of what really matters, of what remains when all else is lost. . . . They know, now, perhaps for the first time, how good a thing cheese is, or an onion, or a peaceful night's sleep on a spring-mattress. This is not an argument in favour of war, but only in favour of individuality as a by-product of one stage of this particular war (Lye, 1935, p. 6).

This statement could be taken as a variation on the 'business as usual' tenet of wartime propaganda. Yet the fact that sounds denoting the peace and quiet of country life should be chosen as the soundtrack for the war is not quite an illustration of the so-called British phlegm or resilience. Lye calls for British citizens not to pretend that war is just another nuisance, or to close ranks with all of their compatriots, but to acknowledge that the pleasures they derive from their own daily life are worth fighting for — something that would speak to the people more than the vague concept of 'defending the nation'.

When the Pie Was Opened, therefore, displays a certain number of thematic and formal similarities with classic informative documentary films of the Second World War. Its 'how to' format and practical purpose, its subdued evocation of war and seemingly unifying soundtrack, qualify it as a piece of propaganda. However, it stands out from similar documentaries insofar as the intention behind its creative and somehow musical treatment of sound is more subversive than it at first appears.

'The rhythm of workaday Britain'[10]

Classifying the film as a mere proponent of the propaganda idea of 'business as usual', or of the 'pulling together' of citizens from all social classes would be missing the point. Beneath the veneer of propaganda, sound experimentation in the film acts primarily as a vehicle for social criticism and the expression of deep wartime social conflicts. It suggests that the middle and upper classes were only sustained in times of war thanks to the working class whose labour is celebrated through an innovative and experimental sound composition.

Len Lye came from a working-class background. He sympathized with Socialist and Communist activists in London, but he was also very suspicious of politicians. Rather than identifying with the British political class, he would rather try to share in the plight of the ordinary people of Great Britain.[11]

Quite significantly, the fact that the orders are given by a disembodied female voice, whose accent is determinedly upper-class, and executed to the recognizable sounds of the working class (farmers, factory workers or shipyard builders) reads as a criticism of the rich and powerful, sheltered from the vicissitudes of war and never really having to cope with shortages or bomb damage.

The first part of the film is characterized by the repetition of the nursery rhymes 'Sing a Song of Sixpence', 'Old Mother Hubbard', and 'Nuts in May', all having to do with food, or the lack thereof, and sung by children's voices. Progressively and throughout the second part of the film, the nursery rhymes (the traditional musical expressions of the people's voice, the 'spiritual lifeblood of the people' as Ralph Vaughan Williams would call them [Vaughan Williams, 1987, p. 23]) are replaced by a new kind of musical leitmotif, namely the voice of the upper-class woman, and the accompanying drum rolls. At the very end of the film when the pie is served and eaten, 'Sing a song of sixpence' is heard again on the soundtrack, but this time the lyrics have changed. 'Four and twenty blackbirds baked in a pie' becomes 'all the season's vegetables baked in a pie'. This could be seen as an illustration of the resilience of the people who, despite the changes and trials brought about by the war, are able to fall back on their feet. But this progressive annihilation of the people's means of expression could also be interpreted as the voice of the governing class, or that of the government and its propaganda discourse glossing over the reality of war.

An earlier sequence in the film has a clearly subversive subtext which, once again, reveals itself through the soundtrack. The sequence is the little girl's fantasy on one of the verses of 'Sing a Song of Sixpence' that reads 'When the pie was opened the

A 'Symphony of Britain at War'

birds began to sing, wasn't that a dainty dish to set before a king'. In the sequence, she is sitting at a table with her father wearing a crown — therefore embodying the king, and the ruling class as a whole. Her father cuts the pie, serves it on a plate, and gestures to hand it to his daughter — who could, by extension, be the personification of the British people (Figures 3 & 4). The slice of pie is topped with a sham blackbird — blackbirds being traditionally seen as bad omens, here the threat of German invasion. When the father-cum-king hands the pie to his daughter-subject, he drops the plate, which crashes to the ground in a cacophony of sound that echoes an aerial attack. Once again, the technique of sound counterpoint is used here: the slow-motion of the plate being dropped is accompanied by the sound of sawing wood (which could be identified as that of the timber industry, the backbone of shipbuilding, which was a staple of warfare). A straightforward interpretation of the sequence would be the king's — and by extension, the government's — inability to feed or help his or its people, who now have to devote their lives to helping the nation win the war.

Len Lye's sound recordist for this film (and for all of his wartime documentaries), Ernst Meyer, came to be particularly known for his use of 'orchestrated sound'. As a Jew and a communist, Meyer had fled Germany for Great Britain in 1933, officially to attend a musicological conference. In Berlin, he had been a student of Hindemith at the Hochschule für Musik, where the lessons included principles of soundtrack instrumentation and composing in counterpoint to the images. One of the instructional shorts he later worked on, *Mobilise your Scrap* (1942), a trailer-length documentary made for Films of Great Britain and sponsored by the Ministry of Information and the Ministry of Supply, was meant to encourage householders to save metal for the war effort. It was made with a soundtrack of factory sounds edited to fit the speech rhythm of the film's slogan, 'Mobilise Your Scrap'. The same rhythm is used over the images of civilians collecting scrap metal and salvage, through to factory workers transforming it into ammunition, and warships firing it at the enemy, once more showing the continuity of the war effort, a sonic device that was prefigured in *When the Pie Was Opened*. Both *Mobilise your Scrap* and *When the Pie Was Opened* seem to have found their inspiration in Walter Ruttmann's *Wochenende* (1930), a purely sonic film without images, or *hörspiel* (radio drama), portraying the rhythm of a Berlin weekend urban landscape. Certain specific sounds used in both films by Lye and Meyer, such as sawing wood, birdsong, the clank of factory machinery, and indistinct shouts, directly call to mind the sounds repeatedly used by Ruttmann in his sonic portrayal of Berlin urban life in the 1930s. *When the Pie Was Opened* plays with the reference to *Wochenende* by

Figure 3: 'Wasn't that a dainty dish . . .' *When the Pie Was Opened* (Lye, 1941), 02:21 © British Film Institute

Figure 4: *When the Pie Was Opened* (Lye, 1941), 02:29 © British Film Institute

making obvious use of sonic material displaying similarities with Ruttmann's *hörspiel*, and by constantly blurring the lines between diegetic and non-diegetic sounds. The film opens with Duke Ellington's song 'Solitude', whose belonging to the diegesis is revealed a few minutes into the film, as the music is shown to emanate from a wireless set. The sounds heard during the pie-making sequence, which we take to be non-diegetic, could therefore be conceived of as radio sounds — a subtle tribute to the innovative sound creations conceived by Meyer's fellow German sound artist. Interestingly, even though nothing proves that Lye and Meyer were aware of it, the first and last parts of Ruttmann's piece — which, of all six parts, are those they seem to have been most inspired by — were entitled 'Jazz der Arbeit' ('Jazz of Work'). The choice of a jazz piece for the film's soundtrack, combined with the sounds of the working-class, comes across as a variation — albeit an unwitting one perhaps — on the idea formulated by Ruttmann.

Both Meyer and Lye were themselves very much attached to the new possibilities offered by sound montage. Together with some of their fellow technicians at Realist, they attempted to patent a new method involving the printing of two sound strips side by side on the soundtrack, one for dialogue, and one for effects, in order to attain greater clarity. Although, because of the lack of investment from the government, the technique was only ever used for their film *Newspaper Train* (1942), this shows how committed to sound experimentation Len Lye was, despite his being more often praised and remembered for his innovative treatment of the image.

After settling in Great Britain, Ernst Meyer had resumed his political activities, joining the Workers' Music Association, and the Freie Deutsche Kulturbund (Free German League of Culture), the political and cultural association of German émigrés in London, which caused him to be under MI5's surveillance. That sound should serve as a conduit for criticism of class relationships in a film about food rationing is therefore far from fortuitous.

Although Len Lye directed seven films for the Ministry of Information, he was also very critical of the values conveyed by British wartime propaganda which, according to him, 'continued to rely upon clichés of nationalism or religion' (Horrocks, 2017, p. 4). The alleged unity of the people and resilience of civilians in the face of adversity — what historian Angus Calder later called the 'myth of the Blitz' (Calder, 1992) — were most likely creeds that Lye did not wholeheartedly embrace. Even though his approach to politics was much less up front than that of his collaborator Ernst Meyer, one could assume that the subtle questioning of propaganda values, and leftist approach to class relations, was something that Lye had deliberately thought out.

Lye, Ellitt and 'sound construction'

Len Lye was politically-minded. He was resolutely anti-Fascist, was sympathetic to Communists (he often took part in the May Day marches) and, as his theory about 'individual happiness' reveals, was well-versed in political reasoning. However, his interest in sound experimentation stemmed from an artistic impulse, more than a political one. As Horrocks (2017, p. 1) states in his introduction to the 'Declaration of Common Purpose', '[Len Lye's] flair was for visual statement . . . not as a hard thinker in social values.'

If we look back to Lye's pre-war productions, whose sound recordist and editor was not Ernst Meyer but his friend and electro-acoustic composer[12] Jack Ellitt, it appears that his experiments in sound were also not far from the later theories behind Pierre Schaeffer's *musique concrète*. As a sound editor, Jack Ellitt had explored the possibilities of 'drawn sound' (just as Lye had perfected the technique of 'drawn film'). As Horrocks explains in his essay on Jack Ellitt,

> He learned to draw his own 'direct' sound-tracks via the variable area system.[13] He modified a hand-cranked Moy camera so it photographed only the soundtrack area, then set it up as a rostrum camera so it could film his hand-drawn soundtracks one frame at a time (1999, p. 25).

In the early 1930s, Ellitt had also devised a concept called 'Sound Construction', a new kind of composition he had described in a 1935 essay. At the core of his essay was the idea of abstract, non-representational sound, a concept that was also at the heart of Pierre Schaeffer's theory of *musique concrète*:

> The word 'abstract' is here used in its common sense of 'nonrepresentational'. . . . An approach towards non-representational music has been made occasionally by certain modern and classical composers . . . [But] the means at their disposal were only meant to be used for the orthodox expression of a musical thought . . . It is therefore apparent that those who are experimentally inclined towards sound should now leave the old musical means of expression (Ellitt, 1935, p. 182).

Although their collaboration had ended before the shooting of *When the Pie Was Opened*, the film bears the traces of Ellitt's theories.

A 'Symphony of Britain at War'

In an experimental short film that they made in 1937 for the GPO Film Unit, entitled *Trade Tattoo*, Len Lye and Jack Ellitt conceived of the British working class as having an overall rhythmic pattern like a tattoo (a military performance of music). The film was based on leftover footage from GPO documentaries showing images of workers in different types of industries — metallurgy, mail-sorting, cargo loading, steel milling, agriculture, railroads — to which Len Lye added animated words and coloured patterns thanks to the colour-separation method ('the rhythm of work-a-day Britain', 'the furnaces are fired', 'cargoes are loaded', 'markets are found', 'the rhythm of trade is maintained by the mails'). The soundtrack was made of excerpts from five songs by the Cuban orchestra Lecuona Cuban Boys, giving rhythm and unity to the different industry bodies. Bestowing 'work-a-day Britain' an inherent rhythm is also the intention behind *When the Pie Was Opened*. In the film, Lye and Meyer sought to highlight the existence of a working-class consciousness and solidarity across the different industries, by endowing them with an independent and idiosyncratic rhythmic pattern, free from all pre-existing canons. This is precisely what Jack Ellitt explains in his essay on 'Sound Construction': 'In speaking of form in sound we mean a construction of selected sound colours used irrespectively of any of those laws and dogmas of harmonic and melodic progression. . . . The ear *can* accept or reject a progression of various sounds without reference to preconceived laws' (Ellitt, 1935, p. 182).

It therefore seems that it was not so much a 'musicalisation of sound' that Ellitt, Lye and Meyer sought to achieve, but rather a more pragmatic approach to music, severed from classical formal canons, such as those of the symphony, whose form a great many wartime films precisely sought to imitate.

Ellitt goes on to state that 'Music is essentially the expression of an inner song. . . . Once the personal sense of song is submerged or replaced by a desire for something more abstract and non-associative, it is then time to think and hear in terms of sound' (Ellitt, 1935, p. 184).

This 'abstract and non-associative' quality of sound is characteristic of the treatment of sound in *When the Pie Was Opened*. Although the various sonic leitmotifs that recur in the pie-making sequence bring to mind certain activities or situations (the cackle of poultry, the drum rolls, the clank of machinery), they are not to be taken as such, but as more comprehensive symbols or concepts. Furthermore, some of the voices and shouts heard on the soundtrack are purposely blurred and indistinct (neither the words nor the context in which they are uttered are discernible), so much so that the message carried matters less than the sound itself.

This idea finds an echo in a comment made by John Grierson in a 1934 article entitled *Introduction to a New Art*, which reads: 'another curious fact emerges once you start detaching sounds from their origins, and it is this. Your aeroplane noise may not become the image of an aeroplane but the image of distance or of height. Your steamer whistle may not become the image of a steamer but of isolation and darkness' (Grierson, 1934, p. 103). This idea was then expanded upon by Paul Rotha, in his 1939 work entitled *Documentary Film*.[14]

What these sounds represent therefore is the idea that the working class has a rhythm of its own, which the governing class, in times of war, strived to annihilate and transmute into a mere 'instrument' of the national war effort, in other words, 'the symphony of Britain at war', with no consideration for those who really strived to feed the nation.

Conclusion

Although *When the Pie Was Opened* was sponsored by the Ministry of Information and it displayed a certain number of typical characteristics of wartime propaganda short films (most particularly the 'pulling together' ethics that were dear to the government), one could call into question its value and efficiency as a piece of propaganda. As Brett Kashmere argues, 'Though Lye's information films were the product of their wartime context, these documentaries contain distinct auteur traces, experimental techniques, and technological innovations that run counter to their training and propaganda objectives' (Kashmere, 2007). That no direct mention should be made of the Blitz or the musical qualities of warfare distinguishes it from most of Jennings's films, for instance. Even though Jennings was a socialist with humanist ideals, who truly believed in the cohesive power of sound, he was sometimes — unfairly — criticized by his contemporaries for being a middle-class artist who only experienced the conditions of the working-class from a safe distance. For instance, his fellow GPO filmmaker Basil Wright (who directed *Song of Ceylon* in 1934), in an interview given in 1974, confessed to having at first dismissed Jennings's film *Spare Time* (1939) on account of its 'patronizing, sometimes almost sneering attitude towards the efforts of the lower-income groups to entertain themselves'[15] (quoted in Sussex, p. 110).

Undeserved though such scathing criticism may be, at any rate, the point of *Listen to Britain* is not to pay tribute to the working class only, but to all British people allegedly sharing a common experience of war.[16]

In contrast, what *When the Pie Was Opened* deals with is not the heroism of the people, 'taking it' bravely in the face of adversity and fighting back, but simply the day-to-day survival of those who had no choice but to continue to work and sustain the nation. It shows a middle-class family going on with their lives unperturbed — the mother manages to bake a pie, almost as in peacetime — thanks to the combined efforts of members of the working-class. Rather than expressing the 'music of a nation at war', the film truly enhances 'the rhythm of workaday Britain' and the subdued yet vital soundtrack of the nation's workforce.

Endnotes

1. This expression is taken from the opening commentary of *Listen to Britain* (Jennings, 1942), spoken by Canadian journalist Leonard Brockington.
2. *Idem*
3. His films *Tusalava* (1929), *A Colour Box* (1935), *The Birth of the Robot* (1935), *Rainbow Dance* (1936), *Trade Tattoo* (1937), *Colour Cry* (1953), and *Free Radicals* (1958), are among the most representative examples of his hand-painted technique.
4. *When the Pie Was Opened* was preceded by *Swinging the Lambeth Walk* (1939) and *Musical Poster #1* (1940), and followed by *Newspaper Train* (1942), *Work Party* (1943), *Killed or Be Killed* (1943), and *Cameramen at War* (1944). Lye also directed short informational films for Realist Film Unit about rationing and salvage, such as *Wheatmeal Bread* (1941), *Collapsible Metal Tubes* (1942), and *Planned Crops* (1943).
5. The passage of the nursery rhyme 'Sing a Song of Sixpence' included in the film is the following one: 'Sing a song of sixpence/A pocket full of rye./Four and twenty blackbirds,/Baked in a pie./When the pie was opened/The birds began to sing;/Wasn't that a dainty dish,/To set before the king.' The meaning of the song is somewhat cryptic. The Oxford Dictionary of Nursery Rhymes states that the rhyme has been tied to a variety of historical events or folkorish symbols (such as the queen symbolizing the moon, the king the sun, and the blackbirds the number of hours in a day), the most probable of which would be an Italian recipe of the Antiquity 'to make pies so that the birds may be alive in them and flie out when it is cut up' (*Oxford Dictionary of Nursery Rhymes* 1952: 394 – 95).
6. Although not a member of the Surrealist movement himself, Len Lye had exhibited his works at the International Surrealist Exhibition in London in 1936 and was friends with such artists as René Magritte and Paul Eluard.
7. The word 'symphony' comes from the Ancient Greek συμφωνία (sumphōnía), composed of the prefix σὖν- (sun-, 'with, together') and the substantive φωνή (phōné, 'sound') meaning 'sounding together'.
8. The melody of the 'mess call' is the following one:

Figure 5: Melody of the 'mess call' used in *When the Pie Was Opened* (Lye, 1941).

9 The only telling visual clue is the newspaper clipping whose headline reads 'How to tackle fire bombs'.

10 This expression is taken from Len Lye's film *Trade Tattoo* (Lye, 1937).

11 I am indebted to Roger Horrocks, Len Lye's biographer, for providing me with an account of Len Lye's political beliefs and activities.

12 The term 'electro-acoustic' here might sound slightly anachronistic, given that the term was not officially used before Pierre Schaeffer's experiments in the late 1940s and early 1950s. However, Jack Ellitt himself talks about 'electro-acoustic sound' as early as 1935, in his essay *On Sound* (1935, pp. 182 – 4).

13 The variable area system is an optical soundtrack in which the audio signal is represented by a line of varying width running the length of the film. This system was still very new at the time, and became common in the 1970s with the advent of the stereo variable-area system.

14 'As soon as sounds are separated from their sources, they become images or symbols of those sources. . . . When separated from its source, a sound will not only become a symbol of that source but a symbol of what that source represents' (Rotha, 1952, p. 221).

15 In the same interview, Wright admitted having been mistaken in formulating this idea: 'I've revised my opinion on that. I think we were a bit too doctrinaire in our attitude in those days . . . I think we may have perhaps missed the point.' (quoted in Sussex, p. 110).

16 A famous example of the 'pulling together' discourse, and of the alleged cohesion of the British nation is to be found in the famous sonic dissolve in *Listen to Britain*, whereby a held top A links the sequence featuring a concert of popular entertainers Flanagan and Allen in a factory canteen, and the following sequence featuring pianist Myra Hess's lunchtime concert at the National Gallery, attended, among other 'ordinary' civilians, by the Queen Mother.

Bibliography

Bergfelder, T., & Cargnelli, C. (2012). *Destination London: German-speaking emigrés and British cinema, 1925 – 1950*. New York: Berghahn Books.

Bijsterveld, K. (Ed.). (2013). *Soundscapes of the urban past: staged sound as mediated cultural heritage*. Bielefeld: Transcript Verlag.

Bouhours, J. M., & Horrocks, R. (2000). *Len Lye [Exhibition catalogue]*. Exhibited at the Centre Pompidou, Paris, 5 – 30 Avril 2000. Paris: Éd. du Centre Pompidou.

Brinson, C., & Dove, R. (2016). *A matter of intelligence: MI5 and the surveillance of Anti-Nazi refugees, 1933 – 50*. Oxford: Oxford University Press.

Calder, A. (1992). *The myth of the Blitz*. London: Random House.

Cantrill, A. (2002). The absolute truth of the happiness Acid. *Senses of Cinema, 19. Retrieved from: http://sensesofcinema.com/2002/feature-articles/lye-2/*

Eisenstein, S. M., Pudovkin, V. I., & Alexandrov, G. V. (1985). A Statement. In E. Weis & J. Belton (Eds.), (1985). *Film sound: theory and practice* (pp. 83 – 5). McGill-Queen's Press-MQUP. (Original work published 1928).

Ellitt, J. (1935). On sound. *Life and Letters Today*, December 1935, 182 – 4.

Grierson, J. (1933). The documentary producer. *Cinema Quarterly*, 2(1).

Grierson, J (1934). Introduction to a New Art. *Sight and Sound*, 3(11): 101 – 4.

Horrocks, R. (1999). Jack Ellitt: the early years. *Cantrills Film Notes, 93 – 100*.

Horrocks, R. (2001). *Len Lye: a biography*. Auckland: Auckland University Press.

Jennings, H. (1942). *The music of war*. Humphrey Jennings Collection, Box 1, Item 7.

Jennings, H. (Director). (1942). *Listen to Britain* [Motion picture]. United Kingdom: Crown Film Unit.

Kashmere, B. (2007). Len Lye. *Senses of Cinema*, 43. Retrieved from: http://www.sensesofcinema. com/contents/directors/07/lye.

Lye, L. (Director). (1937). *Trade tattoo* [Motion picture]. United Kingdom: GPO Film Unit.

Lye, L. (Director). (1941). *When the pie was opened* [Motion picture]. United Kingdom: Realist Film Unit.

Lye, L., Curnow, W., & Horrocks R. (1984). *Figures of motion: Selected writings*. Auckland, New Zealand: Auckland University Press.

Lye, L., & Horrocks, R. (2015). *Zizz!: The life and art of Len Lye : In his own words*. Wellington, New Zealand: Awa Press.

Lye, L., Graves, R., Horrocks, R., & Govett-Brewster Art Gallery. (2017). *'Individual Happiness Now': A definition of common purpose*. New Plymouth, Aotearoa New Zealand: Govett-Brewster Art Gallery / Len Lye Centre. (Essay written 1935)

Mansell, J. G. (2016). *The age of noise in Britain: Hearing modernity*. Urbana: University of Illinois Press.

Ministry of Information (Sponsor). (1942). *Mobilise your scrap* [Motion picture]. United Kingdom: Films of Great Britain.

Opie, P., & Opie, P. (Eds.). (1952). *The Oxford dictionary of nursery rhymes*. Oxford: Clarendon Press.

Robinson, C. (2010). *Light and rhythm: the life and music of Jack Ellitt* (Unpublished doctoral thesis). University of Melbourne, Melbourne.

Rotha, P. (1952). *Documentary film: the use of the film medium to interpret creatively and in social terms the life of the people as it exists in reality*. London: Faber & Faber Limited.

Ruttmann, W. (Director). (1930). *Wochenende* [Radio piece]. Germany: Berlin Radio Hour.

Schaeffer, P. (2012). *In search of concrete music* (North, C. and Dack, J. Trans). Berkeley: University of California Press. (Original work published 1952)

Sussex, E. (1976). *The rise and fall of British documentary: the story of the film movement founded by John Grierson*. Berkeley: University of California Press.

Vaughan Williams, R. (1987). *National music and other essays*. Oxford; New York: Oxford University Press, 1987. (Original work published 1963)

Building a sonic image of a nation: Finnish documentary and propaganda films in the early decades of sound film

Kaarina Kilpiö

This chapter looks into the early non-fiction filmmakers' tools for building a sonic image of Finland around the mid-twentieth century. It outlines the circumstances and tendencies in short filmmaking in Finland from the 1940s to 1950s. The approach is built from the viewpoint of my own background as an ethnomusicologically-oriented social historian — a researcher of different uses of music in an everyday life context, including music in historical advertising, and functional background music.

I am interested in three main points. Firstly, I want to find out what music was chosen for use in the short films, and what its connections are to the musical cultures and soundscapes of Finnish everyday life at the time when the films were produced. Secondly, I wish to shed light on what the filmmakers wished to convey when combining certain music with different non-musical elements (sonic and visual). Thirdly, on the one hand I want to gain an understanding of the lasting elements of the sonic image of the nation presented by the filmmakers, and on the other, of those sonic elements that are present in the films only for certain purposes or for limited times.

The history and nature of Finnish short film production has been studied in several publications (e.g. Sedergren & Kippola, 2009 and 2015; Lammi 2006; Mickwitz 1995). However, the sonic expressive means utilised have only been mentioned briefly or left out altogether in previous studies. To round out understanding of the subject, I have started analysing the short film soundtracks in their historical context. This chapter is one of the first attempts to gather initial observations and findings for this project.

My working method consisted of several phases. Firstly, I found out, from existing research and the database of the Finnish National Audiovisual Institute archives, what films had been made and which of them had been preserved. I then viewed the material extensively in order to gain an understanding of the means of expression used in short film making during the research period. After this, I chose certain films on the basis of their typicality — or atypicality — in their use of sound, judged by the general understanding that I had gained from the viewing sessions. Next, I carried out close-listening sessions of the soundtracks of the chosen films, comparing the sonic execution to the typical solutions of the time. Finally, I undertook a more detailed analysis of some scenes, tracing the decision-making process and the underlying presumptions about the listening audience of the time.

Some special chains of events occurred in the chosen time period (1940s to 1950s). These include World War II — in which Finland fought against the neighbouring Soviet Union and was allied with Nazi Germany — as well as a period of swift urbanization and rise in the standard of living after the war. Within the cinema industry, the time

Building a sonic image of a nation 241

period also coincides with a unique era: movie-going peaked at levels it would never reach again (Keto, 1974, 64), and also, short film making was significantly supported by the state. In 1933, the year following the introduction of sound film in Finland, a new law came into effect offering tax deductions for tickets for film presentations that included domestic short films. The short films warranting deduction had to be at least 200 meters in length and their themes regarded as educational, scientific, or depicting domestic industry and commerce. This law was intended to improve the conditions for producing short films in Finland, which it did in an effective and profound way until its repeal in 1964. This meant short films were not only made in record numbers but also experienced by a significant portion of the population (see Lammi 2006, pp. 39 – 40).

The research material for this chapter consists of samples from short films made in Finland during this time. The thousands of films made during the tax deduction era constitute an extremely valuable body of research material for historians on local industry, commerce and tourism as well as education, science and cultural life. They are useful as sources for studying the audiovisual expression at the time, and to a certain extent, different aspects of Finnish society.

The term 'non-fiction' in the opening of my text is in no way indicative of any truth-value of the content in the films. The narratives are often fictional by nature, and the events staged to a high degree; a war propaganda film may feature the camera backing ahead of a minesweeping soldier on 'a dangerous village road', and a travel film may present a 'tourist' — played by an actor — guiding the camera through the sights and experiences of a certain route or city. The 'non-fictionality' of the films is thus actualized more in their depiction of something — an event, a location, a national achievement — as 'real' and having an effect on life in Finland. The filmmakers have realized this effect by using various means of audiovisual expression. These include writing the speaker's commentary in the present tense, incorporating scenes from public places and of 'everyday people' engaged in their chores, showing an awareness of the camera, and subordinating the occasional narrative human interest elements to the principal aim and theme of the film. The characters are seldom named: they are not individuals but representatives of their place of residence, profession, or other role beyond their personal attributes. This also affects how the sonic elements are situated and mixed in the films. In short, source criticism is essential when studying this type of material.

Sound in 1940s films is almost never completely actuality sound (recorded on location). From the 1950s on, this gradually changes, as lighter and more high-quality field recording equipment became available. Depending on the production company's resources, a clearly audible difference between the sound quality of material drawn from published library recordings and recorded location sound remains until at least the 1960s.

By the 1940s, all music used in Finnish audiovisual productions had to be licensed. This is a feature of Finnish copyright history that helps a historian when using film as research material. Because of these archived licence documents of the Finnish music authors' organisation Teosto (formed in 1928), we have a good understanding of the sonic material used in films and television. It is therefore possible to conduct a study of the 'reception' and interpretation of different kinds of music among filmmakers in twentieth-century Finland. The process of combining data from my two sources — the Teosto archives and the National Audiovisual Institute of Finland — is currently in progress.

I have sampled two sets of films from the National Audiovisual Institute archives more extensively. The first set includes war propaganda newsreels from the Continuation War (1941 – 44), where Finland, after a short 15-month period of peace following the Winter War (1939 – 40), returned to fight against the Soviet Union in WWII, allied with Nazi Germany. The second set consists of educational films from the series *Our Culture and Us* (1938 – 52). I have also viewed other educational short films; because of my overall aim (finding sonic features of the image of Finland) there was an emphasis on travel films, presenting several locations in Finland from the 1940s to the early 1960s.

War propaganda

The 86 publicly shown propaganda newsreels made during WWII were called *Surveys of the Armed Forces* (SoAF). These films had two aims: to evoke goodwill outside Finland; and to strengthen patriotism and trust in victory locally. Every Finnish cinema showed the newsreels, and newspapers estimated 'tens of millions' viewers around the world (Sedergren & Kippola 2009, p. 362).

The soundtracks on the *Surveys* consist of three elements: read commentary from written and carefully inspected manuscripts; rare sound effects (possibly partly from the Finnish broadcasting company Yleisradio, but also staged and taped material); and naturally, music. There is no commissioned music nor exclusive performances included on the *Survey* soundtracks. All music is taken from pre-recorded material — either Yleisradio tapes or commercially available recordings. Very few sound effects were included on the soundtracks, with the notable exception of the sounds of firearms.

Most of the music heard comes from different Finnish composers — classical orchestral repertoire and so-called 'lighter repertoire'. Some instances of lighter orchestral music from other European composers is included, as is popular dance music where entertainment or infrequent cheerful moments are featured. The lighter orchestral music composers are not necessarily the canonical names of today, but 'lesser' composers, perhaps familiar to some viewers of the time from light music concerts, a tradition that had been fading in Finland since the beginning of the twentieth century. Not all music used in war propaganda was necessarily familiar to the majority of viewers in the movie theatres however, and symphonic repertoire certainly was not. Orchestral concerts had mainly been attended by the middle and upper classes, and the movie theatre audience included a wider spectrum of the population than the concerts did. One thing is absolutely indisputable in the Finnish war propaganda soundtracks, and that is the use of Jean Sibelius's music as one of its most defining features. The Teosto documents reveal that his work was heard nearly as much as all the other composers put together. Based on my listening sessions, I would also say that, as a rule, the instances of Sibelius's music are in longer stretches than that of other composers' music. The overall impact of this collective media experience has also extended to later media contents in a powerful way.

The prominence of certain composers or styles in propaganda was possibly derived from the German model, the *Wochenschau* propagandistic newsreel. The German propaganda machinery used music and sound extensively, with one of their main musical categories being orchestral classics — large symphonic sounds written by composers who were not racially 'dubious' and '*völkisch*' in their composing (Chamblee, 2003). In Germany, the most important composer in this regard was Richard Wagner. As frequently as other Finnish composers' work was utilized in the newsreels, none could match Sibelius's significance and fame inside and outside of Finland. In his case, fame and appreciation were more important than the (indisputably anti-modernist) style of the composer's works, or his ancestry. For Finnish viewers of propaganda, an added positive attribute of Sibelius came from his active and visible role in the independence efforts during the late nineteenth century.

Music had several roles in the war propaganda newsreel soundtracks. They included — though often in modified forms — the roles typical of film music: creating and maintaining the defining mood of the film; creating continuity between scenes; and guiding the spectator's interpretation of what is seen and heard. In addition to these basic functions, I will present two attributes that stem from the character of war propaganda — the transformative function and the collectivizing function.

In creating the mood of war propaganda films, music sometimes bypasses the visuals as well as other sonic elements — spoken message and the sound effects. This interesting trait of war propaganda film sound is illustrated with an analysis of a scene from *SoAF 2* (1941) that follows a section where the Finnish army has been shown recapturing a Karelian village and the surroundings subsequently being cleared of possible enemy forces and mines. A Finnish soldier is filmed sweeping mines on a village road. The soldier's movements are cautious and considered. He is using a modest tool, — a stick taken from a tree — to inspect the road from side to side. The scene is clearly staged however: the camera is backing in front of the concentrating soldier on the 'dangerous' road, a setting that would have created a life-threatening situation for the cameraman had the road actually been unswept for mines.

The narration emphasizes the precision and danger involved in the work. But throughout the scene the speaker also continues to relieve the mood with humorous

Image 1: *Survey of the Armed Forces 2*, 1941: the mine-sweeping soldier proceeding carefully on the Karelian village road. © The National Audiovisual Institute, Finland.

Image 2: *Survey of the Armed Forces 2*, 1941: the third 'unhealthy bread loaf', hidden by the Russian forces on the mined road and found by the 'precise and level-headed Finnish soldier'. © The National Audiovisual Institute, Finland.

notions. These include calling the Soviet fighters by the Finnish nickname 'iivana', their mines and ambushes 'pranks', and the mines themselves 'unhealthy bread loaves'.

This kind of boyish adventure book's language is present in many Finnish propaganda films. It counterpoints the general rhetoric of the heroic, morally impeccable Finnish soldier, softening the message and creating the image of warfare as catering to the masculine craving for thrills. No sound effects are audible on the soundtrack and thus probably have not been included in this scene. Musically, however, the scene is constructed as if something — cavalry, a fleet of aeroplanes or boats — was storming victoriously towards the enemy.

The music — a symphony orchestra at full throttle playing the 'Intermezzo' from Sibelius's *Karelia Suite* — certainly undermines the suspense that is being simultaneously built, partly through the verbal message and partly through the visual information of the cautious movements of the minesweeper. This feature of propaganda film music is recurrent and stems from the aims of the audiovisual message. No qualms about the mission, mood or determination of the Finnish troops is permissible in the genre. Even in those cases where there are subtle cues of hardship in the verbal narration, the music eschews any lamenting tones. The closest musical expression to feelings of sorrow or concern are used in a section of *Survey 29* (1942) where wounded soldiers are treated. Here, the elegiac and gentle music of Sibelius's *The Lover* is used. The music is counterbalanced throughout, however, with visual materials and verbal narration that emphasize efficiency and determination.

The transformative function of war propaganda film music is associated with the task of the filmmakers to convey the impression of meaningful action and a sense of coherence. This is especially needed when the visual material presents isolated battle scenes from the front or monotonous routine tasks. The music lends support to the verbal message in turning chaos, violence and hardship into elements of a narrative implying the Armed Forces are in command of the situation. Indeed, an important streak of this function consists of emphasizing the active, forward-looking role of the Finnish forces even when the film material — or the current war — did not convey an active image.

The function of music in the SoAFs that I have called 'collectivizing' underlines the noble cause of fighting. It places the activities of fighting and persevering beyond individuals, on and off screen. This is in no way unique in propaganda music: the uplifting and rousing sounds, mostly produced collaboratively by an ensemble of musicians (solo performances are infrequent), aspire to ring with national consciousness. In the case of Finland, the use of collective musical utterances also aims to reverse or at least relieve the concern brought about by the evident imbalance of a miniature state fighting a superpower. When it comes to using Sibelius especially, the symphonic music also acts to inject historical significance to the fight, with the use of a large orchestral sound and pieces known (at least to upper- and middle-class viewers) for their significant role during the time of Finland's efforts in seceding from Russia around the turn of the century. In my view, this is one important factor in the frequent use of a symphony orchestra sound in Finnish war propaganda: the sound directly implies a social act of a large number of musicians / citizens, working together for a shared goal (cf. e.g. van Leeuwen 1999, pp. 72 – 79).

In the case of Sibelius, and particularly his symphonies, the films also established (temporary) recognizable tropes such as efficiency, perseverance, home front motivation, and gentleness. It was typical for the third symphony, for example, to be combined with scenes of the munition industry or similar tangible war efforts. Another example is the tone poem *The Oceanides* being used in scenes depicting sea transport, the navy, or other conceivable contexts such as the watery chaos resulting from the Finnish troops blowing up a dam in order to drive the enemy out of a village (*Survey 26*, 1941).

Sibelius apparently gave permission not only to use any and all of his work in the war propaganda, but to use it for free. The permission itself does not seem to have been documented in print, but the constant use of his music was, and in a detailed way — it is these archival documents that I am relying upon in my research. However, no financial transactions resulting from the propaganda use took place between Sibelius and Teosto. Before and after the war, this was not the case: it was and is very hard to gain permission to use Sibelius' symphonies alongside moving images, and a fee is always required. (Kilpiö 2017.)

Our Culture and Us: a cultural representation of Finland

Several series of films about Finnish artists, musicians, scientists, and writers were produced during the tax deductions era. In what follows I will draw examples from the first of the 'genre', *Our Culture and Us* — a series of films initiated in 1938 by the folklore scholar Martti Haavio and social scientist Lauri Aadolf Puntila for the Finnish Cultural Foundation (Sedergren & Kippola, 2009, pp. 192 – 4, p. 196). The idea was to exhibit to Finns the literature, art and science of their own country and so these films were not made for promoting Finland outside the country.

The nearly 20 episodes of the series present cultural, historical, industrial, and geographical features of the country. Not all the episodes have been preserved, so for this analysis I have only been able to choose from those films with sound that are still available. They constitute a selection of artists and scientists, and areas such as geology or chemistry, and show people in their working environments and, sometimes, during their leisure time. Each episode is focused on a specific 'advanced' feature of the Finnish culture. Some of the films from 1940s onwards contain sections with on-location sound.

One sonic characteristic of the decade after WWII is the significant use of several trusted (mostly male) voices as narrators. The *Our Culture and Us* series presents a typical example of the abundant use of a narrator's reassuring input on the soundtracks. The narrator would be audible almost throughout the film, providing the spectator with an interpretation of all the events on screen. Foremost of the 'national narrators' was Carl-

Erik Creutz, whose voice, with his slightly Swedish-speaking accent, was omnipresent in Finnish audiovisual products, from newsreels to sports films to the national public broadcasting company — Yleisradio's productions. This feature is close to what Bjørn Sørenssen wrote about Norwegian films in his article 'The Voice of Reconstruction: the Norwegian postwar newsreel' (Sørenssen, 1996).

A closer analysis is presented in episode number 10 (*Kalevala* 1949). The film is definitely one of the most pronouncedly nationalistic in the series, and is scripted by Haavio and Puntila. It features the Finnish national epic *Kalevala* (a work of epic poetry compiled from national folklore and mythology in 1835 by Elias Lönnrot) and its impact on the arts in Finland and around the world. The film opens with a long sequence of nature shots from the 'runo country' of Karelia. It explicitly connects the inspired 'runolahjainen yksilö' (an individual with endowment in poetry) with the Finnish countryside through narration:

> The poetry in our national epic *Kalevala* was sung by common men and women. Nature, in its beauty and magnificence, has inspired poem-making with its wonders, as have adventures on open waters and in endless wild territories experienced or heard by the singers. From these experiences, in a moment of inspiration, the individual with endowment in poetry produced a poem that has travelled from mouth to mouth.

The narration celebrates these individuals not as gifted personalities — that role is reserved for contemporary artists and scientists — but mainly as preservers of a tradition, inspired by nature. No visual material of runo singers is combined with this narration: the film presents images of a stately pine forest and a wide, swirling torrent, matched musically with Sibelius's *Karelia Suite*. The choice of composer and work is self-explanatory: the inspiration for the suite (originally incidental music) was known to have come from the culture and nature of the Karelia district. The runo singers and tradition bearers are here brought out to the spectator as an invisible outcome of the local natural conditions — or perhaps even as a 'spirit of the Finnish nation' that cannot be separated from its source of inspiration. This continuum from nature to oral tradition is then linked to contemporary artists and writers via the Kalevala epic since they are shown, and verbally described as creating significant art that is based on the poems and characters in *Kalevala*.

The sonic image of the nation in this film is the most high-brow of the series. The speaker's tone is ceremonial throughout the film: the chosen social distance from the spectators is one of an assembly hall orator. The music proceeds with a narrative and justification of its own. This is intentional and expressed verbally at the end: '. . . the music of Sibelius, which we have had the chance to enjoy throughout the film'. Perhaps the most interesting detail in the sonic structure of the film is an omission. Runo singing — the origin of Kalevala poetry — had been recorded from the earliest times of sound recording technology. This happened from 1905 onwards, when the first recording devices to be used in Finland were introduced by the Finnish Literature Society. The writers of the film script, Martti Haavio and Lauri A. Puntila, were very well aware of the archives of the Society; Haavio was the Society's director. There is, however, no trace of runo material on the soundtrack. The runo singers on the recordings naturally would not have been those who inspired the compilation of the epic in 1835. However, this oral tradition as a whole is given no voice, and the runo singers are only visible on film as statues created by the 'best of the sculptors' in

Image 3: *Our Culture and Us part 10 (Kalevala)*: nature scenes are shown and the Karelia Suite by Sibelius played when presenting the role of the vernacular runo artists. © The National Audiovisual Institute, Finland.

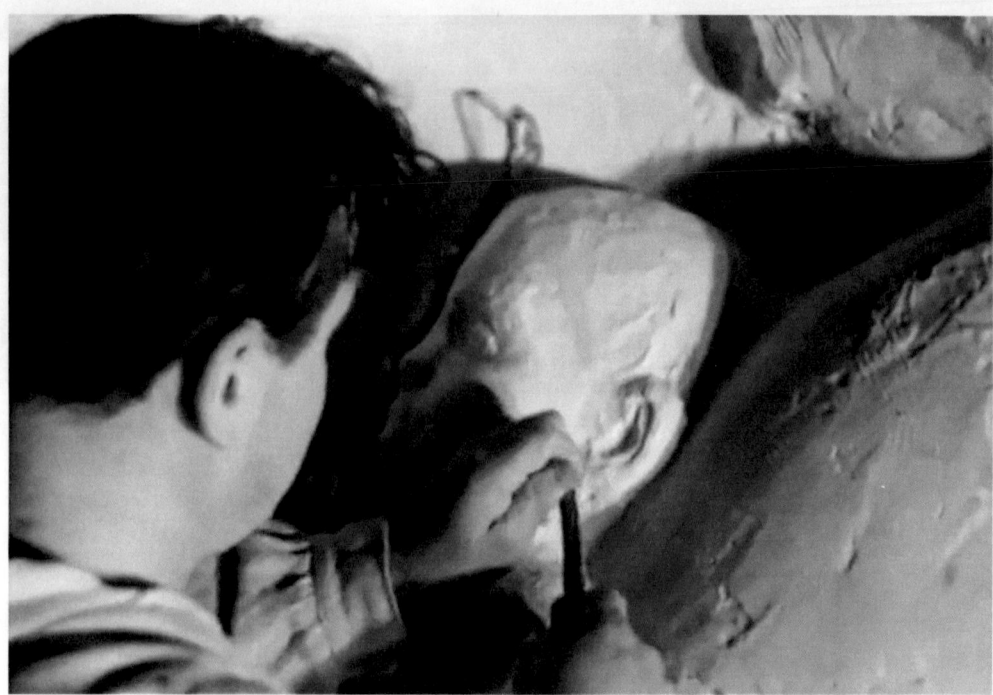

Image 4: *Our Culture and Us part 10 (Kalevala)*: sculptor, professor Väinö Aaltonen using his skills to create 'lasting beauty' inspired by Kalevala. © The National Audiovisual Institute, Finland.

Finland. In addition to the authoritarian voice of the narrator, the soundtrack features — and later in the film, also verbally foregrounds – Sibelius's *Karelia Suite*. Using the nationally important composer's music (titled and themed suitably) is not surprising, but the dominance of the music in the soundtrack is. The runo singers are largely absent from the visual material of the film, and entirely so from the soundtrack.

Since these omissions are conscious choices made by the filmmakers, it is worthwhile considering their meanings and implications. My interpretation is twofold. Firstly, the filmmakers viewed the singers as simply tradition bearers: rather than being portrayed as artists and individuals in their own right, they are seen more or less as 'faceless' carriers of tradition, from the alien era of oral culture. Secondly, since the nationalistic project had been (and continued to be in the 1940s) very tightly associated with written culture, passing over the oral tradition as mere raw material for the veritable artists of the day was a conceivable, even natural, choice. Those constructing national epics had been, in Keith Bosley's oft-cited words, 'concerned less with fidelity to sources than with the validation of a national culture' (Lefevere 1998, p. 79). With its expressive choices, the film carries on validating Finnish national culture, which is especially clear when the treatment of sonic materials is analysed.

In Finnish short films of the late 1940s and 1950s, the frequent use of Sibelius's compositions continues. There are differences, however: those works by Sibelius that are used in *Our Culture and Us* series are not the symphonies used in war propaganda, but smaller compositions and pieces originally composed for the stage. Compared with the war-time films, this means a move back to the pre-war practice of using chamber music pieces and incidental music, and leaving the symphonies to be heard in live performances in concert halls and, of course, from recordings. During peace, the sonic representation of the Finnish nation thus did not require as dramatic and urgent sonic action as using the majestic symphonies of the towering figure of Finnish music: that was reserved for war-time purposes.

The sonic image presented in the *Our Culture and Us* series is also typical of Finnish travel films of the 1940s and 1950s. Sound effects and location sounds are rarely present, Sibelius's ever-present incidental music and a narrator (generally with a formal, even ceremonial public announcer tone) are the recurrent choices for the soundtrack. The influence of the introduction of television into daily life in Finland in the late 1950s, however, is audible in film documentary and especially in films that have commercial significance, such as travel films.

The sonic expression in television, especially advertising, differed from theatre productions in several ways: the loudspeakers were now smaller and thus created a less impressive sound. During the early years, in the late 1950s, television programming was mostly carried out live. Television advertising was costly compared to cinema advertising, and the production processes were hectic. This led to extensive use of two music content providers: 1) small (often jazzy) combos working or long hours with little time for rehearsals, and 2) catalogue/library music collections. Television was also the hot new medium, spreading quickly to Finnish homes. The smaller sound production and quicker pace of television content gradually started seeping into other Finnish audiovisual material of the early 1960s. This is most often audible in films whose content gives reason for advertisement-type expression: travel films, presentations of industries or services, consumer practices such as savings accounts in banks, etc.

Conclusion

The use of music and sound to construct an image of Finland has gone through several phases of which the first significant one was war-time propaganda. The need to create a favourable image of Finland as a western civilization was urgent, since the goodwill and perhaps also the help of some other western nations was at stake. Another crucial function of music and sound was to reassure Finns of the historic significance and shared task of the noble fight. By the final stages of the Continuation War (in 1944 and 1945), voices emerged questioning whether or not it was justified to continue the offensive beyond the old Finnish-Russian border and whether Germany was the best possible choice for comrade-in-arms. All these factors contributed to the main features of soundtrack design for propaganda purposes. Using Jean Sibelius's works extensively has been and remains a hallmark feature in audiovisually representing Finnish nationalism. War propaganda took advantage of the composer's fame and associated goodwill by the practice of using mainly his works for a large symphony orchestra to parallel the social unit of the symphony orchestra on the soundtrack with the Finnish people in the audience. The tone of the Armed Forces newsreels speaker was kept relatively friendly and inclusive (to Finns) — in contrast to the German *Wochenschau* newsreels, where the speakers used a more military-sounding tone.

The second significant phase in constructing the soundtracks can be heard in the reconstruction era, from 1945 to the end of the 1950s. This era features several narrators whose voices built trust about the progress of Finnish society. This era again normalizes a more diverse spectrum of musics: Sibelius's incidental music, chamber music, and light popular classics — but also, little by little, jazz and other popular music genres.

From the introduction of television in Finland at the very end of 1950s, different kinds of influences find their way to the soundtracks. The visual rhythm develops towards quicker cuts and swift changes between shot types. This visual development also affects the tone and pacing of the narration, that evolves with the help of advances in recording technology, bringing the total auditory experience closer to the short and snappy expression of television (see also Kilpiö 2005, pp. 164 – 7, p. 314).

The Finnish professional audiovisual scene, being small but very receptive to new technologies and trends, constitutes a good case study for finding out how sonic expression in non-fiction film has developed during the last 80 years. More detailed research, preferably with a comparative take from several countries, would be welcome to gain a better understanding of the developments and trends in the professional production of documentaries and short films.

Bibliography

Chamblee, C. (2003). The juxtaposition of visual and musical elements in Nazi Films (1933–1945). *Music Research Forum 18*, 2 – 28.

Kalevala – kansallinen, yleismaailmallinen. Kulttuurimme ja me 10 (1949) [Kalevala – national, universal. Our Culture and Us, part 10]. Retrieved from https://www.elonet.fi/fi/elokuva/628740 [18 December 2017].

Keto, J. (1974). *Elokuvalippujen kysyntä ja siihen vaikuttaneet tekijät Suomessa 1915 – 1972* [The demand of movie tickets and factors affecting it in Finland 1915 – 1972]. Acta Academiae oeconomicae Helsingiensis. Series A; 10: Helsinki.

Kilpiö, K. (2017). Jean Sibelius's music in Finnish propaganda films during WWII. In D. Grimley & T. Howell & V. Murtomäki & T. Virtanen (Eds.). *Jean Sibelius's legacy. Research on his 150th Anniversary* (pp. 171 – 80). Newcastle: Cambridge Scholars Publishing.

Kilpiö, K. (2005). *Kulutuksen sävel. Suomalaisen mainoselouvan musiikki 1950-luvulta 1970-luvulle* [Consumer Tunes: music in Finnish advertising films from 1950s to 1970s]. Helsinki: Like.

Lammi, M. (2006). *Ett' varttuisi Suomenmaa. Suomalaisten kasvattaminen kulutusyhteiskuntaan kotimaisissa lyhytelokuvissa 1920 – 1969* [So that Finland would grow. Educating Finns into consumer society in domestic short films 1920 – 1969]. Helsinki: Finnish Literature Society.

Lefevere, A. (1998). The gates of analogy: The Kalevala in English. In S. Bassnett & A. Lefevere (Eds.). *Constructing cultures. essays on literary translation*. Topics in Translation 11. Multilingual Matters.

Mickwitz, J. (1995). *Folkbildning, Företag, Propaganda: Den finska icke-fiktiva filmen på det fält när nationell symbolgods skapades under mellankrigstiden* [Popular enlightenment, entrepreneurship, propaganda: the Finnish non-fiction film on the field of national symbol assets creation in the interwar period]. Historical Research 190. Helsinki: Finnish Historical Society.

Sedergren, J. & Kippola, I. (2009). *Dokumentin ytimessä: suomalaisen dokumentti- ja lyhytelokuvan historia 1904 – 1944* [In the heart of the documentary: the history of Finnish documentary and short film, 1904 – 1944]. Helsinki: Finnish Literature Society.

Sedergren, J. & Kippola, I. (2015). *Dokumentin utopiat. Suomalaisen dokumentti- ja lyhytelokuvan historia 1944 – 1989* [Utopias of the documentary: the history of Finnish documentary and short film, 1944 – 1989]. Helsinki: Finnish Literature Society.

Survey of the Armed Forces 2: Crossing the border of 1940 (1941). Retrieved from http://www.elonet.fi/fi/elokuva/604846 [14 February 2018]

Survey of the Armed Forces 26: The takeover of Poventsa (1941). Retrieved from http://www.elonet.fi/fi/elokuva/640448 [14 February 2018]

Survey of the Armed Forces 29: Transport and treatment of the wounded (1942). https://www.elonet.fi/fi/elokuva/615832 [14 February 2018]

Sørenssen, B. (1996). The voice of reconstruction: the Norwegian postwar newsreel. In R. Smither & W. Klaue (Eds.). *Newsreels in film archives: a survey based on the FIAF Newsreel Symposium*. Cranbury: Associated University Press.

van Leeuwen, T. (1999). *Speech, music, sound*. London: Macmillan.

Raúl Ruiz's *Now We're Gonna Call You Brother* and the problem of the people's sonic representation

Laura Jordán González and Nicolas Lema Habash

A version of this chapter was presented at the Sound and Music Film Symposium at the University of Huddersfield (2017). We would like to thank the audience on that occasion and especially Valeria Sarmiento, who kindly allowed us to reproduce some images from Raúl Ruiz's films in this article. Thanks also to Geoffrey Cox for his comments on our first draft.

Raúl Ruiz is probably Latin America's most prolific filmmaker, with over 100 films shot during his career. Due to the breadth of his *œuvre*, and also to his own particular filmmaking style and methods, many of his works are still to be studied and analyzed. *Ahora te vamos a llamar hermano* (*Now We're Gonna Call You Brother*) is one of his most understudied documentaries.[1] It was made in 1971, on the occasion of Socialist President Salvador Allende's visit to the Araucanía region, home of the Mapuche people, in southern Chile. The purpose of this visit was to announce a new bill that the government was presenting in support of indigenous populations.

Although *Now We're Gonna Call you Brother* explicitly points out at the beginning that it will cover Allende's activities, its real focus is not the President, but the Mapuche themselves. In this chapter we offer a close interpretation of the sonic dynamics present in this documentary. We argue that Ruiz creates a sonic dialectical tension between the sounds of the Mapuche people (expressed in their voices, language and music) and Allende's speech announcing the bill. This artistic strategy supposes a recuperation of those Mapuche sounds often excluded from New Chilean Song and Cinema, two of the most important forms of cultural expression within the leftist cultural establishment in Chile, from the 1950s up to the 1970s.

The article is divided into four sections. Firstly, we present *Now We're Gonna Call You Brother* within the broader context of Ruiz's filmography during this period, which corresponds to the years of the New Chilean Cinema (NCC) movement. Secondly, we introduce the musical counterpart to NCC: the Chilean New Song (CNS). We discuss how this musical movement sought to represent the people, how it became something like the 'soundtrack' of the so-called Chilean Road to Socialism and the specific status given to indigenous sonorities within this New Song project. In the third section we offer a close comparative analysis of *Now We're Gonna Call You Brother* and some other documentaries on the Mapuche and Allende in order to highlight Ruiz's artistic and political innovations vis-à-vis NCC projects about these same subjects. The fourth section studies the sonic dialectical relationship between the two sonorous poles in *Now We're Gonna Call You Brother*: Allende's voice and Mapuche sounds. We stress how Ruiz's critical portrayal of the encounter between the President and this indigenous population contributes to a questioning and renewal of what was understood as 'the popular' within revolutionary art. We thus propose an interpretation of how Ruiz's work in general, and *Now We're Gonna Call You Brother* in particular, can be understood as critical contributions to the artistic cultural establishment during the Allende administration.

Now We're Gonna Call You Brother within Raúl Ruiz's Filmography

Together with other filmmakers such as Sergio Bravo, Patricio Kaulen, Patricio Guzmán, Miguel Littín, Helvio Soto and Aldo Francia, Ruiz was key in the development of what became known as New Chilean Cinema. Unlike similar new cinema experiences in other Latin American countries, the renewal of Chilean cinema during the 1950s and 1960s became inextricably linked to party- and state-based political projects that sought to introduce radical economic and social changes in the country's structure. The first of these projects was undertaken by a centrist political party, the Christian Democracy, and led by Eduardo Frei Montalva, who became president in 1964. Thanks to the approval of a set of legal dispositions favouring filmmaking, national productions flourished during this administration, to the extent that the whole process was described as a 'boomlet' in Chilean cinema. Ruiz's first feature film, *Three Sad Tigers* (*Tres tristes tigres*) was produced in 1968, aided precisely by the abovementioned new legal dispositions on film (Cortínez & Engelbert, 2014, pp. 116 – 133). In 1970, Socialist Salvador Allende won office supported by the Unidad Popular (UP) coalition with an openly socialist revolutionary program. At this moment, New Chilean Cinema became inextricably associated with leftist politics and, regardless of the disagreements that some filmmakers advanced in relation to government policies, the development of NCC became openly militant.

Such militancy on the part of film creators was accompanied by a discourse about what an engaged cinema should involve and the role it should play within the broader revolutionary scenario. The key notions of 'realism' and the 'people' featured as two conceptual axes around which NCC was supposed to gravitate. Filming 'the real' became a duty, since this would contribute to the de-alienation of a national popular culture thought of as being hidden under imperialistic interests, which had become materialized in the film domain by Hollywood culture.[2] Although the precise nature of 'the real' was never exactly defined, the privileged social actor within the phenomenal domain of this 'real' was 'the people.' Imagined to become the main force of the revolutionary process, 'the people' were considered, by the same token, the main object and subject of this new cinema. Film would contribute to audiovisually place the problems of vast masses of the population under a new bright light, proposing an image of the people that they could themselves recognize. Filmmakers thus tended to provide an epic image of the people as the government's main base of support.[3]

Ruiz positioned himself critically vis-à-vis the image and discourse that NCC filmmakers developed concerning the political process the country was experiencing.

In fact, Ruiz showed a critical and skeptical attitude towards some of the main assumptions of the political-cum-filmmaking leftist establishment. This critical attitude comes from a filmmaker who was himself a Socialist militant committed to a programme of radical changes; therefore, we believe it is accurate to describe Ruiz's project during these years as one of 'revolutionary self-critique.'[4] The political nature of Ruiz's films and discourse during the Chilean Road to Socialism lies precisely in how he depicts the tensions, problems and impasses present *within* the left. Considered from this perspective, we propose to distinguish what we call three critical strategies in his œuvre, all of which question different aspects of the ideological imagination supporting leftist politics.

First Critical Strategy: *Desclasamiento*

In some of his films such as *The Expropriation* (*La expropiación*, 1971 – 1973), and *Socialist Realism* (*Realismo socialista*, 1972), Ruiz depicts people who are supposed to behave according to Marxist standards, but do not. In *The Expropriation*, peasants massacre the government official in charge of taking over a private *hacienda*, so that it may be exploited for and by the people. In turn, *Socialist Realism* shows the story of a proletarian man who shifts to the right and a bourgeois publicist who radicalizes to the left, all of which happens under the Allende administration. *Little White Dove* (*Palomita blanca*, 1973) also shows a similar phenomenon: in the manner of Romeo and Juliet, two youngsters fall in love with one another, although each belongs to a different social class. All of these films portray the political, social and sentimental activity of subjects who leave their class interests behind, a process that in Spanish is called *desclasamiento*. They advance a problematization of some presuppositions lying at the very heart of the leftist political establishment: namely, that the proletariat and the peasantry should automatically support the government and its policies; but in these films they do not.

Second Critical Strategy: Critique of Direct Cinema

During this time, Ruiz developed an acute and refined critique of the filming method that became known as 'direct cinema' (*cine directo*) during the New Latin American Cinema period. Ruiz argued that direct cinema sought to 'idealize' political revolutionary processes and, in his ironic words, he preferred to 'document' them. Such a critical attitude can be traced back to the months during which he studied at the Escuela de Cine Documental de Santa Fé, Argentina, a film institute led by one of the founders of New Latin American Cinema, Octavio Gettino. There, Ruiz remembered, he was taught that the duty of every Latin American was to shoot documentaries in a direct cinema style (Ruiz, 1970). In a 1972 interview, Ruiz straightforwardly targeted this (to his eyes) naïve conception of cinematic realism, by referring to the actual impossibility of filming things exactly as they are:

> . . . in film, I do not believe in the myth of a perfect mirror, a myth in which many filmmakers believe, especially Chilean filmmakers. Besides, the mirror gives us the face of reality, but inverted. I would be interested in using cinema as a mirror, but as a mirror that would give me reality as it is. And this, I believe, is impossible. Therefore, I use cinema as a mirror, through which I obtain an inverted face of reality, and I also use cinema as a deforming mirror. I start from the fact that I see reality with my eyes and that cinema, through distortion, may help me capture elements of reality that escape oneself.[5]

The upshot of this statement was to be the development of what Ruiz calls an 'inquiry' or 'investigative cinema' (*cine de indagatoria*), a notion that announces much of his ideas on the nature of film advanced in his *Poetics of Cinema* (2000), but in a politically charged context.

Third Critical Strategy: Displacement of the Popular (*desplazamiento de lo popular*).

Whilst the first two strategies have already been studied by scholars and critics (Lema Habash, 2006 and 2009; Pinto & Horta, 2010; Cortínez & Engelbert, 2011, pp. 63 – 83; Goddard, 2013, pp. 17 – 31), the third is a less acknowledged one. Although we find its traces in many of his fiction films, we believe its main mode of presentation can be more clearly discovered in the two documentaries Ruiz made during the UP years: the lost *Little Wild Dove* (*Palomilla brava*, 1973) and the film on which this article focuses: *Now We're Gonna Call You Brother*. We would like to suggest that the specific critical approach Ruiz advanced in these films lies in what we may call a 'displacement' or 're-placement' of the popular. Such a displacement consists of a focus of attention on subjects who are conceived of as belonging to 'the people' within the imagination of the left and the rhetoric present in revolutionary processes, but who do not conform to the traditional standards that have modeled or 'stylized' what a popular subject should look like, how it should sound and what it should do. Although *Little Wild Dove* is lost, we know that it focused on the youngsters who attended the casting for the main roles in *Little White Dove*. It showed, amongst other things, the desire to become a film 'star.' In addition, it depicted (just as *Little White Dove* does) how rooted 'pop' culture can become in a Latin American society through media devices such as music and television. It would seem as if Ruiz wished to emphasize that, regardless of the leftist purist discourse in relation to the popular milieu, 'pop' culture had also become part of that sphere of society.[6]

In a radically different manner, Ruiz's focus on the Mapuche indigenous population is also a clear example of this critical attitude towards the stylization of the people within the left-wing imagination. Through a variety of cinematic devices, Ruiz openly breaks with the image of an indigenous Mapuche population simply becoming subsumed under the standard category of 'the peasantry.' In contrast to other films about the Mapuche made during this time (such as *Amuhuelai-mi*, 1972, by Marilú Mallet), Ruiz focuses on the differential and non-epic status of the Mapuche as a people, rather than on their incorporation as masses that support the UP government (Aguirre, 2015).

The foremost element Ruiz uses to displace the traditional view of the people and to emphasize the specificity of the Mapuche is an alternative regime of sounds, music and language from the one that has traditionally accompanied the representation of the people in New Latin American and Chilean Cinema. The sounds in *Now We're Gonna Call You Brother* correspond to a mixture of languages (where Mapudungun prevails over Spanish) and to a music that bypasses the repertoire of the New Latin American Song movement, which, as we will argue, was developing its own representational strategies to depict the people as a revolutionary subject, just as filmmakers were.

New Chilean Song and Indigenous Sonic Representations

The music created by the CNS movement during the 1960s and 1970s has usually been conceived of as the soundtrack of the Chilean Road to Socialism. Its main features may be described in terms of the conjunction of international protest song and a vocal-instrumental hybrid style nourished by rhythms and musical forms from all over the continent. Not surprisingly, the development of New Song movements has been labeled as an eminently Latin-Americanist project. Such a project was seen as an artistic statement concerning the internationalist ethos traditionally associated with socialism, which, in the Chilean case, was opposed to other currents of popular music considered to be nationalist and conservative. The musical repertoire included a great variety of songs, instrumental pieces, albums, cantatas, oratorios, masses and even a number of film scores.[7]

In terms of its lyrics, one of the key features of the CNS was, as Rodrigo Torres has pointed out, the 'systematic incorporation of current human realities and viewpoints that until then had been marginalized or relegated into very small circuits within the realm of Chilean music' (1980, p. 18). If in the context of this political-cum-artistic project the portrayal of various 'popular' subjects became a goal, it was certainly the miner who turned out to be the figure *par excellence* to embody the revolutionary subject. Such a trend can be traced through a plethora of songs and musical works depicting the life and struggles of the working class (Jordán González, 2014). Through a reading of a specific notion of 'the revolutionary subject' (informed by Marxist intellectuals), the proletariat was imagined as belonging to a more advanced historical stage than the peasantry. In fact, songs referring to rural life often played a denunciatory role concerning the precarious conditions of the lower classes rather than portraying the peasants as agents of revolutionary change. By the same token, indigenous peoples were usually illustrated as part of the peasant community, thus lacking the agency to generate specific sovereign demands pertaining to their particular needs as a social-cum-cultural group. .

Indeed, when treated in their ethnic specificity, indigenous populations became preferentially linked with the so-called 'Andean region,' a transnational area including Chile, Argentina, Bolivia, Peru and (sometimes) Ecuador. Within this representational paradigm, the so-called 'Andean sounds' acquired a salient role within the New Song's style in order to portray various elements representing the cultural diversity of the continent and its peoples. Instruments whose origins may be traced back to this Andean region, such as the *quena*, *charango* and *zampoña*, came to simultaneously symbolize a certain *ethos*, as it were, pertaining to indigenous cultures in general. Interestingly enough, such a symbolic attachment appeared simultaneously as the index of a transnational culture (Andean region) and, more importantly, as the representational embodiment of the people as a whole, summoned to become the protagonist of a new social and political order (Fairley, 1989).

Contrary to what happened with such Andean sounds, the culture of the Mapuche people was barely recuperated by the political and hybridizing project of the CNS. Apart from a few terms in Mapudungun used to designate some specific artistic endeavours,[8] the references to Mapuche culture are meagre. Mapuche instruments — not to mention their rhythms and forms — only feature in a few songs that portray specific political struggles of this people[9] or as a vague reference to southern Chile in rare instrumental pieces.[10]

As an exception, we may mention the singer-songwriter Violeta Parra, undoubtedly considered as the 'mother' of the NCS (Rodríguez, 1986), who during the 1950s developed fieldwork in Mapuche territory collecting songs and interviewing *ülkantufe* (singers). She registered 39 songs about love, spirituality, collective work and female self-determination, as well as a number of lullabies. Although much of Parra's work on the Mapuche has only recently become available for the wider public, it is certain that through her research it was possible to appreciate the great musical creativity of this people via the recording of their rhythms, voices and singing inflections (Miranda et al., 2016, p. 21). Unfortunately, she recorded neither cover versions of the collected songs nor early arrangements of her own work including Mapuche instruments. However, there seems to be enough evidence to state that her own creations were significantly informed by this fieldwork.

According to this discussion, we may therefore argue that the virtual lack of Mapuche sonorities within the NCS can be explained through two main interpretations. Firstly, Andean sounds were able to symbolize an indigenous *ethos* sufficiently whilst at the same time sidelining nationalist discourses. Secondly, the proletariat (true protagonist of the revolution, paradigmatically embodied in Chile by the miner) was too distant from the popular subject represented by the peasantry, let alone that represented by the Mapuche people. Although we do not claim that this twofold argument is exhaustive, these two interpretative strands will allow us to propose a reading of *Now We're Gonna Call You Brother* that puts into question some of the assumptions present both in the NCS and NCC concerning the Mapuche.

Music and the Representation of the People in Documentary New Chilean Film

Now We're Gonna Call You Brother may be placed within two streams in the history of Chilean film. In the first place, it belongs to the history of documentary filmmaking on the Mapuche. Amongst the works created on this theme during the NCC period we can count Sergio Bravo's *Aquel nguillatun* (*That Nguillatun*, 1960 – 2000) and Marilú Mallet's already mentioned *Amuhuelai-mi*.

Bravo's and Ruiz's films both show an interest in capturing the sounds proper of the Mapuche. Bravo sought to register the direct sounds born out of the ritual context of the *nguillatun*, a traditional Mapuche ceremony. But the final cut of the documentary also incorporates avant-garde style extra-diegetic music, which establishes a clear distinction between Mapuche and non-Mapuche sounds. In Ruiz's film, on the contrary, the soundtrack is only composed of direct sounds, both of the Mapuche and of Allende's allocution. *Now We're Gonna Call You Brother* thus inscribes this direct-sound register within an explicitly political context. Such politicization of the Mapuche can also be found in Mallet's work, but through a completely different strategy. While Mallet seeks to subsume the Mapuche cause under the larger category of the people who support the UP government, Ruiz uses the encounter of two different sound registers (those created by the Mapuche and Allende's discourse) in order to problematize the standard relationship between this indigenous population and the left.

Secondly, Ruiz's film may be placed within the history of 'official' documentaries made to promote and support a specific government or political project.[11] Indeed, Ruiz's documentary was made under the auspices of Chile Films (the state-owned film company) and the purpose of this project was to document *in situ* the announcement of a government bill. Seen from this perspective, the film can be related to one of the most iconic documentaries made by Chile Films to support the UP: *Compañero presidente* (1971), by Miguel Littín, which registers the famous interview between Allende and French intellectual Regis Debray held in Santiago in 1970 – 1971 (Debray, 1971). Since both films feature Allende's voice and its relationship with the people as their main axis, a brief comparison between them is appropriate.

As an official documentary on the UP, it is possible to argue that *Compañero presidente* crystallizes the linkage between the somewhat clichéd image of the people, as represented both in the NCC and the CNS. It is probably the film that most clearly merges the UP, as a political project, with the CNS movement. In fact, the CNS is *literally* used as the soundtrack of the revolutionary struggle which, in Littín's film, is carefully explained through Allende's voice.

Compañero presidente's whole soundtrack consists of the Allende's and Debray's chatting voices, a selection of musical excerpts taken from the official Presidential campaign and a set of propaganda songs. As we mentioned, the CNS sought to create a hybrid musical expression by mixing and juxtaposing subcontinental rhythms and timbres. But it is also the case that some of its most representative songs were based on Western musical genres, traditionally associated with politics, such as the anthem over a rhythmic march form. In *Compañero presidente*, we repeatedly hear the pro-government anthem 'Venceremos' (Ortega, 1970) with its characteristic martial rhythm sung by a male choir, which typically represents the people's voice. The film similarly includes excerpts of the *Cantata Santa María de Iquique* (Advis, 1969), a musical work that narrates a brutal 1917 massacre of miners. Thanks to the cantata's arrangements, the timbre of its Andean instruments becomes charged with an eminently political meaning.

In an analogous manner to the tone of Allende's discourse in Littín's documentary, the soundtrack depicts a triumphalist perspective of the Government's political project. Therefore, Allende's discourse blends with the multiple images of the people represented in demonstrations supporting him as a politician and with the Government being represented as leading the revolutionary struggle. By the same token, Allende's voice and message are mirrored in the lyrics and sounds of the CNS, interpreted by its two most iconic bands, Quilapayún and Inti Illimani. We may say then that Littín portrays one large *fresco*, as it were, of the revolutionary process in Chile, where image, voice and music reinforce each other.

The displacement of the popular in *Now We're Gonna Call You Brother* begins with a displacement of the sounds — and the devices used to play sounds — created by the people. If, from an official perspective, *Compañero presidente* had linked up the whole cinematic representation of the UP's project to the artistic representation of the people as developed in the NCS, Ruiz, also filming from an official perspective, does the opposite: he moves the soundtrack away from the familiarity and representational stability that the NCS had developed in relation to the people.

Filming in an indigenous territory different from the Andean region, Ruiz shifts attention away from politically charged instruments such as *charangos, quenas* and *zampoñas* (pan-pipes) to a novel portrayal of typical Mapuche instruments like the *trutruka, pifilka* flute and *kultrun* drum. While Andean sonorities had been adapted, through a series of mixing practices, for Western listeners (in terms of scales, tuning, and forms) and had been interpreted by a music intelligentsia mostly educated according to the Western canon, Mapuche instruments are here presented as directly issuing from their indigenous source without passing through processes of mediation and stylization. A clear example of this contrast is shown in the way the *trutruka* (an animal horn) and the *pifilka* (a vertical flute whose sound is characterized by the production of multiphonics) feature as components of a heterogeneous soundscape, intertwined with street noise and vociferations, rather than appearing as part of standardized arrangements. The same can be said about the *kultrun* (a kettledrum) which is played as one sound among others in a political rally (images 1, 2, 3 and 4).

Some of these Mapuche instruments had featured in nationalistic operas and symphonic pieces created by indigenist composers during the twentieth century.[12] Ruiz further breaks with this model and shows these instruments explicitly played by the Mapuche themselves. The rather long scene where a *trutruka* is ceremoniously played at the end of the demonstration where Allende has spoken illustrates this gesture

Image 1: Mapuche instruments: *pifilka* flute and *kultrun* drum. Reproduced with the permission of Valeria Sarmiento

Image 2: Mapuche instruments: *trutruka*. Reproduced with the permission of Valeria Sarmiento.

Image 3: Mapuche instruments: *trutruka*. Reproduced with the permission of Valeria Sarmiento

Image 4: Mapuche instruments: *kultrun* drums. Reproduced with the permission of Valeria Sarmiento

of placing this instrument in its communal context (that is, played collectively by the Mapuche themselves), but exposing it in a politically charged urban space. If, as our argument has intimated, the CNS had failed in providing a scenario for the Mapuche to express their own sonorities,[13] Ruiz's soundtrack offers a radical displacement of the usual sonic tropes more commonly imagined by Chilean people employing a 'direct' documentary method.

In addition, *Now We're Gonna Call You Brother* establishes a sharp contrast with the way in which *Compañero presidente* had portrayed the relationship between Allende (and his voice) and the people. As we pointed out, Littín had blended Allende's image with the representation of the people, precisely through the mediation of a CNS soundtrack. Ruiz's film, on the contrary, refuses to establish an explicit fusion of the political leader and the mobilized Mapuche people. In fact, precisely through the dialectical use of the two sonic registers, Ruiz portrays a problematic encounter between Allende and the Mapuche. We now turn to this issue as the closing section of the article.

Sonic Dialectics

Now We're Gonna Call You Brother generates a dialectic between two sonic regimes — that of the Mapuche people and that of Allende proclaiming the speech that announces the new bill. We can distinguish two aspects of this dialectical tension between these two poles. Firstly, there is a tension characterized by a specific relationship with space. Allende's speech sounds — as is usual in the case of political speeches — are amplified by a microphone. The camera focuses on him from a low angle shot, at a certain distance, without moving (image 5). The frame itself of Allende is mostly static. All in all, this framing and the use of loudspeakers stress a sense of 'distance' between the politician and the camera, the people and the place where he speaks. Thus the *modus operandi* of his speech and performance does not crystallize in an intimate relationship with the territory upon which he speaks. Allende talks as a 'distant' speaker and, by the same token, his speech could be cut off from the film and placed anywhere else in the world. Allende as a speaker becomes sonically isolated from the site. His visit is the excuse to make this film but his speech becomes something like a 'parenthesis' in the documentary.

A relevant device reinforcing the sense of distance between Allende's vocal sounds and the site where he speaks concerns amplification. We hear his voice mediated by a double set of microphones: one in front of his mouth and another capturing the sound for the film. The final soundtrack reveals the distortion produced by the loudspeakers and the reverberation of Allende's noisy voice across the public space,

Image 5: Low-angle shot of Salvador Allende speaking. Reproduced with the permission of Valeria Sarmiento

thus exalting his 'piercing' timbre through amplifying technics.[14] The gap between the site and Allende is therefore given, not only by the visual framing of his body, but also by the exacerbation of the mechanisms through which the voice is mediated from the speaker up to the listeners.

On the opposite pole, we find Ruiz's portrayal of the Mapuche. From the first image onwards their voices are heard right next to the camera. Close-up shots of their faces when speaking emphasize a sense of closeness and intimacy between them as speakers and us as listeners/spectators.

Likewise, from the first sequence of the film the camera alternates big long shots of the territory which they inhabit with the abovementioned facial close-ups (image 6). Although we see that their voices literally come out of their bodies because they are closely framed, those voices then become voice-over — thanks to the montage — when we move to seeing these long shots.[15] The intimacy of their voices vis-à-vis the camera and the symbiotic relationship between these sounds and the landscape produce a sense of closeness with the territory. Contrary to Allende's speech, this is a 'situated' discourse intimately attached to the land, but whose demands are universal as they refer to the vital needs of any human animal who has become impoverished.

Image 6: Close-up shot of a Mapuche woman. Reproduced with the permission of Valeria Sarmiento

The second sonic dialectical tension is found in the modalities that speaking itself assumes. On the pole of Allende's speech — as is usual in the case of party political rhetoric — what is relevant is the 'content' of what he says. Although Allende was an outstanding orator, the emphasis of his voice is placed on 'what' he says, namely, on the *logos* of his discourse. The amplifying devices that distort the quality of the sound do not overshadow the content of what it is being said, but they do reveal Ruiz's efforts to show the whole of the politician's 'performance.' It is here, again, that we find the excuse to make this film: the content of Allende's speech focuses on the need to integrate the Mapuche people into the revolutionary process through specific policies that may help unite them with the larger revolutionary forces of Chilean peasantry.

In contrast, when depicting the Mapuche speaking, Ruiz illustrates a specific performance of the voice that stresses, not simply its content, but the sonic materiality that allows the *logos* to be expressed. Ruiz illustrates a *non-logical* mode of speaking. Voices here are presented via a polyphonic strategy, which also involves a reflection on the sonic-cum-musical quality of language and not simply on its content. If Allende's speech appeared straightforward, Mapuche voices tend to overlap upon one another. Interestingly, such a procedure takes place not only when the characters sing, but also when they speak.

This polyphonic treatment of speaking voices clearly appears in a key scene, where Ruiz shows an old man talking directly to the camera. As his words progress, a second voice coming from a woman sitting next to him is added upon his (image 7).

Although her voice may be audible, it could be argued that most Chilean listeners could not understand what she says because she murmurs in Mapudungun. The use of this language and the need for Spanish subtitles reinforce the sonic focus on language, whose logical content becomes clear only through a detour via the materiality of its expressive form, namely, via its sounding itself.

This sonorous quality of speaking with its polyphonic expression implies a specific articulation of the two voices, that of the old man and that of the old woman. More specifically, the particular relationship between these voices obeys a logic of an 'imitative counterpoint.' In musical terms, this technique refers to the mimicking of

Image 7: Mapuche elders speaking to the camera. Reproduced with the permission of Valeria Sarmiento

a first melody by a second one, in such a way that the two overlap. In this scene the imitative counterpoint is accomplished by the voice of the woman, who seems to repeat what her male counterpart says but in a delayed fashion.

Moreover, the polyphonic tendency goes beyond the relationship between the two voices. Through montage, Ruiz proceeds to rhythmically link up the vocal imitative counterpoint with music stemming from Mapuche instruments captured *in situ*. The soundtrack of the scene thus integrates Mapuche language with Mapuche instruments in a sequence that produces an epic feeling through the construction of a *crescendo*. The rhythmic fusion of voices and musical instruments is mirrored by the visual montage which alternates shots of the old Mapuche speaking with those of a demonstration in support of the Government taking place in Temuco. The musical *crescendo* is visually replicated by accelerated camera movements in both shooting sites. In the case of the demonstration, the camera moves more rapidly than in the rest of the film as if marching along with the people. In this key scene, the soundtrack stemming from the people supporting the UP has been created entirely with Mapuche documented sounds, a creative procedure which stands in contrast with the traditional representation of the people advanced by Andean music.

If the sonic registers conform a dialectical tension, do we have a resolution? While in *Compañero presidente* the anthem of the UP works almost as the leitmotif of the film, *Now We're Gonna Call You Brother* shows Allende's political encounter with the people accompanied by a fanfare-like melody played by a Mapuche *trutruka* (see figure 1). We may therefore argue that this Mapuche instrument plays the role of a trumpet closing a political traditional speech (images 2 and 3). Via this specific use of the *trutruka*, the montage expresses, if not a proximity between the two sonic poles, at least a desire of closeness. While the timbre of the *trutruka* works as an index referring to the Mapuche, its melodic content evokes a musical convention that relates the sound of horn instruments to heroism and bravery. By playing a succession of thirds forming a basic triad (with some added passing notes), the *trutruka* thus enacts the role of a device that ceremoniously closes the political event we have just witnessed:[16]

Figure 1: Trutruka melody used in *Now We're Gonna Call You Brother*

The two sonic poles — Allende's political speech and Mapuche sounds — converge here in a sort of sonic dialogue. If the speech of the President could seem devoid of a sense of territorialization, the actual dialogue between Allende's and the Mapuche's sounds integrate a sonorous realm where the *popular* is convincingly reinvented. This reinvention of the popular refers to the way in which Ruiz portrays the Mapuche. Whereas he depicts these people in their cultural specificity (and not simply as part of Chilean peasantry and proletariat) the film does not collapse its perspective about this indigenous population into a romanticization of a group totally detached from the political institutions proper to a modern nation state.

What we have dubbed as a 'sonic dialogue' points to the possibility of cinematically rethinking the relationship between political institutional establishment and the people it aims at representing, by way of maintaining a critical attitude towards the danger of a uniform representation of the sphere of society traditionally referred to as 'the popular.' In this context, the Mapuche appear as direct agents — by directly performing their music and sounds — and not simply as represented subjects mediated by sonic stereotypes.

As such, *Now We're Gonna Call You Brother* is pivotal in what we described as Ruiz's revolutionary self-critique. For it is a documentary that, in spite of presenting a critical attitude towards the leftist cultural establishment (as expressed, for example, in NCC and CNS), it still seeks to renew a properly *political* representational strategy based on the problematization of the idea of realism and the depiction of the people, in general terms, and the support of the Chilean Road to Socialism, in particular.

The analysis of this particular film also points to understudied aspects concerning both the musical and cinematic projects developed during the Allende administration. For one thing, *Now We're Gonna Call You Brother* destabilizes the conventional musical structures through which the NCS had created its sonic language in support of the UP. The inclusion of Mapuche sounds and, more importantly, of the Mapuche as a music-making people stands for the absence of the self-representation of this part of the population within the musical establishment. In addition, this documentary provides new elements for aiding towards a different understanding of an aesthetics of 'direct cinema,' one that does not mystify its objects and that makes use of direct sound as a powerful creative and political device.

Endnotes

1. Three of the most comprehensive studies on Raúl Ruiz (Ríos & Pinto, 2010; Cortínez & Engelbert, 2011; and Goddard, 2013) mention this documentary only in passing. Aguirre (2015) is probably the most complete study of this film, where it receives a comparative analysis from a post-colonial perspective. Although *Now we're gonna call you brother* does not receive a substantial treatment by Malcolm Coad, he does mention an important element concerning the use of the voice in the documentary, an issue which will be further explored in this article: '*Ahora te vamos a llamar hermano* (1971) [is] reputedly one of the best of the didactic shorts of the period (according to Ruiz, because it was one of the few in which the protagonists spoke for themselves without voice-over commentary)' (1981, p. 72; 2010, p. 72).

2. On the filmmakers' ideas about the filming of the real, see Lema Habash (2006); on realism more generally in NCC, see Corro et al. (2007); and on the penetration of Hollywood into Chilean society, see Purcell (2012).

3. The paradigmatic example in this regard is the 1971 documentary *Compañero presidente* by Miguel Littín, which we also study below.

4. On this critical dimension of Ruiz's cinema during these years, see Pinto and Horta (2010), Aguirre (2014) and Lema Habash (2008).

5. '…en cine yo no creo en el mito del espejo perfecto, mito en el cual tantos cineastas creen, especialmente chilenos. Por lo demás, el espejo nos da la cara de la realidad, pero invertida. A mí me interesaría usar un cine como espejo, pero como espejo que me diera la realidad tal cual es. Y eso creo que es imposible. Por lo tanto uso al cine como espejo, con lo cual obtengo una cara invertida da la realidad, y uso también al cine como espejo deformante. Parto del hecho de que la realidad la veo como los ojos y que el cine, mediante la distorsión, me puede ayudar a captar elementos de la realidad que a uno se le escapan' (Ruiz, 1972, p. 9; our translation).

6. This idea was then developed in Latin American cultural studies, during the 1990s, under the concept of a 'hybrid' culture (García Canclini, 1990).

7. For a recent overview of the CNS, see Karmy and Farías (2014); for a view on the continental new song movement, see Vila (2014). Regarding the specific contribution of the CNS on cinema, Osvaldo Rodríguez mentions his own pieces composed for Raúl Ruiz, as well as Angel Parra's songs for the film *Eloy* (Humberto Ríos, 1969), (Rodríguez, 1986, pp. 97 – 98).

8 The name of one of the most prominent New Song bands is Quilapayun, which means 'three beards' in Mapudungun. Similarly, the name of the duet Quelentaro is a toponym from the Mapuche region, signifying the tail of a local bird called *traro*.

9 For example, Violeta Parra's song 'Arauco tiene una pena' and Víctor Jara's 'Angelita Huenumán.'

10 This is the case of Victor Jara's 'Cai cai vilú.'

11 Here we may mention Sergio Bravo's *Las banderas del pueblo* (*The Flags of the People*, 1964), made to support Allende during the 1964 presidential campaign, and two documentaries by Alvaro Covacevich, *El diálogo de América* (*The Dialogue of America*, 1972), which shows a conversation between Allende and Fidel Castro held in Santiago, and *Chile, el gran desafío* (*Chile, the Great Challenge*, 1973), a film which follows Allende during his 1973 tour out of Chile.

12 For an overview of the uses of Mapuche sounds in written music during the twentieth century, see González (1993). On the presence of Mapuche instruments and devices in contemporary music, see Díaz (2008a and 2008b).

13 For a reading of the reception of CNS by Mapuche listeners, see Mularski (2014, pp. 162 – 164).

14 Interestingly enough, this piercing timbre has become, in collective imagination, a distinctive feature of Allende's voice through his famous radiophonic last speech, where, in addition, he describes his own speaking as literally containing a 'tranquil metal.' The complete Spanish quote is: '*el metal tranquilo de mi voz*'. The complete version of this last speech is available at https://vimeo.com/14889196 (accessed 7 April 2018)

15 Juan Pablo Silva (2006) points out that there is a widespread tendency present in Chilean documentary films on indigenous populations to produce a split between their voices and their images. If such a thesis is correct, we may say that Ruiz does the complete opposite by emphasizing the intimate relationship between speaking bodies and the landscape they inhabit when filming the Mapuche.

16 In the transcript of the *trutruka* sounds we present here, pitches have been approximated to the standard Western tuning, while the original *ad libitum* rhythms have been adapted to mensural notation.

Bibliography

Aguirre, C. (2014). Una imagen no mistificadora de la Unidad Popular: El filme *Realismo Socialista* de Raúl Ruiz como espacio de autocrítica política de la vía chilena al socialismo. Unpublished paper presented at the 4th Jornadas de Historia de las Izquierdas, Universidad de Santiago.

Aguirre, C. (2015). Complacencias y desacoples temporales con la imagen-pueblo: *Amuhuelai-mi* (Marilú Mallet, 1972) y *Ahora te vamos a llamar hermano* (Raúl Ruiz, 1972). *Revista Faro* 2(22), 47–60.

Coad, M. (1981). Great events and ordinary people. *Afterimage* 10, 72–77.

Coad, M. (2010). Grandes acontecimientos y gente corriente. In V. De los Ríos & I. Pinto (Eds.), *El cine de Raúl Ruiz. Fantasmas, simulacros y artificios.* 71–79. Santiago: Uqbar.

Corro, P., Larraín, C., Alberdi, M. & van Diest, C. (2007). *Teorías del cine documental chileno.* Santiago: Universidad Católica de Chile.

Cortínez, V. & Engelbert, M. (2011). *La tristeza de los tigres y los misterios de Raúl Ruiz.* Santiago: Cuarto Propio.

Cortínez, V. & Engelbert, M. (2014). *Evolución en libertad: El cine chileno de fines de los sesenta*, volume 1 Santiago: Editorial Cuarto Propio.

Díaz, R. (2008a). Poética musical mapuche: Factor de dislocación de la música chilena contemporánea. El caso de 'Cantos ceremoniales', de Eduardo Cáceres. *Revista Musical Chilena* 62(210), 7–25.

Díaz, R. (2008b). La excéntrica identidad mapuche de la música chilena contemporánea: del estilema de Isamitt al etnotexto de Cáceres. *Cátedra de Artes* 5, 65–93.

Debray, R. (1971). *The Chilean Revolution: conversations with Salvador Allende.* New York: Vintage Books.

De los Ríos, V. & Pinto, I (Eds.) (2010), *El cine de Raúl Ruiz. Fantasmas, simulacros y artificios.* Santiago: Uqbar.

Fairley, J. (1989). Analysing performance: narrative and ideology in concerts by ¡Karaxú!. *Popular Music* 8(1), 1–30.

García Canclini, N. (1989). *Culturas híbridas. Estrategias para entrar y salir de la modernidad.* Mexico: Grijalbo.

Goddard, M. (2013). *The cinema of Raúl Ruiz: impossible cartographies.* London: Wallflower Press.

González, J. P. (1993). Estilo y función social de la música chilena de raíz mapuche. *Revista Musical Chilena 47(179),* 78 – 113.

Jordán González, L. (2014). Les travailleurs au sein de la Nouvelle Chanson Chilienne: la représentation du mineur et l'incarnation du travail musical. *MUSICultures 41(1),* 132 – 150.

Karmy, E. & Farías, M (Eds). (2014). *Palimpsestos sonoros. Reflexiones sobre la Nueva Canción Chilena.* Santiago: Ediciones Ceibos.

Lema Habash, N. (2006). Pensamientos sobre un nuevo cine. Los cineastas de izquierda en el contexto revolucionario de la Unidad Popular. In R. Sagredo (Ed.), *Seminario Simon Collier 2006.*149 – 183. Santiago: Universidad Católica de Chile.

Lema Habash, N. (2009). Una dialéctica dispersa. Desbordes lingüísticos en *Palomita blanca* de Raúl Ruiz. In M. Alvarado (Ed.), *Segundo simposio internacional estéticas americanas 2008.* 401 – 411. Santiago: Universidad Católica de Chile.

Miranda, P., Ramay, A. & Loncón, E. (2016). *Violeta Parra en el Wallmapu. Su encuentro con el canto mapuche.* Santiago: Pehuen Editores.

Mularski, J. (2014). *Music, politics, and nationalism in Latin America.* Amherst, New York: Cambria Press.

Pinto, I. & Horta, L. (2010). Vías no realizadas en el cine político chileno. Parodia, extrañamiento y reflexividad. *Aisthesis 47,* 128 – 141.

Purcell, F. (2012). *¡De película! Hollywood y su impacto en Chile 1910 – 1950.* Santiago: Taurus.

Rodríguez, O. (1984). *Cantores que reflexionan. Notas para una historia personal de la Nueva Canción Chilena.* Madrid: LAR.

Ruiz, R. (1970). Trabalenguas de tragos y tigres: Entrevista con Raúl Ruiz. *Hablemos de cine 52,* 48 – 54.

Ruiz, R. (1972). Prefiero Registrar antes que mistificar el proceso chileno. *Primer Plano 4,* 3 – 21.

Ruiz, R. (2000). *Poética del cine.* Santiago: Sudamericana.

Silva, J. P. (2006). Campo de poder: los pueblos originarios en el cine de ficción y en el documental chileno. *Boletín del Museo Chileno de Arte Precolombino 11(1),* 45 – 54.

Torres, R. (1980). Perfil de la creación musical en la Nueva Canción Chilena desde sus orígenes hasta 1973. Santiago: CENECA.

Vila, P. (Ed.). (2014). *The militant song movement in Latin America. Chile, Uruguay, and Argentina.* Lanham, MD: Lexington Books

Afterword

John Corner

Working as co-editor on the compilation of this book, I was prompted to recall many moments of viewing, of study and of reflection in my own engagement with documentary over nearly 45 years. In particular, I remember my first encounter, at a 1970s weekend film school, with John Grierson's *Coalface (1936)* and Humphrey Jennings' *Listen to Britain (1942)*, both screened in the same afternoon. What struck me most powerfully was not just the aesthetic richness of which documentary was capable, but also the way in which music played a vital part (in the two films, a very different part of course) in the construction of this richness. Whatever the diversity of musical approach, both films had a 'strangeness' given to them by their music. In the case of *Coalface*, this resulted from the harsh modernist tones of Benjamin Britten's score over the shots of slagheap, working processes, mining communities and uses of coal. At many points, the music partly imitated the sounds of the machines and processes it was looking at (the sounds of 'the real' itself), at other points it set up dissonant emotions about what 'coal mining' was all about as an industry and an occupation (the sounds appropriate to *considering* this bit of 'the real'). In *Listen to Britain*, the movement in sonic relationships was from an alignment with what the audience was hearing at a London lunchtime concert to an overlay, variously sourced and inflected in its associations and tones, across a range of scenes of the 'wartime everyday'. This intermittent musical frame pushes and pulls a viewer's sense of that everyday into what is first of all a quiet sense of positivity, a recognition of calm and even of beauty in ongoing life, and finally into a strong current of national resolve.

In both cases, this was not music as background so much as music as a key part of the documentary foreground (importantly, connecting both with images and speech, as do many of the analyses in these chapters). A few months later I started using a range of documentary films in my own teaching on aspects of media, using the BFI's good stock of 16mm copies, this being well before VHS and DVD options.

I make these points, with no originality beyond their biographical embedding, because they connect powerfully with my sense of what has been achieved in this book and my sense, too, of the kinds of thinking about documentary to which its chapters lead. Such thinking would, in some cases, be a part of developments within 'documentary studies', but in other cases it would be taking the instance of documentary work to make more general connections concerning the range of mediated sounds, our uses of them within different combinations of other elements and, more broadly, the changing profile of audiovisual culture.

I want, first of all, to note how the 'aesthetic' character of documentary work has variously figured, or not, in academic engagement with it. There is a long, and continuing, history of documentary productions from different periods being used in a largely 'transparent' way as forms of visual and verbal documentation to support work in, say, history and the social sciences, as well as in some other disciplines. There is no need for usage of this kind to be naively realist about the 'truth' of documentary but certainly there is little time to consider the *forms* in which 'the real' is articulated, the emphasis being on that 'real' itself. As we know, the gradual inclusion of documentary within the research and teaching of Film Studies shifted the analytic approach and the scale of engagement. Often, in my recollection, critical work on documentary was considered a rather poor second best to the serious business of grappling with the symbolic densities of cinematic fiction! Many studies, including some in my own earlier writing, attempted to connect both with the thematics of documentary work (as an attempt to show aspects of the world and to say something about them) and with its rich and imaginative recipes for undertaking this business. The essentially *referential* project of documentary (however complicated, indirect and perhaps even self-critical this project was) needed to be inter-related to its diversity of forms. These forms have nearly always been in some kind of relationship (embrace, critique, denial, alternative) with ideas of 'realism', ideas which lie at the centre of any thinking about documentary, as the Introduction noted, and are the focus of most debates about it, including those in the previous pages.

Form sometimes conceals itself and needs excavating by analysis. Across the history of documentary expression, nowhere is this more true than in the forms of 'direct cinema' (or later versions of that troublesome category, 'vérité') where alignments with ideas of transparency are strongest and, not surprisingly, the use of non-diegetic music has been the most minimal and cautious. In some documentaries, however, particularly those from strands of a more experimental, avant-garde character, it is impossible to view a documentary without consciously taking into account its formal construction, sometimes a quite challenging task for the viewer. Not surprisingly, such work has figured prominently in scholarly accounts, including mine, on the grounds that its relative complexity and cultural ambition, in the use of speech and music, for example, gives greater room for analytic play than is to be found in more conventionally 'realist' productions. This is understandable, although it can lead to neglect of the more popular modes of documentary, including those of television, which also hold formal interest.

I think the sharpness of the division between popular and 'art' documentary has reduced in recent years, as part of a broader cultural shift in which aspects of postmodern thinking have been active in relation not only to ideas about the 'true' but also to ideas about generic propriety and to how 'playful' and 'entertaining' a documentary can be allowed to be. Certainly, there is now a very wide diversity of documentary aesthetics at work internationally, often drawing extensively in their aural as well as their visual styling from a broad inter-generic palette, one to which the affordances of digital production have added considerably. We know that 'documentary' has never been any kind of firm generic marker, even though largely futile debates about its definition continue to give some scholars a topic for conference papers. Instances of 'documentariness', sometimes in sustained form, are now widespread across audiovisual activity, and only in some of these instances do productions work self-consciously under the label of 'documentary'. Of course, many of the pieces in this collection focus on aspects of this increasing heterogeneity.

I think what I want to say by way of final reflection, in part picking up on what has been said by the contributors themselves, can be organised well under three headings — 'Cognition and affect', 'Listening as cultural practice' and 'Producing documentary sounds'. All three, but the first two in particular, connect with a developing research perspective internationally — the exploration of the terms of documentary spectatorship or, as we should say here, listenership.

Cognition and Affect.

What we think about what we see and what we feel about what we see are clearly interconnected. This interconnection is a recurrent theme in film and television analysis, and one given sharper profile by those studies taking a self-consciously 'cognitive' approach to the viewing experience. Clearly, sound is deeply involved in helping to manage the emotional frames within which we view documentary scenes, with music — given its capacity to generate mood, its associational resonances and its appeal to memory — to the forefront here, just as speech is often to the forefront in managing the 'knowledge yield' of a documentary. But, as Geoffrey Cox pointed out in his introduction and as many of the contributors show, to split off the consequences of speech and music too firmly risks foreshortening a sense of the way in which music connects with the incremental processes of 'knowing' through the length of a documentary, modifying our sense of 'what is going on' and positioning us at different vantages from this — at one end of the scale 'immersive', at the other coolly distant. Meanwhile, speech carries its own affective alignments, signalling not only the social and perhaps regional position of speakers but also, in the case of commentary and direct address, the kind of communicative relationship they are attempting with us, the viewers. There may also be clues as to the speakers' own emotional state, however reduced in projection compared to the dialogue of feature film. The character of the speech, its vocabulary and phrasing, is also clearly of great importance to our reading of the image, as many of the writers here have discussed. It can tightly localize our perception of meaning (as, for instance, in a brief account of the building of a castle spoken across a sequence of shots of its principal features) or can expand and disperse it, taking it 'higher and broader' (as in the words of a poem spoken across what appears to be a routine shot of a busy city centre). It can prompt us to reflection or it can attempt to persuade us of a certain evaluation and judgement, possibly using propagandist strategies to 'enforce' this. In that sense it can either 'open up' the space for thought or variously 'close it down' and music can support it in either task.

As some of the chapters bring out very well, it has been a feature of much documentary which has taken itself seriously as aesthetic production to foreground these sonic inter-relationships across knowledge and emotion, perhaps at least temporarily 'disturbing' the viewer by placing things out of alignment or in tension or contradiction with each other. The condition of being 'unsure' about the knowledge to take from a scene or the appropriate emotions to feel in response to it is quite frequently a consequence of such a practice, pulling the viewer into acts of viewing and hearing that become acts of vigorous questioning, both of what the film is doing and of their own relationship to the persons, acts, circumstances and issues that its images and sound purport to depict. Even in television, where relative simplicity and clarity of development are given emphasis by the terms of a broad audience demographic and levels of casualness in viewer engagement, there is now greater willingness to provoke and to challenge than once there was.

Afterword

Listening as a Cultural Practice.

Much of this book is the result of 'careful listening', often in the context of specialist skills, of analysis or of production. It has posed documentary viewing as 'listening' as well as 'spectating' and it has refused the tendency to hide questions of sound partially within the terms of questions concerning the image. But listening to a range of media in different contexts, alone and with others, is, clearly, an everyday cultural practice too, of which current strands in Cultural Studies have made us more aware. One way for research to push further here would be to explore a little more the kinds of 'ordinary listening' which documentaries receive. This is something of a challenge. There is only a modest literature on the reception of documentary by audiences and quite of lot of this is strongly thematically, rather than formally, oriented, such as the work on modes of reality television. It is possible to find indications of how people have listened to documentaries and what they have made of what they have heard by looking at the postings on film and television websites, but this is a scattershot approach. Nevertheless, it shows some of the difficulties that may be experienced in 'navigating' a documentary across its diverse sounds as well as indicating some of the productivity and pleasure of what is heard. More investigation of how viewers 'follow' a documentary through the sounds it offers would, I think, prove interesting. How conscious are they of music and how does their awareness of it, and its various resonances and connotations, vary across the documentary? How does it figure in their sense of the images that are shown and the speaking being done? Its function as an important indicator of time-values, both in its rhythm and tempo and its role in the organisation of temporality and duration across a whole film or programme, can really only be confirmed by evidence from non-specialist experience. There is the distinctive case of documentaries which are partly or even largely *about* music, some examples of which have been discussed. Here, the foregrounding of the music is explicit as it becomes itself the subject of commentary and appraisal or provides a thematically illustrative accompaniment for biographical references to specific composers or musicians. Such work is often quite marked both in its sound structures and in the modes of listening which it receives.

An inquiry of the kind proposed might have to work partly through special screenings or with viewing diaries, with the problems of sensitization that these approaches produce, but if combined with the textual approaches demonstrated here, it could sharpen our sense of the producer-text-spectator relationship, of the processes of listening *subjectivity*, and further weaken the idea of some homogenous 'viewer' to whom '*the* meaning' of a documentary is directly available. Listening out of general interest and listening out of professional research interest are, of course, very different modes of orientation and we know how critic/scholar perspectives and 'ordinary' perspectives can differ across a whole range of cultural production.

Producing documentary sounds.

A number of chapters take the reader inside the process of documentary's sonic production. They discuss the framing ideas at work, the more specific plans of approach, the recording and editing phases. In a more explicit way than most analytic work can achieve, they testify to the 'materiality' of sound, its *physical* presence as music, speech or 'noise', and its capture by particular pieces of equipment. Such materiality poses a challenge for the sound designer and recordist, perhaps also for composers and musicians working on a score, but it is also a factor in the satisfaction of listening, first of all to production workers at the stage of building what will be heard in a film and then to audiences. We can be sure that the technical resources for sonic design will continue to increase and that their employment in the creation of innovative ways to build a documentary soundtrack will draw for its inspiration across a wide generic array. Production studies have developed strongly in media scholarship over the last decade although the problem of access still remains, with only a few practitioners themselves prepared to write in detail about their work in other than a 'handbook' style. This book has certainly helped to extend our knowledge of the perspectives and practices involved. Of course, just as textual analysts are at risk of bracketing out both production and audience phases, and audience researchers are at risk of minimising issues of production design and textual system, so producers can remain relatively ignorant of just how their work has been received both by audiences (beyond the broadest indicators) and by those with an academic interest in the area. It is likely they can therefore benefit from knowing a little more about issues of viewer engagement and understanding.

This collection clearly picks up on the achievements of a wide range of previous scholarship but, as I hope to have indicated, it poses many further questions for exploration, ones which suggest connections across humanities scholarship, pressing further into an understanding of the role played by sound in the media arts.

Contributors

Ana Berkenhoff is a German theatre director, actress and musician. She studied post-dramatic theatre at Gießen/D and contemporary dance at the CNSMD Lyon. In the team Berkenhoff/Siegwald she directs music theatre and has staged shows, installations and films in St. Petersburg, Praha, Lyon, and Berlin. As an actress she has worked at venues including HAU Berlin, Kampnagel Hamburg, and Berliner Festspiele. Recently Berkenhoff started working on music as ERA GELDES. Last year she received the Francis Chagrin Award for Sound and Music and her work has featured on Radio Wave Farm NY, BBC Radio 3, Resonance Extra, and NTS London.

Jude Brereton is Senior Lecturer in Audio and Music Technology in the Department of Electronic Engineering, University of York where she teaches virtual acoustics and auralization, music performance analysis and voice analysis/ synthesis. In 2013 she founded the department's successful MSc in Audio and Music Technology. She has degrees in German and Linguistic Science (BA(Hons), York), Speech and Language Processing (MPhil, Trinity College, Dublin) and Music Technology (PhD, York) and her research reflects this varied background. She is dedicated to public engagement and outreach through exciting research-inspired events which combine art and science.

James Bulley is an artist, composer and researcher whose practice explores place-specific composition, locative sound and sound sculpture. His work has been featured by the BBC, ITV, the New York Times and the Guardian. Recent artworks include *Tactus* (2015–), a touch–sound landscape (exhibited at Kaunas Biennial, Lithuania) and *Living Symphonies* (2014–), a forest–located sound installation by Jones/Bulley. In 2016 Bulley collaborated with composer Shiva Feshareki to realise the world premiere of Daphne Oram's *Still Point* for double orchestra and turntables with the London

Contemporary Orchestra. Bulley is a member of the New Radiophonic Workshop, graduate representative for Goldsmiths Sound Practice Research Unit and a trustee of Jem Finer's *Longplayer*.

Simon Connor is a sound designer, multimedia composer and Lecturer in Music Technology at the University of Salford. Performances and screenings of works have taken place at the Flatpack Festival (Birmingham), ICA (London), The Whitworth (Manchester), Leeds International Film Festival, Alta Schmiede (Vienna) and FILAF, the International Art Book and Film Festival (Perpignan). Simon is currently undertaking his PhD at the Sound Music Image Collaboration (SMIC) research centre at the University of Huddersfield. His research explores the evocation of place through sound, and new approaches to the artistic landscape through spatial and interactive audio.

John Corner is Visiting Professor in Media and Communication at the University of Leeds and Professor Emeritus of the University of Liverpool. He has published widely since the 1970s in international journals and in books with aspects of documentary history and form a regular theme alongside theories of media power and the forms of political mediation. Edited collections relevant to this book include *Documentary and the Mass Media* (1986) and the co-edited *New Challenges for Documentary* (second edition, 2005). His monographs include *The Art of Record* (1996) and more recently *Theorising Media* (2011) and the co-authored *Political Culture and Media Genre* (2012).

Geoffrey Cox is a Senior lecturer in Music and a filmmaker and composer of both acoustic and electronic music with a focus on its application to documentary film sound. This has resulted in a number of solo and collaborative film projects: *Cider Makers* (Marley and Cox, 2007), *No Escape* (Cox, 2009), *A Film About Nice* (Marley and Cox, 2010) and *Tree People* (Cox, 2014). He has recently finished working with Marley on *Mill Study* (2017), a short film about a working textile mill in Slaithwaite, West Yorkshire, which receives its overseas premiere at Ethnografilm, Paris in April 2018. He has published articles in *The Soundtrack*, *The New Soundtrack* and *Contemporary Music Review* on the contextual underpinning of his work. His most recent *Organised Sound* article (2017) links the pioneering approach to sound of pre-WWII British documentary filmmakers, with Pierre Schaeffer's *musique concrète*.

Will L. Finch is a PhD student at the University of Bristol supervised by Dr Guido Heldt and Dr Angela Piccini. His research explores music in the BBC documentary series *Arena*—on the means by which *Arena* constructs ideas about music, and on the uses the series itself makes of music. Will previously studied at Royal Holloway and the University of Cambridge where he completed research on jazz in the French New Wave.

Laura Jordán González teaches musicology at the University of Chile, Catholic University of Chile and ARCOS Institute in Santiago. She earned a PhD in Musicology from Laval University (Quebec, Canada). Her doctoral thesis focused on the relationship between singing and social representations associated with the use of the voice in the Chilean *cueca*. She has published on Latin American popular music, music and political resistance, film and sound, and music in exile.

Nicolas Lema Habash is a doctoral candidate in philosophy at the University of Paris 1, Panthéon-Sorbonne. He also holds a Masters in Ancient Philosophy from the University of Oxford. He previously studied philosophy, aesthetics and history. His research focuses on Spinoza and contemporary French philosophy. He has published on the history of philosophy, film and art theory, and Latin American cinema.

Anita Jorge studied English at the École Normale Supérieure of Lyon. Since 2014, she has been preparing a thesis in British cultural history at the Université de Lorraine, France. She currently lectures at the Université de Poitiers. Her PhD thesis examines how British civilians perceived and reacted to their sonic environment during the Second World War in the context of the emergence of new listening practices and of a new culture of aurality. It looks into the role of documentary films in the establishment of a British national identity based on the fundamental musicality of the nation and the aural and musical resistance of Great Britain to Nazi assimilation. Her previous research dealt with the soundscapes of Michael Powell and Emeric Pressburger's wartime films.

Kaarina Kilpiö is a Doctor of Social Sciences, presently working as a university lecturer in the Sibelius Academy of the Uniarts Helsinki (Finland). Her research interests have focused on the ways music has been used in different (mainly historical) audiovisual cultural products and contexts, as well as on users of music and sound technologies. She has recently studied the history of music and sound in commercial background music products, and in films for advertising, educational and propaganda purposes, as well as the C-cassette culture in Finland.

Lars Koens is a sound designer, music composer, and experimental filmmaker. Since receiving his PhD in 2015 from the University of Edinburgh he has directed and collaborated on films, dance performances, and art installations. He teaches at Liverpool John Moores University in film and art

Demelza Kooij is a filmmaker, artist, and senior lecturer in filmmaking at Liverpool John Moores University. She works in documentary, fiction, and hybrid film forms. Her films re-imagine landscape; depict engagement with technologies, and are studies of interactions between human and non-human animals.

Andrew Kötting is an award winning artist-filmmaker who, after leaving school, worked as a scrap metal dealer and then a lumberjack before completing an MA in Fine Art at The Slade. He made his first feature film *Gallivant* in 1996. Subsequent feature films, installations and performances include This *Filthy Earth, Ivul, Mapping Perception, In The Wake of a Deadad, This Our Still Life, Swandown, By Our Selves* and *Edith Walks*. The final part of his Earthworks trilogy, *Lek And The Dogs*, is released in June 2018. He currently lives and works between Hastings in England and Fougax-et-Barrineuf in the French Pyrenees.

Dr Rosa Nogués is an Associate Lecturer in Art Theory at the Chelsea College of Arts (London). She obtained her PhD in 2013 at the Centre for Research in Modern European Philosophy (Kingston University). She has lectured at Central Saint Martins (London), Middlesex University (London) and the Universität für angewandte Kunst (Vienna). Her writing has been published in n-paradoxa, Revista Mundo Crítico and the current issue of MIRAJ.

Dr Radoslaw Rudnicki is Lecturer and Major Coordinator of Music Practice at the School of Music & Creative Media Production, Massey University, Wellington, New Zealand. Working as sound designer and music composer he collaborates with synthesiser manufacturers, visual artists and as Deputy Director of Precyzja Foundation and Director of Wave Folder Records he curates and funds new media art projects. In 2008 Radoslaw was shortlisted by SPNM (UK), as one of the most interesting emerging composers living in the UK. In 2013 he was announced Ambassador of Jazz in the North of England with the project Space F!ght. Radek performs regularly, his work gaining exposure at festivals and art galleries worldwide.

Tsung-Han Tsai is currently an independent scholar based in Taiwan, having previously received his PhD from the University of St Andrews and taught in the UK and China. His research interest is in the relationship between music and modernist literature, focusing particularly on the contentious relation between music and politics. He is finishing a book on E. M. Forster and music and developing a new project on the ways in which a diverse range of ideas about music informed modernist experiments in life-writing.

Index

A Colour Box 48, n. 234

A Diary for Timothy 11, 204–16

Action Space (arts collective) 10, 86–8, 90, 92–8, 101–2

Action Space (documentary film) 10, 85–105

Addinsell, Richard 207, 209, 215

Allende, Salvador 12, 256–8, 262–4, 267–72, n. 274

Altman, Rick 86, 92, n. 103

Ambassador Magazine, The 37, 38–41, 44, 45, 63, n. 64

American Dream 10, 109–10

American pavilion 117

American Zoetrope 93

Amis, Martin 126, 141

AMM 10, 94–5, 100–1

Amuhuelai-mi 260, 262

Anderson, Lindsay 7

Animal Farm 41

Anstey, Edgar 4, 135, 141, n. 147

anti-propaganda 206, 211

Apocalypse Now 86

archival turn 20, 28, 30–1

archives 9, 18, 20–32, n. 64, 88, 89, 95, 96, 97, 99, 100, 102, 126, 127, 141, 144, n. 146, 240, 242

Arena 9, 18, 20–3, 26, 28–32, n. 33

Arena Hotel 9, 17–36

Aristotle 187–8

Arnhem 204, 208–10

asynchronicity 1, 4, 11, 100, 118, 222

Auden, W. H. 132, n. 146

Babyshambles 26–7

Bauhaus School 38, 44

Bazin, André 6, 7

BBC 205, 208, 209, 211–12, 214

Beethoven, Ludwig van 11, 47, 189, 204, 205, 207, 209–11, 213–15

   Piano Sonata No. 23 in F minor, Op.57 'Appassionata' 203–16

   Symphony No. 5 in C minor 213

BFI. See British Film Institute

Big Mill, The 47, 62
Birtwistle, Andy 4, 5
Boyle, Rory 47, n. 65
BP. See British Petroleum
Bravo, Sergio 257, 262, n. 274
Brecht, Bertolt 7
Breitrose, Henry 118
Bresson, Robert 6
British Film Institute (BFI) n. 146, n. 148, 279
British Petroleum (BP) 126, 135, 136, 139
Britten, Benjamin 3, 41, 132, n. 146, 279
Broadcasting of Music, The 133
Bryars, Gavin 25, 193
Burroughs, William 18, 22, 23, 28
Burtt, Ben 92

Cage, John 184
calypso 137, 138, n. 147, n. 148
camera work 44, 52, 55, 57, 90, 100, 112–3, 118, 132, 154, 157, 160, 162, 166, 168, 175–6, 204–5, 208, 210, 230, 241, 244, 267–8, 271
Canboulay 136–7, 138
Canemaker, John 41
Cardew, Cornelius 95
Cariso music 136
Carson, Anne 189
Cashmere is Scottish 62
Central Office of Information 40–1, n. 64
Chanan, Michael 6, 7

Chelsea Hotel 21, 22
Chile Films 263
Chilean cinema 256, 257, 260
Chilean New Song (CNS) 256, 260–1, 263–4, 267, 272, n. 273, n. 274
Chilean Road to Socialism 256, 258, 260, 272
Chion, Michel 10, 24, 91, n. 148, 153, 155–8, 160, 166
  acousmêtre 153, 157, 162–4, 166, 169
  added value 160
  de-acousmatization 157, 164
  Materializing Sound Indices 91
  Mickeymousing 158
  suspension 166, 168
Cinema Quarterly 8
cinéma vérité 113, 114
Clarke, Shirley 10, 108–9, 111–121
CNS. See Chilean New Song
Coalface 279
Coleman, Ornette 10, 107–16, 118–22
Communism 221, 226, 227, 230
concrete music. See *musique concrète*
Connection, The 108, 113, 114, 117
Connor, Steven 2, 3, n. 13
Cool World, The 113, 116–7
Coppola, Francis Ford 86
Cormorant 11, 174–7, 179
Coull, Gordon 43, 45, 62
Crown Film Unit 207, 208, 220, 221

curating 28

David Holzman's Diary 113
Davis, Miles 111, 120
Derbyshire, Delia 2
Derrida, Jacques 31, 108, 110, n. 146
Doherty, Pete 18, 19, 26, 27, 31
Donald, Henry 51–2, 57
Donaldson, Lucy 2, 91, 98

Ellington, Duke 224, 229
Ellitt, Jack 230–1
    Sound Construction 230–1
Emmer, Luciano 133, 134
Empire Marketing Board (EMB) n. 64, 132
End of Time, The 168–70
Eno, Brian 194
Enthusiasm 4
Episode Metallic 141
Export or Die 41
Expropriation, The 258

Fawlty Towers 29
Ferguson, Howard 210
Films of Scotland 5, 9, 40–2, 44, 47, 48, 59
Finland 11–12, 240–3, 246–7, 249–52
Fluxus 88
Folk, Ethan 11, 174, 175, 177, 179, 180
Forster, E. M. 11, 207, 208, 211–13, 215
    Howards End 213

Foster, Hal 144
Foucault, Paul-Michel 31

Gambling, Gods and LSD 152, 153, 157, 162, 168, 169
Gerhardt, Elena 204, 211
Glas 47, 133, 140
Glasgow School of Art 44
glitches 75, 76
Godfather Part II, The 86
Goethe, Johann Wolfgang von 189
Goldsmiths, University of London 126, 127, 131, n. 146
Goya 133
GPO Film Unit 132, 221, 231
Grant, John 44, 62, n. 64
Graves, Robert 225
Grierson, John 3–4, 7, 41, 44, 47, 52, 62, n. 64, 90, 131–2, 140, n. 147, 221, 232, 279

Halas and Batchelor 41, 43, 48
Hamilton, Iain 42
Hamilton, Richard 21, 22, n. 33
    Just what is it that makes today's homes so different, so appealing? 21, 22
Haanstra, Bert 47, 133, 140
Haavio, Martti 247, 248, 249
Handke, Peter 176, 179
Hand of Adam, The 47
Hardy, Forsyth 40, n. 64, n. 65

Harmolodics 115
Heart of Britain, The 207
Heart of Scotland, The 42, 47
Heidegger, Martin 176–8
Henry Cow 10, 94
Henson, Laurence 42, 47, 62
Hess, Myra 11, 204–11, 215, n. 235
Hoffman, Kathelin 111–2
Holliday, Jason 113–4
Hollywood 86, 89, 92, 93, 99, n. 103, 257
Hörspiel 179, 227, 229

Innocents, The 134
Inter-Action 88
interactive spatial sonification 70, 73
Introduction to a New Art 232

jazz 10, 43, 47–8, 51, 52, 55, 57, 108–11, 116–21, 229, 252
    bebop 52, 109, 120
Jennings, Humphrey 11, 131, 132, 204, 205, 206–8, 210, 212, 220, 222, 232, 279
Jones, Geoffrey 10, 126, 131, 133–5, 138–40, 143–4, n. 146, n. 148
Juda, Elsbeth 38, 39, 44
Juda, Hans 38, 41–2, 44, 58, 63

Kalevala 248–50
Kitchener, Lord 136, 137, n. 147
Kulezic-Wilson, Danijela 3

L'arrivée d'un train à La Ciotat 169
Leacock, Richard 108, 114, 117
Lipari, Lisbeth 5
listening 1–9, 12, 23–5, 97, 162, 189, 205–6, 209–10, 212, 240, 281, 283–4
Listen to Britain 132, 206–8, 210, 220, 222, 224, 232, n. 235, 279
Littín, Miguel 257, 263–4, 267
    Compañero president 263–4, 267, 271
Little White Dove 258, 260
Little Wild Dove 259
Logan, Philip C. 207, 212
Lumière, Auguste and Louis 169
Lye, Len 11, 41, 47, 131, 132, 133, 221, 224–32, n. 234, n. 235

McAllister, Stewart 207
McBride, Jim 113
McClary, Susan 210
McConnell, Edward 9, 41–4, 58, 62–3, n. 64–5
McLaren, Norman 131–4
Mallet, Marilú 260, 263
Manufactured Landscapes 152
Man With A Movie Camera 131, 140
Mapuche people 12, 256, 260–72
    Mapuche musical instruments 261, 262, 264–6, 271, 272, n. 274
Marzola, Alessandra 206
mas 136–8, n. 147
Mathieson, Muir 208

Index

memory 30, 32, 184–5, 282
cultural memory 31, 32
Mettler, Peter 10, 151–70
Meyer, Ernst 221, 227, 229, 230, 231
microphone use 90, 91, 92, 94, 96, 133, 138, 154, 267
Mighty Sparrow 127, 137
Ministry of Information 41, 207, 220, 221, 222, 224
Minton, Phil 10, 94–5, 100, 101
mise-en-bande 86, n. 103
Mitchell, William 38
Mobilise your Scrap 227
Murch, Walter 86, 91, 92, 93, 98, 99
music
    improvisation 48, 52, n. 65, 80, 90, 94, 95, 100, 108–9, 115–6, 121
    jazz. See jazz
    leitmotif 226, 231, 271
    modernism 9, 43, 47, 52, 279
    motif 204, 209, 214
    serialism 47, 52, 55, 133
musique concrète 5, 97, 126, 141, 230, 286

narration 25, 132, 135, 152, 153, 168, 244, 246, 248, 252
NASWM. See National Association of Scottish Woollen Manufacturers
National Association of Scottish Woollen Manufacturers (NASWM) 39–40, 59, 63
National Gallery n. 147, 204, 214–15, n. 235

nationalism 12, 212, 214–5, 229, 248, 250, 260, 262
Nazi Germany 240, 242
NCC. See New Chilean Cinema
New American Cinema 109
New Chilean Cinema (NCC) 256–7, 262, 263, 272, n. 273
New Latin American Cinema 258–9
Newspaper Train 229, n. 234
newsreels 242, 243, 248, 252
Nietzsche, Friedrich 170
Night Mail 3, 42, 132, 140, n. 146
Nisbet, Alan 85, 97–101
noise 1, 3, 4, 11, 63, 80, 139, 155, 162, 164, 185, 187, 195, 196, 220, 232, 264, 284
nostalgia 9, 20, 30–31, n. 65, 207
Now We're Gonna Call You Brother 12, 259–72, n. 273
Nucleus 141

Ono, Yoko 116, 119
Oram, Daphne 10, 125–8, 131–41, 144, n. 146–8
    BBC Radiophonic Workshop 126, 135, n. 147
    and electronic music 134, 141, n. 146
    Oramics Machine 134, n. 147
    Tower Folly 126, 134, 140
oscillator 75–6
Ornette: Made in America 10, 108–21
Our Culture and Us 242, 247–51

Parker, Charlie 110, 120
Parra, Violeta 262, n. 273, n. 274
PBL. See Public Broadcasting Laboratory
Pennebaker D. A. 108, 114, 117
Petropolis: Aerial Perspectives on the Alberta Tar Sands 152, 153, 166–9
Picasso, Pablo 44
Picture of Light 152, 153–8, 160, 162, 166, 168, 169
Plato 188
Poetics of Cinema 259
Pop Art 21, 24
Port of Spain 137, 138, 140
Portrait of Jason 108, 113
postmodernism 195, 281
Prévost, Eddie 95
Progress Music 10, 125–45
propaganda 7, 132, 220, 222, 225, 226, 230, 251–2
propaganda films 11, 226, 232, 241–7, 251–2
    Wochenschau 243, 252
Public Broadcasting Laboratory (PBL) 111, 116
Puntila, Lauri Aadolf 247, 248, 249

Rail 141
Rangan, Pooja 2, 6, 8
realism 7, 28, 257, 259, 272, 280
Realist Film Unit 221, n. 234
Redgrave, Michael 11, 207, 212, 214

Rogers, Holly 4, 7, 8, 90, 91, 101, 102, 144
Ruby, Jay 7
Ruiz, Raúl 12, 255–72, n. 273, n. 274
    direct cinema 12, 108, 114, 117, 258–9, 272, 280
runo singing 248–50
Rydstrom, Gary 93

Schaeffer, Pierre 3–4, 97, 133, 230, n. 235
Schlegel, Friedrich 3
Schopenhauer, Arthur 3, 7
Scottish Sinfonia 48
Seawards the Great Ships 42
Shadow of Progress, The 141
Shell Film Unit 134
Shell Panorama 134
Shell Spirit 134
Sibelius, Jean 12, 243, 245–53
    Karelia Suite 245, 248–50
    Lover, The 246
    Oceanides, The 247
    Symphony No. 3 in C major 246
signal processing 75
Skies of America 109, 110, 115, 119
Skyscraper 118
Snow 135, 147
Socialist Realism 258
sonic dialectics 256, 267–70, 272
sonic dialogue 272

Index

sonification 70–1, 73, 76, 79, 80, 81

Sound and Music in Documentary Film Symposium (SMDF) 1, 8, 9

sound
    concrete sound. See *musique concrète*
    diegetic 1, 6, 11, 108, 114, 117, 152, 157, 164, 169, 229
    electronic 55, 76, 135, 141
    exodiegetic 24
    extra-diegetic 152, 209, 262
    kinediegetic 24
    location sound 70, 71, 73, 75, 76, 79, 81, 144
    non-diegetic 101, 118, 177, 229, 280
    sound collage 86, 95, 97, 99, 222, 225
    sound effects 1, 86, 92, 93, n. 103, 134, 141, 158, 214, 222, 224, 242, 244, 245, 251
    sounds of warfare 220, 224
    spatial sound 70, 75, 79

sound design 9, 10, 24, 70, 75–6, 78, 81, 86, 92–3, 98, 99, 101, 102, n. 103, 152, 284

Sound of Insects: Record of a Mummy, The 153

soundscape 2, 23–4, 75, 126, 139, 164, 185, 196, 206, 264

sound synthesis 75

soundtrack 1, 10, 11, 12, 27, 42, 45, 47, 51, 86, 90, 99, 100, 102, 114, 116– 17, 131, 133–5, 137, 140–1, 225–7, 229–31, 233, n. 235, 242–3, 245, 250–2, 262, 264, 267, 271, 284

soundworld 4, 25, 70, 71, 75

Spare Time 232

Spedding, Frank 9, 42–3, 45–7, 51, 54, 55, 58, 61–3, n. 65

speech 1, 152, 156, 158, 160, 178, 206, 208, 215, 216, 267, 269, 270, 272, 279, 281, 282, 284

Star Wars 92

steel pans 128, 137, 138–9, 140, 141

Stockhausen, Karlheinz 133

storytelling 152, 176

Styrene, Poly 19, 26–7, 31

Suschitzky, Wolfgang 135, 136, 138–40, n. 147

Swan Neck, Edith 197–9

Taxi Driver 156

Teen Beat 135

television
    documentary 5, 9, 18, 21, 282, 282, 283
    in Finland 251–2

Templar Film Studios 39, 62

Teosto 242, 243, 247

That Nguillatún 262

This is Shell 134

Three Sad Tigers 257

Tilbury, John 95

To Hell With Culture 89

Toop, David 189, 196

Trade Tattoo 231, n. 234

Trinidad and Tobago 10, 126, 128, 131, 136–41, 144, n. 148

Turner, Ken 86, 88, 90, 93, 95, 97, 98, 101–2

Turner, Mary 86, 88, 90

Unidad Popular (UP) 257, 271, 272

UP. See Unidad Popular

Van Dyke, Willard 108, 114, 117, 118

Vaughan Williams, Ralph 207, 226

Vaughan, Dai 6, 102

Vertov, Dziga 4, n. 64, 131–2, 139, 140

video 10, 11, 70, 78–81, 108, 112, 114, 115–16, 118, 145

video-games 23–4, n. 33, 118

voice

creative use of voice in film 151–70, 175, 176–8, 186, 204–5, 208–9, 212, 214–5, 222, 226, 231, 247–8, 250, 252, 256, 262, 263–4, 267–71, n. 273, n. 274,

voice of God commentary 4, 11, 152

voice-over 10, 11, 45, 100, 152–7, 161–2, 168–70, 175, 176, n. 268

Vortex Concerts 134

Wahl, Huw 10, 86, 88, 89, 94, 101, 102

Wall, Anthony 20, 26, 29–30

Warhol, Andy 18, 19, 22, 23, 28, 116

Watt, Harry 4, 42, 132

Weave Me a Rainbow 9, 37–63, n. 64

Wenders, Wim 175, 176, 178–9

When the Pie was Opened 11, 219–33, n. 234

Williams, Derek 141

Winehouse, Amy 19, 25–6, 30

Wings of Desire 175, 176

Wochenende 227

Wolff, Christian 95

women

portrayal of 62, 210–11

World War II 132, n. 147, 204, 206, 225, 240

Wright, Basil 86, 132, 207, 212, 213, 232, n. 235

Yleisradio 242, 248